Criminal Law in China

Criminal Law in China

Shizhou Wang

This book was originally published as a monograph in the International Encyclopaedia of Laws/Criminal Law.

General Editor: Roger Blanpain
Founding Editor: Frank Hendrickx
Volume Editors: Frank Verbruggen & Vanessa Franssen

Wolters Kluwer

Published by:
Kluwer Law International B.V.
PO Box 316
2400 AH Alphen aan den Rijn
The Netherlands
Website: www.wolterskluwerlr.com

Sold and distributed in North, Central and South America by:
Wolters Kluwer Legal & Regulatory U.S.
7201 McKinney Circle
Frederick, MD 21704
United States of America
Email: customer.service@wolterskluwer.com

Sold and distributed in all other countries by:
Quadrant
Rockwood House
Haywards Heath
West Sussex
RH16 3DH
United Kingdom
Email: international-customerservice@wolterskluwer.com

ISBN 978-90-411-9527-2

e-Book: ISBN 978-90-411-9528-9
web-PDF: ISBN 978-90-411-9529-6

This title is available on www.kluwerlawonline.com

The Author

Professor Shizhou Wang (born 20 June 1953) studied at the Law Faculty of Peking University (1978–1985), where he received his LLB and his first LLM degree, he then went on to the Law School of the University of California at Berkeley, USA (1987–1988), where he received his second LLM degree. From 1994 to 1996 he worked on a research project as Alexander-von-Humboldt's Research Fellow at Max-Planck-Institute of Foreign and International Criminal Law in Freiburg and at the University of Augsburg, Germany. He has worked at the Law Faculty of Peking University since 1985 and is currently a Professor of Law and LLD Supervisor, while he is a visiting scholar in many countries, such as K C Wong Research Fellow in Advanced Legal Studies at London University, UK and Van Calker Research Fellow in Swiss Institute of Comparative Law (ISDC) in Switzerland. Since 2007, he has been engaged as Visiting Professor at both Stanford University, as part of their Beijing Programme, and at Huaqiao University. He has been a legal consultant for Chinese legislation in the fields of anti-security fraud, copyright protection, the Chinese Criminal Code of 1997, women's rights protection, anti-domestic violence, anti-terrorism, national security and sports law.

Prof. Wang holds memberships of Societies including, China Law, China Criminal Law, AIDP (International Association of Penal Law China Branch), Western Returned Student and Sports Law. Since 2013 he has acted as the arbitrator for the China International Economic and Trade Arbitration Commission (CIETAC). He was the winner of the Humboldt Research Award in 2009 and has been the Scientist Ambassador for the Alexander-von-Humboldt Foundation since 2011. He is the author of numerous books and articles on criminal law, economic crime, comparative criminal law, international criminal law and criminology in China and has also published in the USA, Germany, Russia, Holland, Great Britain, Poland, Korea, Japan, Turkey, Italy, Chinese Taiwan, Spain and South America. These publications are translated into a variety of languages, including English, German, Russian, Turkish, Korean, Ukrainian, Japanese, Spanish and Chinese.

The Author

Table of Contents

List of Abbreviations

Glossary

Art.	Article
CCC	Criminal Code of the PR China
CCP	The Code of Criminal Procedure of the People's Republic of China (Version of 14 March 2012, Unless Specifically Indicated Otherwise)
CIETAC	China International Economic and Trade Arbitration Commission
Civil Law	General Principle of the Civil Law of the People's Republic of China
CNY	Chinese currency, Yuan (1 USD = 6.6 CYN (as of 23 September 2017))
Code of Conduct	The Code of Conduct for the Prisoners Issued by the Chinese Ministry of Justice in 2004
Const.	Constitution of the People's Republic of China
CPL	Chinese Prison Law of 26 October 2012, when Not Specifically Indicated
Decision on Judicial Authentication	Decision of the Standing Committee of the National People's Congress on the Administration of Judicial Authentication
Electoral Law	Electoral Law of the National People's Congress and Local People's Congresses of the People's Republic of China
Expl. of SPC	Explanation of the Supreme People's Court
GDP	Gross Domestic Product
Juvenile House	Management and Education Houses for Juvenile Delinquents
NPC	National People's Congress
OLPC	Organic Law of the People's Court (Version of 31 October 2006, Unless Indicated Otherwise)
OLPP	Organic Law of People's Procuratorates
PAPF	People's Armed Police Force
para.	paragraph
paras	paragraphs
PLA	People's Liberation Army

List of Abbreviations

PRC	People's Republic of China
Provision of 2013	Provisions of the Supreme People's Court, the Supreme People's Procuratorate, the Ministry of Public Security, the Ministry of State Security, the Ministry of Justice, and the Legislative Affairs Commission of the Standing Committee of the National People's Congress on Several Issues Concerning the Implementation of the Criminal Procedure Law, Effective as of 1 January 2013
SPC	Supreme People's Court

General Introduction

§1. The General Background of the Country

I. Geography and Climate

1. The People's Republic of China (the PRC) is situated in East Asia, on the western shores of the Pacific Ocean. China is the largest country in Asia and also one of the largest countries in the world by land size. It stretches from 53 degrees 30 minutes to 4 degrees 15 minutes north latitude with an extent of more than 5,200 kilometres, and from 74 degrees to 135 degrees east longitude with an extent of more than 5,500 kilometres. It covers about 9.6 million square kilometres. China has a continental land boundary of more than 20,000 kilometres and a coastline of more than 18,000 kilometres. The PRC borders the Democratic People's Republic of Korea in the east, the Russian Federation in the north-east and north-west, Mongolia in the north, Kazakhstan, Kyrgyzstan and Tajikistan in the north-east, Afghanistan, Pakistan, India, Nepal, Sikkim and Bhutan in the west, Burma, Laos and Viet Nam in the south, and looks across the seas towards the Republic of Korea, Japan, the Philippines, Malaysia, Indonesia and Brunei. Off the coast, there are more than 5,000 islands, including for instance the Diaoyu Islands. Of them, the largest is the Island of Taiwan and the second largest is the Island of Hainan.

Geographically, China can be divided (west to east) into three terraces. The highest one is the Qinghai-Xizang (Tibet) Plateau with an average elevation of 4,000 metres, famously known as 'the roof of the world'. Mount Qomolangma (Mount Everest) (8,848 metres above sea level), the highest point of China and also the number one summit in the world, is located on the border between Tibet and Nepal. The second terrace is composed of the plateau and basin approximately 1,000–2,000 metres above sea level. The ruggedness of the Yunnan-Guizhou Plateau, the criss-cross ravines of the Loess Plateau, the gentle terrain of the Mongolian Plateau, the grace of the Sichuan Basin, the desert of the Tarim Basin and the grassland of the Zhungeer Basin shows the great diversity and the magnificent scenery of the landscape. The lowest point in China (155 metres below sea level) rests on the Turpan Basin in this terrace. The lowest terrace is found to the east of the Greater Xing'an Mountains, Taihang Mountains, Wu Mountain and the eastern fringe of the Yunnan-Guizhou Plateau. Within this terrace there are great plains with an elevation of less than 200 metres, i.e., the Northeast Plain, the North China Plain and the plain of the middle and lower reaches of the Yangtse River. In the Southeast, there is a hilly land with some less than 1,000 metres high.

2. The diversity of the climate in China is a result of being a particularly expansive country with such a varied topography. The greater part of China is situated in the northern temperate zone and subtropical zone and so enjoys the monsoon climate. However, there is no summer at the top of the north-east area of China and no winter on the Hainan Island. While it is like spring all year round in the Yunnan-Guizhou Plateau (in the south-west) and the Huai River basin (in the middle of China) enjoys clear seasons, the north-west desert is warm in the daytime and cold at night and snowy mountains are the typical scenery of the Qinghai-Xizhang (Tibet) Plateau. Generally, the summer temperature is high throughout the country, but the winter temperature is vastly different from north to south. The annual average precipitation is equally as diverse, running from 1,500 mm in the south-east area to 50 mm in the north-west area.

II. Population and Nationalities

3. According to the data of the National Bureau of Statistics of China, the country had a population of 1,360,720,000 in the mainland part by the end of 2013. Of them, 53.73% i.e., 731,110,000 belong to urban resident populations. The population density in China varies greatly from west to east. More than 90% of the population lives in the area of the lowest terrace. The north-west covers 64% of the national land but only has a 5.8% population density.

In 2013, the birth rate in China was 12.08% and the death rate was 7.16%. In other words, the rate of natural increase was 4.92% meaning that China will grow by 6.68 million people annually. Population statistics have become very difficult in China over recent years, because people move from one city to another easily for new jobs or better living in a freer society. In 2013, it is reported that 2,890 million people are living in places where they are not registered as a permanent resident but have been living there for more than six months. Of those people, 2,450 million are living in the places other than where they registered.

4. China is a multinational country containing fifty-six nationalities (i.e., minorities or ethnicities – but in China the term 'nationalities' is preferred). Of them, the Han people cover about 93.3% of the whole national population. The Zhuang (Chuang), the Hui, the Uygur (Uighur), the Yi, the Miao, the Zang (Tibetan), and the Menggol (Mongolian) are the minorities with a relatively large population. Generally, the minority people live in the north-east, north-west and the south-west, while the Han people live in the central and south-east area.

III. Economy

5. The PRC carried out the system of a planned economy for thirty years after the founding of the socialist system in 1949. After 1979, the planned economy of over-centralisation had shown its disadvantage in terms of ossified management. It hindered the development of the productive force. The policy of opening up to the outside world and reforming this outdated system were considered and carried out by the leading party, the Chinese Communist Party. The system of a planned economy is gradually being replaced by the socialist market economic system. In accordance with the Constitution of the PRC, China now practices a socialist market economy (Article 15 of the Const.). The socialist market economic system is linked to the basic system of socialism. It upholds the principle of taking the publicly owned sector as the mainstay, while striving for a simultaneous development of all economic sectors. Both public and non-public ownership are key components of China's socialist market economy. China has taken the socialist market economy as the orientation of its reform for the past thirty years. More recently, China has been improving its basic economic system and will make the market play a more decisive role in resource allocation. For this purpose, China has made efforts to build a market system that is uniform but open, orderly and competitive. Besides public ownership, the Chinese socialist market economy requires an income distribution system which values the principle of 'to each according to his work' as its mainstay (Article 6 of the Const.), gives priority to efficiency, while also taking fairness into account so as to encourage some localities to become prosperous first while adhering to the road to common prosperity. The Chinese socialist market economy also requires a social security system.

China has carried out an open and reform policy for more than thirty years and made great achievements. For example, the Chinese Gross Domestic Product (GDP) has seen an increase from CNY 1.958 trillion in 1991 to CNY 56.8845 trillion in 2016.

6. The Chinese economy now contains various kinds of ownership, as follows.

The *state-owned economy*, namely, the socialist economy under ownership of the entire nation, is the leading force in the national economy (Article 7 of the Const.). The state ensures the consolidation and growth of the state-owned economy. While state-owned enterprises are still the backbone of the Chinese economy, the state-owned economy no longer exclusively refers to enterprises which are purely owned by the state's capital. Indeed, today, state-owned enterprises may be classified in three categories. The first category includes the purely state-owned enterprises, which are 100% owned by the state. The second category of state-owned enterprises refers to state absolute or relative holding companies. The former refers to those in which the state holds more than 50% of the shares; the latter are those in which the state either is the largest shareholder, though not exceeding 50%, or possesses the actual controlling power according to the contract. The third category consists of state-owned shareholding companies, i.e., companies in which the state has some but not the controlling part of the capital.

Next, the *collective ownership by the working people* forms an important part of the basis of the socialist economy system in the PRC. After three decades of reform, the sectors of socialist economy under collective ownership by the working people are now largely taking the household-responsibility system as their forms. This system shall link remuneration to output, while the farmers shall enjoy the rights of independent management, though they obtain their land by contract to the collective units they belong to. Between farmers or their families, they may take forms of co-operative economy, such as the co-operatives of producers, supply and marketing, credit and consumers, in rural areas. In the cities and towns, the collective ownership by the working people is usually taking various forms of co-operative economy. These forms are more common for in the business such as handicraft, industrial, building, transport, commercial and service trades. In accordance with the Constitution of the PRC, the state protects the lawful rights and interests of the urban and rural economic collectivities and encourages; it guides and helps the growth of the collective economy (Article 8 of the Const.).

Furthermore, the privately owned economy is deemed as an important sector to the socialist public economy. In accordance with the Constitution of the PRC, the state protects the lawful rights and interests of the private economy and guides, supervises and manages it (Article 11 of the Const.). China has tried to improve the legal protection for the privately owned economy. On 1 January 2000, the Law on Individual Proprietorship Enterprises went into effect.

Finally, the PRC also permits foreign enterprises, other foreign economic organisations and individual foreigners to invest in China and to enter into various forms of economic co-operation with Chinese enterprises and other Chinese economic organisations in accordance with the law of the PRC. Since 1979, Chinese-foreign equity joint ventures, Chinese-foreign contractual joint ventures, and wholly foreign-owned enterprises have appeared in China. In accordance with the Constitution of the PRC, all foreign enterprises, other foreign economic organisations as well as Chinese-foreign joint ventures within Chinese territory shall be protected by the law of the PRC.

In sum, according to the state's statistics at the end of 2001, 12.2% of all Chinese enterprises were state-owned enterprises, 28.3% collective enterprises, 43.7% private enterprises, 9.9% shareholding enterprises, 1.9% enterprises with foreign investment, 2.7% enterprises with investment from Hong Kong, Macau and Taiwan, and 1.3% other enterprises.

7. In order to develop external economic co-operation, technical exchanges and to promote the socialist modernisation programme, China has delineated since 1980 certain areas to form special economic zones. There are five of these areas so far, three of which are located in Guangdong Province: Shenzhen, Zhuhai and Shantou. Xiamen is another special economic zone, located in Fujian Province, and the final special economic zone is the whole province of Hainan.

In the special zones, foreign citizens, overseas Chinese, compatriots in Taiwan, Hong Kong, Macao and their companies and enterprises are encouraged to open factories or set up enterprises and other establishments with their own investment or undertake joint ventures with Chinese investment, and their assets, due profits and other legitimate rights and interests will be legally protected. In addition to the special economic zones, there are fourteen cities along the coastline, fifteen economic and technical development zones, five cities along the Yangtze River, and four cities along the boundary which are opening to the world. In short, the Chinese economy is no longer isolated. By April of 2013, China had cumulatively absorbed foreign investments worth more than USD 1.3 trillion. It is said that China absorbed foreign investments of more than USD 130 billion in 2016 and became the third among those countries that attracted the most foreign investment in the world.

Besides that, China has begun to invest outwardly into foreign countries and foreign enterprises. By the end of 2013, China had cumulatively made a direct foreign investment of USD 525,000 billion in the non-banking fields. In 2013 alone, USD

90,170 million was made by the Chinese investors to 5,090 foreign enterprises in 156 countries and districts in the world.

IV. Political System and Administrative Structure

A. *Introduction*

8. The PRC is a socialist state under the people's democratic dictatorship led by the working class and based on the alliance of workers and peasants. The socialist system is the basic system of China. These basic characteristics of the Chinese national and political system have remained unchanged in the consecutive Constitutions of the PRC.

The Constitution states that the state respects and protects human rights (Article 33 of the Const.) and that it shall practice the rule of law to construct a socialist country ruled by law (Article 5 of the Const.).

9. In accordance with Article 31 of the Const. the state may establish special administrative regions when necessary. The systems to be instituted in those special administrative regions shall be prescribed by law enacted by the National People's Congress (NPC) in the light of special conditions.

Based on this provision, the PRC established the Hong Kong Special Administrative Region on 1 July 1997 and the Macao Special Administrative Region on 20 December 1999, while it continues to exercise sovereignty over each of them. According to the policy of 'one country with two systems', Hong Kong and Macao not only retained their capitalist system after reunification, but can also enjoy their high degree of autonomy according to the Basic Law of Hong Kong Special Administrative Region and the Basic Law of Macao Special Administrative Region, which includes legislative power and the power of final judicial instance. The governor of Macao even has the power to enact administrative regulations and to enforce them.

Taiwan is part of the sacred territory of the PRC. It is the inviolable duty of all Chinese people, including our compatriots in Taiwan, to accomplish the great task of reunifying the motherland. It is well known that Taiwan may enjoy a different social and political system from that of the mainland when China will be reunified. China's policy of being 'one country with two systems' has been consistently used by the Chinese government to resolve the Taiwan problem.

B. *Main Institutions*

10. The Constitution of the PRC provides that all power in China belongs to the people. The NPC and the local people's congresses, at various levels, are the organs through which the people exercise state power.

11. The NPC is the highest organ of state power and its permanent body is the Standing Committee of the NPC. The NPC and its Standing Committee exercise the legislative power of the state. The NPC has the power to amend the Constitution and to enact and amend basic laws governing criminal offences, civil affairs, the state organs and other matters, while the Standing Committee can only interpret the

Constitution and partially supplement and amend laws enacted by the NPC, when the NPC is not in session. However, the laws enacted by the NPC are not supposed to contravene the basic principles of those supplemented or amended laws. The legislative amendments and legislative explanations made within the framework of Chinese laws are part of the key sources of Chinese criminal law (*see also infra*, paragraph 44).

The NPC also has the power to elect the leaders of the state, such as the President and the Vice-President of the State, the Chairman of the Central Military Commission, the Chief Judge of the Supreme People's Court (SPC) and the Procurator-General of the Supreme People's Procuratorate (*see infra* paragraphs 16, 32 and 35). For the position of the Premier of the State Council (i.e., the head of the Central People's Government; *infra*, paragraph 12), the person selected shall be nominated first by the President of the State. Upon nomination by the President of the state, the Congress has the power to decide on the choice of the Premier of the State Council, and upon nomination by the Premier of the State Council, on the choice of the Ministers. Logically, the NPC shall also possess the power to remove from office the persons mentioned above.

The NPC is elected for a term of five years. Its Standing Committee is elected for the same duration and it shall exercise its functions and powers until a new Standing Committee is elected by the succeeding NPC. The Chairman and Vice-Chairman of the Standing Committee shall serve no more than two consecutive terms.

12. The State Council, that is, the Central People's Government of the PRC, is the executive body and the highest organ of state administration.

The Premier assumes overall responsibility for the work of the State Council and the Ministers assume overall responsibility for the work of the ministries and commissions.

The State Council has the power to adopt administrative measures, enact administrative rules and regulations and issue decisions and orders in accordance with the Constitution and the laws, as well as to exercise unified leadership over the work of the ministries, commissions and local organs of state administration at various levels throughout the country. The administrative regulations enacted by the State Council are important parts of Chinese law but they shall not provide direct regulation for the matters of crime and criminal punishment (Article 8 of the Legislation Law of the PRC; *see also infra*, paragraph 42).

It is the State Council's function to direct and administer the affairs of economy, foreign affairs, national defence, education, science, culture, public health, physical culture, urban and rural development, finance, civil affairs, public security, nationalities affairs, judicial administration, supervision and family planning. Definitions in the administrative regulations enacted by the State Council or in the rules adopted by the ministries of the State Council may be useful in the context of Chinese criminal law.

The term of office of the State Council is the same as that of the NPC. The Premier, Vice-Premiers and State Councillors shall serve no more than two consecutive terms.

13. Since the end of 1999, China has been composed of thirty-four territories which have the constitutional status of 'province'. Of them, there are four municipalities directly under the Central Government: Beijing (Peking), Shanghai, Tianjin and Chongqing; five autonomous regions: the Nei Monggol (Inner Mongolia) Autonomous

Region, the Ningxia Hui Autonomous Region, the Xinjiang Uygur (Uighur) Autonomous Region, the Guangxi Zhuang Autonomous Region and the Xizang (Tibet) Autonomous Region; twenty-three provinces: Hebei, Shanxi, Liaoning, Jilin, Helongjian, Shaanxi, Gansu, Qinghai, Shandong, Jiangsu, Anhui, Zhejiang, Jiangxi, Fujian, Taiwan, Henan, Hubei, Hunan, Guangdong, Sichuan, Guizhou, Yunnan, and Hainan; and two special administrative regions: Hong Kong and Macao.

At the provincial level, there are thousands of counties, cities, municipal districts, townships, so-called nationality townships and towns. People's congresses and people's governments are established at various local levels.

14. Local people's congresses at various levels (*see also infra*) are local organs of state power, which establish standing committees. The people's congresses of provinces and municipalities work directly under the Central Government and their standing committees may adopt local regulations, which must not contravene the Constitution and the law and administrative rules and regulations; they shall report such local regulations to the Standing Committee of the NPC. Local people's congresses at and above the county level have the power to alter or annul inappropriate decisions of their own standing committees. The people's congresses at their respective levels elect their leaders and have the power to recall the leaders they have elected. Local people's congresses at and above the county level elect, and have the corresponding power to recall, the Chief Judge of the people's courts and the chief procurators of the people's procuratorates at the corresponding level. However, the election or recall of chief procurators of the people's procuratorates shall be reported to the chief procurators of the people's procurates at the same level for submission to the standing committees of the people's congresses at the corresponding level for approval. The term of office of the people's congresses of provinces, municipalities directly under the Central Government and cities which are divided into districts is five years. By contrast, the term of office of the people's congresses of counties, cities not divided into districts, municipal districts, townships, nationality townships, and towns is three years.

15. Local people's governments at various levels are the executive bodies of local organs of state power as well as the local organs of state administration at the corresponding levels. Governors, mayors and heads of counties, districts, townships and towns assume overall responsibility for local people's governments at various levels.

16. National autonomous regions (*supra*, paragraph 13) establish their own organs of self-government, exercising the functions and powers of local organs. At the same time, they exercise the power of autonomy within the limits of their authority as prescribed by the Constitution, the Law on Regional National Autonomy and other laws. These national autonomous regions will then implement the laws and policies of the state in the light of the existing local situation.

17. The residents committees and villagers committees established among urban and rural residents on the basis of their place of residence are mass organisations of self-management at the grass-roots level, including sub-committees for people's mediation, public security, public health and other matters in order to manage public affairs and social services in their areas, mediate civil disputes, help maintain public order and convey residents' opinions and demands and make suggestions to the people's government. The heads and the working staff of these committees are, formally speaking, not public officials. They are elected by the local people. But when they assist the people's government in exercising certain administrative tasks, such as managing funds and materials for disaster relief, emergency rescue, flood prevention and control, special care for disabled servicemen and aid to the poor and social relief, they shall become the 'state functionaries who perform public services according to law' (Article 93, paragraph 2, *see infra* paragraph 289). Therefore, when they are in the course of performing certain public services, they will fall into the scope of certain criminal law provisions which are specifically provided for the state officials.

C. Parties

18. The Communist Party of China has held the leadership of this country since 1949 when the PRC was established. However, there are in fact eight democratic parties participating in government and political affairs. They are:

- Jiu San (i.e., September Third) Society.
- Taiwan Democratic Self-Government League.
- Revolutionary Committee of the Chinese Kuomingtang (RCCK).
- China Association for Promoting Democracy (CAPD).
- China Democratic National Construction Association (CDNCA).
- China Democratic League.
- Chinese Peasants and Workers Democratic Party (CPWDP).
- China Zhi Gong Party (China Public Interest Party).

In the long period of revolution and construction, before 1949 (*see infra*, paragraph 24), a broad patriotic united front was formed under the leadership of the Communist Party of China. This party is composed of the democratic parties and people's organisations; item braces all socialist working people, all patriots who support socialism and all patriots who stand for the reunification of the motherland. The Chinese People's Political Consultative Conference, a broadly based representative organisation of the united front which has played a significant historical role, plays an important role in the country's political and social life, in promoting friendship with other countries and in the struggle for socialist modernisation and for the reunification and unity of the country.

V. The Judicial System

19. The people's courts are the judicial organs of the state, whereas the people's procuratorates (i.e., the Chinese public prosecution service; *infra*, paragraphs 35 et seq.) are state organs which ensure the correct enforcement of laws. The people's courts and the people's procuratorates exercise their respective judicial and prosecutorial power independently, in accordance with the provisions of the law; they are not subject to interference by any administrative organ, public organisation or individual. However, the people's courts, the people's procuratorates and the public security organs (i.e., the Chinese police; *infra*, paragraph 34) shall, in handling criminal cases, divide their tasks, each taking responsibility for their own work; they shall co-ordinate their efforts and check each other to ensure the correct and effective enforcement of the law.

Under Chinese law and in Chinese legal practice, the term 'judicial personnel' usually refers to personnel engaged in the functions of investigating, prosecuting, adjudicating, supervising and controlling offenders (Article 94 of the CCC (Criminal Code of the PR China)), which will include police, prosecutors as well as penitentiary staff working in prisons (*see also infra*, paragraph 44).

20. The judicial authority of China (*see also infra*, paragraphs 56 et seq.) shall be exercised by the following people's courts:

(1) the Supreme People's Court;
(2) special people's courts; and
(3) local people's courts at various levels.

The SPC is the highest judicial organ. Its judgments and orders are deemed to be final. However, the Chinese SPC does not have the power to rule on the constitutionality of acts passed by the Legislature, i.e., the NPC. It is the NPC Standing Committee's function and power to interpret the Constitution and supervise its enforcement (*supra*, paragraph 11). It should be noted, though, that Hong Kong and Macao enjoy their own power of final instance according to their respective Basic Laws.

The special people's courts encompass military courts, maritime courts and railway transport courts. In 2014, the specialised intellectual property rights was established in Beijing, Shanghai and Guangzhou according to a special decision of the Standing Committee of the NPC.

The local people's courts shall be divided into three levels: the higher people's courts, the intermediate people's courts and the basic people's courts. There are thirty-one higher people's courts, which are established at the provincial level. Taiwan, however, has no people's court. The intermediate people's courts are established at the level of the prefectures in a province or an autonomous region or in a municipality directly under the Central Government. The basic people's courts are established at the level of county and at the level of the city and the municipal district. Furthermore, a basic people's court may set up a number of people's tribunals according to local conditions, population and cases. A people's tribunal shall be part of the basic people' court, and its judgments and orders are considered to be judgments and orders of the basic people's court.

People's courts at all levels may set up criminal divisions, civil divisions, economic divisions, and when necessary, other divisions. For example, the Beijing Intermediate People's Court has set up additional tribunals to try the cases of juvenile delinquency and intellectual property.

21. Finally, it should be noted that there are no specific appeal courts in China. Actually, the courts at and above the level of intermediate people's court shall be the appellate courts for the courts immediately subordinate to them.

§2. THE HISTORICAL BACKGROUND

I. The Classical Development

22. The classical origins of Chinese criminal law might be traced back to as early as the Xia Dynasty (2095 B.C.–1711 B.C.). It was recorded in the Zuo Zhuan, one of the Expositions of the Spring and Autumn Annals, a very famous ancient Chinese history book, that 'There are disorders in Xia Dynasty and Yu (the reputed founder of the Xia Dynasty) makes the law to suppress them'. In like manner to the history of other countries, the earliest Chinese laws were not written laws. The movement of codification began in the Spring and Autumn Period (722 B.C.–221 B.C.). It was said that the earliest written laws were engraved or casted on the surface of a tripod or quadripod in the Kingdoms of Zhen (536 B.C.) and Jin (513 B.C.). After that, Chinese law came out of its secret status and became accessible to the public. Today, we only know fragments of the contents of the earliest written laws through early Chinese publications, some of which were even written on animal bones, tortoise shells and bamboo slip.

Fa Jing, the Book of Law compiled by Kui Li, the Premier Minister of the Kingdom of Wei in the Warring States Period (475 B.C.–221 B.C.), is said to be the earliest Chinese code we have ever known. However, we only know the structure of this code and have to leave its details for further research. There are only six chapters in this code: Theft, Robbery, Arrest, Custody, Miscellanies, and Adjustments. Obviously, this law combines substantive criminal law and criminal procedure. However, it established the basic principles and structure which acted as the foundation for the Chinese feudalist criminal law until the end of the nineteenth century.

23. After the Opium War (Britain's invasion of China, 1840–1842), China gradually changed into a semi-colonial, semi-feudalist society. It was semi-colonial because China had lost its jurisdiction over many areas of foreign concessions, and semi-feudalist because many capitalist elements were introduced into China. The Qing Dynasty began to contemplate legal reform in order to save the Dynasty from being overthrown. Shen Jiaben, the first Chinese jurist with modern democratic ideas, was appointed to be responsible for the drafting of the new criminal code. He invited a Japanese legal scholar, Ogadachotailo, to assist with the creation of a new code in 1907. The New Criminal Code of the Great Qing Dynasty was eventually published on 25 December 1910. However, the Qing Dynasty, the last feudalist dynasty in Chinese history, was overthrown in the revolution of 10 October 1911 and so the aforementioned Code was not actually put into effect. This Code provided, for the first time in Chinese history, a substantive criminal code.

Shen Jiaben also created the draft code of Criminal and Civil Procedure of the Qing Dynasty on 24 January 1911 and although the draft was not published because of the collapse of the Qing Dynasty, the Beijing Government, at the beginning of the Republic of China, adopted it and published it as the Regulation of Procedure.

In the Criminal Code, Shen Jiaben made an extensive reform of the traditional Chinese criminal law system and adopted many legal principles from western countries such as *nullum crimen, nulla poena sine lege*, the concept of specific crimes and the concept of minimum age of criminal responsibility. The western ideal of a punishment system itself was also reflected and incorporated into the Chinese Law. The Code consisted of a General Part and a Specific Part with 53 chapters and 411 articles. However, the reform made the people who insisted on the old systems very angry. They insisted on those provisions which aimed to protect the old feudalist rules and orders. Under the pressure of these 'old liners', Shen Jiaben had to compromise and so constructed a Temporary Provision with five articles as a supplement to the Code, which would, for instance, enhance the punishments for the offences against the royal family and limit the use of self-defence by descendants against their ascendants. These provisions were an embodiment of feudalism and were contrary to the majority of principles of the General Part of the Code.

II. The Period of the Republic of China

24. The revolution of 10 October 1911 led to the fall of the feudal monarchy and gave birth to the Republic of China. However, in the early days of the Republic, China had to practice the law of the Qing Dynasty. Even the name of the New Criminal Code of the Great Qing Dynasty was not changed until later, when it was modified into the Interim New Criminal Code.

On 10 March 1928, the Nanjing Government of the Kuomintang (KMT), after making some revisions to the New Code, published the Criminal Code (now referred to as the Old Criminal Code of the Republic of China). In December 1931, the Nanjing Government established the Committee of the Criminal Code Drafting. Its Draft of the Criminal Code was completed in October 1934 and became law on 1 January 1935.

The Code of Criminal Procedure of the Republic of China (CCP), published on 28 July 1928, was formulated on the basis of the Regulation of Criminal Procedure made by the Beijing Government in the early times of the Republic of China (*supra*). This CCP was re-examined in 1933. In 1935, on the same date as the Criminal Code was published, the new CCP was also published.

In addition to the Codes, the KMT government also made many separate criminal regulations, secretly or openly, whose principles were inconsistent with the Codes.

The Criminal Code and the Criminal Procedure of the Republic of China, as well as its entire legal system, were abolished by the success of the Chinese people's New-Democratic Revolution led by the Communist Party of China in 1949 when the Republic of China was overthrown, and the PRC was established.

III. The Period of the PRC

25. The development of the criminal law of the PRC has experienced a zig-zag course since its founding in 1949.

26. The first stage of the development was from 1949 to 1956. During this stage, the new criminal law for the PRC was established which completely negated the criminal law of the old regime in China and indiscriminately copied the experience of the Soviet Union. On 25 July 1950, the Legal Affairs Committee of the Central

People's Government presented the Draft Outline for the CCC, which signified the start of criminal law in the new China. During the first three years, several criminal regulations were published. Among them, the most influential publications were, first, the Regulation Concerning the Punishment of Counter-Revolution (February 1951) and second, the Regulation Concerning the Punishment of Embezzlement (April 1952).

Chinese legal research and legal education at this stage were subject to very strong Russian influence. A large amount of Soviet articles and books on criminal law and criminal procedure were translated and introduced into the new China, forming the fundamental basis for Chinese criminal law science and legal education. However, after the publication of the first Chinese Constitution of 1954, the Chinese scholarly circle began to explore the legal principles based upon the experiences of the Chinese themselves.

Theoretical research in the criminal law field focused on the drafting of the Criminal Code. From 1950 to June 1957, as many as twenty-two drafts of that code were elaborated. Quite a lot of legislative suggestions were made and many specific issues were discussed in detail.

Generally, at this stage, Chinese criminal law and its academic research remained able to positively influence the development of the Chinese criminal law. However, the strong influence of the ultra-'left' school of thought, which insisted that the theory of criminal law should serve the need of the political regime, negated the independence of this discipline and so prevented the progression of any further and systematical research into the theory of criminal law.

27. The second stage of the development of the new Chinese criminal law was from 1957 to 1966, which was a very depressing period for Chinese legal scholars.

The ultra-'left' school of thought considering that law would be useless for a new China and should be replaced by policy, was rampant. Legal academic research initially continued only in a small circle and eventually stagnated. Except for very few articles and translations in the early stages, there were hardly any academic publications. Even the drafting of the Criminal Code was put on hold until 1962.

Significant criminal laws of this stage were the Decrees Concerning the Special Amnesty of the War Criminals, Counter-Revolutionaries and Ordinary Criminals. Other criminal punishments were provided in new economic and administrative regulations.

28. The third stage was a very miserable one. This stage took place during the so-called Cultural Revolution, and lasted for ten years, from 1966 until 1976. Within this period, the legal journals were stopped; the law faculties were closed, except for those of Peking University and Jilin University; the theory of criminal law was criticised by the revolutionaries at that time; academic research was inexistent, and even the very notion of criminal law science was replaced by criminal policy. In sum, the Chinese criminal justice system and its legal doctrine were totally destroyed. The Chinese Communist Party and the Chinese people had to suffered great pains and losses from this lawless state.

29. A new era began in 1976, when the Chinese Communist Party advocated the rule of law after correcting the serious mistakes of the Cultural Revolution. With the promulgation of the Criminal Code and Criminal Procedure of the PRC in 1979, the great development of Chinese criminal law started. Dozens of law faculties, institutions, and colleges were recovered or newly established, legal periodicals were re-opened and hundreds of books and thousands of articles on law began to appear. The Chinese academic circle of criminal law, like the whole legal circle, was able to flourish once again.

Today, law faculties and law schools are the most popular departments in Chinese universities, Chinese society is developing, and its planned economy is transitioning into a market economy. The principle of ruling by law and the ambition to develop a country governed by the rule of law have been added to the Constitution of the PRC. In 1997, the Chinese Criminal Code was revised and re-promulgated. The Chinese criminal law is moving towards a modern legal system which will be able to suit the needs of a socialist market economy. Chinese criminal law scholars play an important role in helping develop this new system.

§3. Criminal Law, Criminal Justice and Criminal Science

I. Definitions of Criminal Law

A. Criminal Law

30. Criminal law in China can be briefly described as the body of laws which define criminal offences and criminal punishments.

In accordance with the guiding ideology of Marxism-Leninism-Mao Zedong, the ruling class considers Chinese criminal law as a branch of law which shall be used for safeguarding the interests of state, society and people.

Article 28 of the Const. sets that the state maintains public order and suppresses treasonable and other criminal activities that endanger national security, it penalises criminal activities that endanger public security and disrupt the socialist economy as well as other criminal activities, and it punishes and reforms criminals. In accordance with this provision, Article 2 of the CCC of 1997 (the Chinese Criminal Code) defines the task of Chinese criminal law as follows:

> The tasks of Chinese criminal law are to use criminal punishments to fight against all criminal acts in order to defend the national security, to safeguard the regime of the people's democratic dictatorship and the socialist system; to protect property owned by the state and property collectively owned by the working people; to protect the citizens' privately owned lawful property; to protect the citizens' rights of the person and their democratic and other rights; to maintain social order and economic order; and to safeguard the smooth progress of the cause of the socialist construction.

This provision clearly shows the understanding of the intrinsic value of criminal law in China.

B. *Criminal Offence: Definition and Characteristics*

31. According to the principle of legality, a harmful act shall not be judicially dealt with as a crime unless it is set as so in the criminal law. Prior to the enactment of criminal legislation, an act may already be considered a crime due to its high degree of social harmfulness. The definition of a crime which has not yet become a legal one is of a political nature, because it mainly explains 'why' an act shall be dealt with as a crime. Once defined by the criminal law, a crime becomes a real crime. The statutory definition determines what act is criminal and will be directly used by the judicial personnel, especially by judges to convict (or acquit) suspects.

32. Interestingly, the CCC gives a general legal definition of a crime. According to Article 13 of the CCC:

> A crime refers to an act that endangers the sovereignty, territorial integrity and/or security of the state, divides the state, subverts the state power of the people's democratic dictatorship and overthrows the socialist system, undermines public and economic order, violates state owned property, property collectively owned by the working people, or property privately owned by citizens, infringes on citizens' civil (or 'personal') rights, their democratic or other rights, and any other act that endangers society and is subject to punishment according to law. However, an act that is clearly of minor importance and little harm shall not be considered a crime.

33. In accordance with the current theory of Chinese criminal law, a crime shall bear the following three characteristics.

First and foremost, a crime should be harmful to society. Without social harmfulness, no conduct can be deemed to be a crime. The harmfulness may be caused to the state, the collectivity or an individual; however, it should attain a certain degree of seriousness. It is indeed one of the most important aspects of Chinese criminal law to determine the degree of social harmfulness which has been caused by a crime.

Second, a crime should violate the criminal law. This characteristic actually reflects in the law the requirement of social harmfulness. Violating the criminal law means that the behaviour should be in conformity with not only the objective elements, i.e., an act or omission, but also with the subjective elements, i.e., intent or negligence, which are prescribed by the criminal law. However, a mere violation of an economic or administrative regulation is not deemed to be a crime.

Third and finally, a criminal offence should be a violation so serious that it attracts criminal punishment. This characteristic is also clearly reflected in the criminal law. In the whole Specific Part of the Chinese Criminal Code, the degree of the social harmfulness and thus seriousness of the offence is, for instance, signalled by the following elements: serious or flagrant circumstances, serious criminal consequences, serious danger, a relatively large amount of money or serious damage, a certain capacity or function of a perpetrator, a criminal method described by law, a specific mental state, a specific intention, and the fact that the perpetrator is acting as the ringleader.

34. China is a developing country even in the sense of the rule of law. The division of various concepts of crime helps people understand the different characteristics of the acts before and after the enactment of criminal legislation and enhance their sense to the principle of legality. People can then easily understand that a crime in the Chinese criminal law can only be referred according to the legislative definition. The reason why this point is important in Chinese criminal law theory is that the theory was founded at a time when the principle of legality was not recognised. According to the new understandings, the judicial concept of crime shall take the violation of criminal law as its first characteristic, though the social harmfulness took the first position in the old understanding. The nature of social harmfulness still plays important role in the legislative concept of crime, but in the judicial concept, it can only play a secondary role in nature, though not totally disappeared.

II. Characteristics of Criminal Law

35. Criminal law in China is substantive law. It is concerned with the general conditions of criminal liability, deals with definitions of specific criminal offences, and includes the types of criminal punishment and the principles for imposing them.

Chinese substantive law is laid down in the Chinese Criminal Code of 1997, which is a revised version of the Criminal Code of 1979, and in separate criminal laws which have amended and supplemented the 1997 Criminal Code.

36. Criminal procedure is regarded as a separate discipline, even though it is closely linked with criminal law. Chinese criminal procedure concerns the principle of criminal proceedings, the organisation and the procedure of the criminal investigation, prosecution, trial, and execution.

Chinese criminal procedure can be found in the Chinese Criminal Procedure of 1996, which is a revised version of the Criminal Procedure of 1979.

37. Criminal law in China is punitive law. When an act fulfils the requirements provided by the criminal law, according to the rule of *nulla poena sine lege*, and when this act should therefore be subject to some type of criminal punishment, criminal punishment will be imposed.

In light of Article 13 of the CCC (*supra*, paragraph 32), an act that is clearly of minor importance and causes little harm, as defined by the criminal Law itself or, more often, by the judicial explanations (*infra*, paragraph 60), shall not be considered a crime. The difference between crime and non-crime, or guilty and innocent, is called the 'guilty line' or threshold of a crime in Chinese criminal law theory.

For those acts which are below the guilty line, they might be treated as violation of laws or disciplines and subject to administrative sanctions or disciplinary measures, which are issued by the central government, corporations, units and parties.

The possibility to deprive a person of his personal freedom is not a unique characteristic of criminal law. A deprivation of freedom may also be the result of administrative sanctions. Before the end of 2013, there was the so-called system of Education through Labour within the administrative sanction, which could deprive people of personal freedom for up to four years. Fortunately, this system was abolished. However, administrative sanction today still includes the sanction which can deprive people of personal freedom for fifteen to twenty days. This type of sanction is decided by policeman, without judicial trial or legal defence, though an afterward judicial review is possible. The reform of administrative sanction is still going on in China.

38. Chinese criminal law is also educational and reformative law. Ancient Chinese legal philosophy advocates that it shall abolish punishment by applying punishment and stop killing by inflicting killing. In modern time, Article 46 of the CCC sets that anyone with the ability to work shall take part in labour, receive education, and undergo reform.

In practice, education and reform of criminals is a comprehensive programme. It is composed of the requirements of labour and a systematic education in ideology and politics, pleading guilty and observing the law, acquiring literacy as well as some professional training (*infra*, paragraph 599). Labour helps the criminal cultivate a good working behaviour and learn some manufacturing skills.

Through labour and education criminals might correct their attitudes towards the commission of crime and thus abstain from further crime. The policy of education and reform has achieved very good results in China: not only ordinary criminals, but also the last Chinese Emperor and Japanese war criminals were reformed to be new men, committed to the modernisation and construction of the PRC.

39. Furthermore, by punishing individual criminals, Chinese criminal law aims to encourage ordinary people in society to fight crime in all respects, to strengthen their confidence in the rule of law and to greatly deter potential criminals from committing crimes.

III. The Forms of Criminal Law

40. In the broadest sense, criminal law in China can be subdivided into three types of criminal law.

41. The first type of criminal law is the Chinese Criminal Code which was adopted during the Second Session of the Fifth NPC on 1 July 1979 and revised during the Fifth Session of the Eighth NPC on 14 March 1997. The revised Code has been in force since 1 October 1997. Informally, people refer to these two versions of Criminal Code as two codes: the Criminal Code of 1979 and the Criminal Code of 1997.

42. The second type of criminal law consists of separate criminal laws. They are regulations or decisions supplementing the Criminal Codes. Between 1979 and 1997, the Standing Committee of the NPC enacted twenty-three separate criminal laws, which can be divided into two groups. According to Article 452 of the 1997 CCC, the laws in Group One were totally incorporated in the revised Criminal Code of 1997 and are no longer be applicable as of the entry into force of the Criminal Code. According to the same article, the laws in Group Two were maintained as special laws, as far as the provisions containing administrative penalties and administrative measures are concerned. By contrast the provisions on criminal responsibility in those laws shall be prevailed by those of the CCC as of the date the CCC went into effect, since they had been incorporated in the Criminal Code. In what follows, we give an overview of these two groups of separate criminal laws:

– Group One:

(1) Interim Regulations on the Punishment of Servicemen Who Commit Crimes Contrary to Their Duties (adopted on 10 June 1981 and effective as of 1 January 1982).
(2) Decision Regarding the Handling of Criminals Undergoing Reform Through Labour and Persons Undergoing Rehabilitation Through Labour Who Escape or Commit New Crimes (adopted on 10 June 1981 and effective as of 10 July 1981).
(3) Decision Regarding the Severe Punishment of Criminals Who Seriously Sabotage the Economy (adopted on 8 March 1982).
(4) Decision Regarding the Severe Punishment of Criminals Who Seriously Endanger Public Security (adopted on 2 September 1983).
(5) Supplementary Provisions Concerning the Punishment of Crimes of Smuggling (adopted on 21 January 1988).
(6) Supplementary Provisions Concerning the Punishment of Crimes of Embezzlement and Bribery (adopted on 21 January 1988).
(7) Supplementary Provisions Concerning the Punishment of Crimes of Divulging State Secrets (adopted on 5 September 1988).
(8) Supplementary Provisions Concerning the Punishment of Crimes of Catching or Killing Precious and Endangered Species of Wildlife under Special State Protection (adopted on 8 November 1988).
(9) Decision Regarding the Punishment of Crimes of Insulting the National Flag and the National Emblem of the PRC (adopted on 28 June 1990).
(10) Supplementary Provisions Concerning the Punishment of Crimes of Unlawfully Excavating the Sites of Ancient Culture or Ancient Tombs (adopted on 29 June 1991).
(11) Decision Regarding the Punishment of Criminals Who Hijack Aircrafts (adopted on 28 December 1992).
(12) Supplementary Provisions Concerning the Punishment of Crimes of Counterfeiting Registered Trademark (adopted on 22 February 1993).
(13) Decision Regarding the Punishment of Crimes of Manufacturing and Trading in Counterfeit and Inferior Goods (adopted on 2 July 1993).
(14) Decision Regarding the Punishment of Crimes of Infringement of Copyright (adopted on 5 July 1994).
(15) Decision Regarding the Punishment of Crimes Against the Company Law (adopted on 28 February 1995).

– Group Two:

(1) Decision Regarding the Prohibition of Drugs (adopted on 28 December 1990).
(2) Decision Regarding the Severe Punishment of Criminals Who Smuggle, Manufacture, Sell and Disseminate Obscene Articles (adopted on 28 December 1990).
(3) Decision Regarding the Severe Punishment of Prostitution and Visiting Prostitution (adopted on 4 September 1991).
(4) Decision Regarding the Severe Punishment of Criminals Who Abduct, Sell and Kidnap Women and Children (adopted on 4 September 1991).

(5) Supplementary Provisions Concerning the Punishment of Crimes of Tax Evasion and Refusal to Pay Taxes (adopted on 4 September 1992).
(6) Supplementary Provisions on the Severe Punishment of Crimes of Organising or Transporting Other Person(s) to Illegally Cross the National Border (adopted on 5 March 1994).
(7) Decision Regarding the Punishment of Crimes Disrupting Financial Order (adopted on 30 June 1995).
(8) Decision Regarding the Punishment of Crimes of Falsely Making or, Forging or Illegally Selling Special Invoices for Value-added Tax (adopted on 30 October 1995).

However, after the promulgation of the Criminal Code of 1997, the Chinese legislature improved its legislative skills and promulgated the Legislation Law of the PRC in 2000. As a result, the use of supplementary regulations and decisions, which had been so popularly adopted after 1979 and before 1997, became very rare. After 1997, only one such decision was adopted: the Decision Concerning Punishment of Criminal Offences Involving Fraudulent Purchase, enacted by the NPC Standing Committee on 29 December of 1998. After 2000, the main methods to revise or supplement the Criminal Code are amendments and legislative explanations. By the end of 2016, nine amendments of the Criminal Code were enacted by the Standing Committee of the NPC: the amendment of 1999, August and December of 2001, 2002, 2005, 2006, 2009, 2011, and 2015. Besides that, thirteen legislative explanations were provided by the Standing Committee of the NPC. The amendments revise, add or delete the provisions in the Criminal Code, while the legislative explanations only interpret the existing wording of the provisions in the Criminal Code.

43. The third type of criminal law is composed of criminal provisions in Chinese economic, administrative and even civil regulations, such as the Environmental Protection Law, the Law on the Protection of Cultural Relics, the Food Hygiene Law, the Patent Law and the Trademark Law. There are dozens of criminal provisions of this kind. However, these criminal provisions do not provide for detailed definitions of specific crimes, nor for the specific applicable sanctions. Therefore, these criminal provisions cannot be directly and independently applied without the guidance from the Chinese Criminal Code, because they are designed in the form of either principled provisions, which generally prescribe certain conduct as criminally punishable, or merely refer to provisions in the Criminal Code.

IV. Overview of the Criminal Justice System

44. The criminal justice system of the PRC is generally similar that of most countries and comprises authorities in charge of law enforcement, adjudication and the execution of judicial decisions. It consists of the police, the public prosecution service, judicial authorities and correctional agencies. The 'judicial personnel' has a general meaning and refers to personnel engaged in the functions of investigating, prosecuting, adjudicating, supervising and controlling offenders (Article 94 of the CCC).

In what follows, we will briefly present these different actors. More details can be found in Part II of the monograph.

A. The Police

45. In China the term 'police' first of all refers to public security organs. Besides that, the term police statutorily also covers those working in State security organs, prisons and organs in charge of re-education through labour, as well as judicial policemen working at the people's courts (*supra*, paragraphs 18 et seq.) and the people's procuratorates (Article 2, paragraph 2 of the People's Police Law; *see also infra*, paragraphs 48 et seq.). These different types of policemen only work in their specific areas, where they shall exercise their functions and powers in accordance with the respective provisions of relevant laws and administrative rules and regulations.

It should be noted that the term police does not cover the People's Armed Police Force (the PAPF), which is an integral part of the country's armed forces (Article 2, paragraph 2 of the Law of the PAPF).

46. Moreover, in particular, the public security organs of the PRC consist of the Ministry of Public Security, the local public security organs, the public security organs in various ministries and basic public security organs.

The Ministry of Public Security is responsible, under the leadership of the State Council, for the national public security and commands the public security force of the whole country.

The local public security organs are a component of the local governments at the various levels and shall be subject themselves to the hierarchic professional leadership.

The basic public security organs are the public security stations in townships, towns, and sub-district offices in cities.

Furthermore, public security organs are also established in the Ministries of Railway, Communications, and Forestry as well as in the General Administration of Civil Aviation. They shall also be subject to the professional leadership from the Ministry of Public Security.

47. A public security organ is a state organ specialised in maintaining public order and safeguarding public security. Within a public security organ, there are units of public order, household register, traffic, fire arms, economic and cultural protection, departure and entrance registration, criminal investigation and preliminary examination.

In criminal proceedings, a public security organ is responsible for carrying out, in accordance with the law, the criminal investigation, preliminary examination, arrest and detention. It advises the people's procuratorate (*infra*, paragraphs 48 et seq.) on whether the prosecution should be launched, executes judgments and supervises criminals who are given a non-custodial sentence.

48. The public security organs are usually responsible for domestic affairs only. There is another state security organ specialised in dealing with matters of national security, such as espionage. That being said, the public security organs and the national security organs shall take the responsibility of criminal investigation, each respectively according to the law.

Unlike the armed police in the People's Liberation Army (hereinafter: PLA), the public security organ is not in the array of the PLA. The armed police's tasks generally include protection and safeguard of the important objects, such as factories, bridges, tunnels, and governmental offices. Normally, the armed police do not get involved in a criminal investigation.

B. The Prosecution Service

49. The public prosecution service is called the people's procuratorate in the PRC.

In the Chinese criminal justice system, the public security organ (the police) does not retain the power to launch prosecution by itself but it merely investigates cases and advise the people's procuratorate with respect to initiating the public prosecution (*supra*, paragraph 47). Article 167 of the Chinese Criminal Procedure sets that all cases requiring initiation of a public prosecution shall be examined and decided by the people's procuratorates.

50. The power of prosecution shall be exercised by the following people's procuratorates:

(1) the Supreme People's Procuratorate;
(2) special people's procuratorates, including the military procuratorate and the railway transport procuratorate; and
(3) local people's procuratorates at various levels.

Furthermore, the local people's procuratorates at various levels shall be divided into:

(a) the people's procuratorates of provinces, autonomous regions, and municipalities directly under the Central Government;
(b) branches of the people's procuratorates of provinces, autonomous regions, and municipalities directly under the Central Government, and people's procuratorates of autonomous prefectures and cities directly under the provincial governments; and
(c) people's procuratorates of counties, cities, autonomous counties and municipal districts.

People's procuratorates at the provincial or county level may, according to work requirements and upon the approval of the standing committee of the people's congress at the corresponding level, set up people's procuratorates as their agencies in industrial and mining areas, agricultural reclamation areas, forest zones, etc.

51. The Supreme People's Procuratorate shall direct the work of the people's procuratorates at various local levels and of the special people's procuratorates; the people's procuratorates at higher levels shall direct the work of those at lower levels.

People's procuratorates at all levels shall each have a chief procurator, a number of deputy chief procurators and procurators. The chief procurator exercises unified leadership over the work of the procuratorate. People's procuratorates at all levels shall each set up a procuratorial committee. The procuratorial committee shall apply the system of democratic centralism and, under the direction of the chief procurator, hold discussions and make decisions on important cases and other major issues. In the case of the chief procurator disagreeing with the majority's opinion over a decision on an important issue, the matter may be reported to the standing committee of the people's congresses at the corresponding level for a final decision.

52. People's procuratorates at all levels exercise various functions and powers. They shall:

(1) exercise procuratorial authority over cases of treason, cases involving acts to dismember the state and other major criminal cases severely impeding the unified enforcement of state policies, laws, decrees and administrative orders;
(2) conduct investigations on criminal cases directly handled by themselves;
(3) review cases investigated by public security organs and determine whether to approve arrest, to prosecute or to exempt from prosecution; and exercise supervision over the investigator activities of public security organs to determine whether they are in conformity with the law;
(4) initiate public prosecutions of criminal cases and support such prosecutions; exercise supervision over the judicial activities of people's courts to determine whether they conform to the law; and
(5) exercise supervision over the execution of judgments and orders in criminal cases and over the activities of prisons, detention houses and organs in charge of reform through labour, to determine whether such execution and activities conform to the law.

C. Investigating Jurisdiction

53. As mentioned above (*supra*, paragraphs 33 and 36), both the public security organs (the police) and the people's procuratorates are responsible for the criminal investigation. Investigating jurisdiction in China is thus divided among the public security organ and the procuratorate.

Besides that, Article 18, paragraph 3 of CCP also sets that cases of private prosecution (*infra*, paragraphs 376 and 461) shall be directly accepted by people's courts.

Special investigating powers apply to offences committed in the Army or in prison (*infra*, paragraph 56).

54. In accordance with Article 18 of the CCP, investigation in criminal cases shall be conducted by the public security organs, except when otherwise provided by law. Crimes of embezzlement and bribery, crimes of dereliction of duty committed by state functionaries, and crimes involving violations of a citizen's civil or personal rights (such as illegal detention, extortion of confessions by torture, retaliation, frame-up and illegal search) and crimes involving infringement of a citizen's democratic rights committed by state functionaries taking advantage of their functions and powers shall be put on file for investigation by the people's procuratorates. If cases involving other grave crimes committed by state functionaries taking advantage of their functions and powers need to be handled directly by the people's procuratorates, they may be placed on file for investigation by the people's procuratorates upon decision by the people's procuratorates at or above the provincial level. This statutory provision is necessary to deal with the cases where the state functionaries concerned are hierarchically at the higher position than the police or the prosecutor who have duty to investigate.

55. In accordance with Article 4 of the CCP, state security organs shall, handle cases of crimes that endanger state security, performing the same functions and powers as the public security organs. Accordingly, cases involving crimes of plotting to subvert the government or dismember the state and to overthrow the socialist system, joining an espionage organisation or accepting a mission assigned by the espionage organisation or its agency, stealing, secretly gathering, buying or supplying state secrets, instigating, luring or bribing a state functionary to defect to the enemy, and other sabotage activities endangering the state's security shall be investigated by the state security organs.

56. Furthermore, in accordance with Article 290 of the CCP, the security departments of the Army shall exercise the power of investigation with respect to criminal offences that have occurred in the Army. Crimes committed by criminals in prison shall be investigated by the prison.

Of course, the security department of the Army and the prison shall handle the criminal cases also in accordance with the CCP.

D. *Trial Jurisdiction*

57. As can be seen above (*supra*, paragraphs 19–20), trial jurisdiction in China is divided among the SPC, higher people's courts, intermediate people's courts and basic people's courts, as well as special people's courts.

58. The SPC is the highest judicial organ of the state. In addition to supervising the administration of justice by the local people's courts at various levels and by the special people's courts, it shall handle the following cases:

(1) cases of first instance which are assigned by laws and decrees to its jurisdiction or which are in principle major criminal cases of national significance;
(2) cases of appeals lodged by the accused and of protests lodged against judgments and orders of higher people's courts and special people's courts lodged by the prosecutor; and
(3) cases of protests lodged by the Supreme People's Procuratorate in accordance with the procedure of judicial supervision.

59. The special people's courts are established for specific industries such as military, railway transportation, maritime and intellectual property. However, the special people's courts which have jurisdiction over criminal cases are only the military and railway transportation courts. And these courts shall only handle the cases within those special industries.

60. The higher people's courts and the intermediate people's courts shall handle the following cases:

(1) cases of first instance assigned to its jurisdiction by laws and decrees;
(2) cases of first instance transferred from the people's courts at lower levels when necessary; in recent years, this is often for trying corruption cases;

(3) cases of appeals and of protests lodged against judgments and orders of people's courts at lower levels; and
(4) cases of protests lodged by people's procuratorates in accordance with the procedures of judicial supervision.

61. Basic people's courts shall adjudicate criminal and civil cases of first instance, except for cases which are assigned to other courts by laws or decrees. In addition, basic people's courts shall settle civil disputes and handle minor criminal cases not requiring a trial and direct the work of people's mediation committees and the local judicial assistants (cf. *infra*, paragraph 386).

If the basic people's court or the intermediate people's court considers that a criminal or civil case which it is handling is of major importance and requires a trial by a people's court at a higher level, it may request that the case be transferred to that court for trial.

62. The people's courts of China shall in principle apply the system whereby the second instance decision is final.

However, cases involving death sentences shall be reported to the SPC for examination and approval by the SPC, no matter whether the accused has appealed. The procedure for review of the death sentence is provided in Chapter 4, Part Three of the Code of Criminal Procedure. In 2006, the Chinese legislature revised the Organic Law of the People's Court (OLPC). Since then, the SPC may no longer authorise lower courts such as higher people's courts of provinces, autonomous regions, and municipalities which are directly under the Central Government to exercise this power and to approve cases involving the imposition of death sentences.

Furthermore, for a situation involving error in the determination of facts or the application of the law in a final judgment or order, there is a procedure for trial supervision available for retrial, which is provided in Chapter 5, Part Three of the Code of Criminal Procedure.

E. Prison System and After-Care

63. The prison institutions used to have a common name: labour reform organs. The system of the labour reform organs was formally founded in 1951. In accordance with the PRC Regulation on Reform through Labour of 1954, the labour reform organs included prisons, supervision teams of reform through labour, management and education houses for juvenile delinquents (the juvenile house), and jail. However, after the promulgation of the Chinese Prison Law (CPL) in 1994, the prison system in China has been reformed and the term now only refers to prisons and management and education houses for juvenile delinquents.

64. As a consequence, prisons are now the main organs of the state in charge of executing criminal punishments (Article 2 of the Prison Law). According to the provisions on management by classification (meaning that inmates shall be categorised in different custody and control regimes) set in the CPL, Chinese prisons can be roughly classified into three categories: (1) prisons for felons who were sentenced to the death penalty with a two-year suspension, to life imprisonment or to a fixed-term imprisonment of more than ten years; (2) prisons for normal prisoners who were sentenced to fixed-term imprisonments of less than ten years; and (3) prisons only for female adult prisoners. Foreign prisoners, prisoners who were convicted as accomplices and the prisons with minority nationality are usually placed in a separate team (*infra*, paragraphs 581 et seq.). By 2012, there were 681 prisons in China with 1.64 million prisoners, of whom 30% were in prison for committing felonies. There were around thirty prisons for female prisoners with 93,051 inmates by 2011. With the abolition of the system of Education through Labour (*supra*, paragraph 37), 351 places thereof have been gradually closed or transformed into places specifically dealing with drug addicts or sexual offenders (*infra*, paragraph 604).

65. Management and education houses for juvenile delinquents were principally designed for juvenile criminals and juvenile delinquents (*infra*, paragraph 604). After the promulgation of the 1994 CPL, they became a type of prison only for minor inmates, which include those who have reached the age of 14 but not yet the age of 18 (*infra*, paragraph 118) and who were sentenced by the people's courts to a fixed-term imprisonment or life imprisonment. If a juvenile delinquent has reached the age of 18 and the remaining term of his sentence does not exceed two years, he may still be kept in the juvenile house for the execution of the remaining term of his sentence.

Currently, those who cannot be criminally punished because they have not reached the age of 16 shall be taken in by the government for re-education in accordance with the regulation of the Chinese Criminal Code and can be held in a juvenile house. A new arrangement is, however, under consideration.

The policy of the juvenile houses is that they 'rely mainly on reform through education while making light work subsidiary'. The reasoning underlining the punishment of juvenile delinquents is different from that for the adult. The main objectives of this punishment shall be to acquire an elementary education and production skills: Article 75 of the CPL explicitly provides that the execution of criminal punishments imposed on juvenile delinquents shall be focused on education and reform, and that labour for juvenile delinquents shall be adjusted to the characteristics of minors.

The basic policy for juvenile delinquency was formulated in early 1980s and has been applied ever since. Accordingly, juvenile delinquency shall be treated in a similar way to how parents treat their children who suffer from infectious diseases, or as medical doctors treat their patients or as teachers treat their pupils who have made mistakes, so that the juvenile delinquent shall be educated, reclaimed and saved. The working time for juvenile delinquents shall not be more than four hours per day and not more than 24 hours per week and those who have not yet reached 16 years old shall not work. In the Outline of Education and the Reform of Prisoners compiled by the Chinese Ministry of Justice, it is set that the teaching hours for the minors shall not be less than 1,000 class hours per year, while the teaching hours for adult prisoners are not less than 500 class hours per year.

The policy and practice of educating juvenile delinquent work well. During the period of 2002–2012, the recidivist rate of juvenile delinquents was below 2%. The population of juvenile delinquents in juvenile houses was 18,450 in 2010 and 16,701 in 2011 (i.e., according to the most recently available statistics).

66. The prison system is under the leadership of the Administration of Labour Reform, which is now a department of the Ministry of Justice of the PRC. There are offices of this Administration at the provincial level. The Administration of Labour

Reform and its offices at various levels have divisions of political work, prison management, education, productive affairs, finance, after-care and other professional divisions.

In China, criminal detention is a kind of criminal punishment with a short term of more than one month and less than six months (*infra*, paragraph 328). According to the CCL, criminals who are serving their term of criminal detention may return home for one or two days per month and receive suitable compensation for their works. In places where prison is too far away, criminal detention may be served in a jail, which is not a prison, under the control of the public security organ.

67. The system of after-care in China is called the '(re)settlement of a prisoner after release' (*infra*, paragraph 68). It is an important part of the policy of maintaining social public order in a comprehensive way, which is the basic policy to prevent and control crime in order to maintain social public security in China.

Before the early stage of the opening and reform period at the beginning of the 1980s and under the restrictions of the planned economy model, the method of employment inside the place for reform through labour after serving a sentence had been adopted. The system of after-care then used to be composed of two parts: settlement through social employment or through employment in the place where the prison was located. The latter is for those who had no home in their original place of residence or were afraid that their victims might make reprisals upon them. The compulsory permanent employment, which is based on the Decision Regarding the Handling of Criminals Undergoing Reform Through Labour and Persons Undergoing Rehabilitation Through Labour Who Escape or Commit New Crime and applicable to those criminals such as recidivists, is no longer a practice, especially after 1997 when the new Criminal Code explicitly invalidated the Decision (Article 452 in Appendix I).

Following the opening and reform period, China has been moving towards a market economy and the settlement after completely serving the term of a sentence has been moving in line with the direction of marketisation and socialisation. Article 35 of the 1994 CPL illustrates the trend, by providing that the prison shall release those whose sentences have been completely served and issue them a certificate of release in a timely manner. Today, China releases about 200,000–300,000 prisoners annually. The good work of settlement after release from punishment is significant for China's social security.

68. Although improvement keeps going on, the current after-care system consists of three stages.

The first stage begins at three months before the planned release. Prisons shall provide some education regarding release to the prisoners who will soon be completing their terms, then make an appraisal of their performance during their time in prison, inform the public security authorities of the places where they will return, and co-ordinate with other units and organisations to resolve specific problems in the settlement and the education through assistance. For those prisoners who have seriously evil habits, whose educational effects are not satisfactory and who therefore have recidivist tendencies, the prison shall alert the local public security of the necessity of careful management, ensuring the maintenance of supervision following a release from prison. Before releasing a prisoner, the prison shall issue a certificate of release when he has completed service of his sentence (Article 35 of the CPL). After he is released, the public security organ shall make a residence registration for him on his certificate of release (Article 36 of the CPL).

The second stage is resettlement. In accordance with the Prison Law, the local people's government shall assist the person who is released after serving his sentence. If the person has lost his ability to work and has no statutory supporters or basic source of income, the local people's government shall offer him relief including, for instance, when necessary, an allowance or a place to live (Article 37). After 2009, when the system of community correction was introduced nationwide into trial use, settlement became the most important part of that system at the local level. Various governmental agencies are involved in assisting released persons who have not found a job. Labour offices shall provide them with employment guidance and skill training and issue doles according to the regulations applicable to those who have participated in the programme of unemployment insurance. Offices of industrial and commercial administrations shall offer equal treatment to the applications submitted by those who want to open an individual business or other economic entities and shall protect their lawful interests. These offices shall also work with other organisations in order to ascertain the security responsibility system and to ensure their operations are complying with law. Offices of civil administration shall encourage local economic entities to help with the settlement. Public security stations shall establish a responsibility system to help and educate the released persons. Prisons shall carry out a system of regular inspection and local feedback for those who are released during the first three years. In sum, all these elements show that China is trying to establish a system which is organised by prisons, local governments, employment units and the families of the released persons, so that they can receive better help and education.

Finally, the third stage is to help the released persons resolve various specific problems in order to encourage them to integrate more easily into society. It is true that, according to the law, a person released after serving his sentence shall enjoy rights that are equal to other citizens. Furthermore, there are certain informal practices in China to help released persons avoid committing new crimes. The most common one is to conclude a joint agreement of assistant education by the prison, the local government, the employer and the family of the released. This may ensure that the released persons receive some help in getting accommodation as well as regularly get education in observing the laws and regulations, to avoid reoffending. By 2011, there were 3.8 million released persons, of whom 1.95 million received help and education and 1.68 million were effectively settled. The settlement of released persons is very difficult. However, the crime-preventive effects of this system are significant: the recidivist rate of released persons is only 0.9%.

F. The Bar

69. The Bar is evidently an important institution in relation to the criminal justice system. It is generally acknowledged that Deng Xi (BC 545–501), an official of the Kingdom of Zhen in the Spring and Autumn Period, was the first (practising) lawyer in China. However, it was not until 1906 that the position and function of a lawyer was recognised by the Criminal and Civil Procedure of Great Qing Dynasty.

After the foundation of the PRC, in the mid-1950s, the new Chinese Bar was established. However, the Bar was abolished at the end of 1957 due to the emerging beliefs that the lawyer played the role of absolving the criminal from guilt, leading to the lawyer's loss of position in society. Until 1979, the Chinese Bar therefore did not play a role in the criminal justice system.

A new era began at the end of the 1970s. The Constitution of the PRC of 1978 reestablished a defence system in the legal system of this country. The Code of Criminal Procedure of 1979 explicitly provided the principle that a defendant should have the right to a defence Lawyer and contained a special chapter on 'Defence'. In 1980, the Interim Regulation of the PRC on Lawyers was promulgated, providing the legal foundation for re-establishing the Chinese Bar.

In 1996, the Lawyers Law of the PRC was promulgated, contributing to the further development of a Bar with Chinese socialist characteristic. By now, the Lawyers Law has been revised three times (in 2001, 2007 and 2012), and Chinese practising lawyers play an even more important position in the Chinese justice system. Chinese law firms are nowadays no longer only state-owned; they can also be a co-operation or a partnership. Foreign law firms are also allowed to open their office in China.

70. In accordance with the Lawyers Law, the term 'lawyer' refers to a practitioner who has acquired a lawyer's practice certificate pursuant to law and provides legal services to the public (Article 2). To be eligible as a PRC lawyer, a person shall uphold the Constitution of the PRC, pass the examination of the Bar and possess the qualification as a lawyer, have practical experience at a law firm for a full year, and be a person of good character and conduct (Article 5). A person having no capacity for civil acts or having limited capacity for civil acts, having been subjected to criminal punishment with exception for a crime of negligence, having been discharged from public employment, or having his lawyer's practice certificate revoked shall not be issued a lawyer's practice certificate (Article 7).

A lawyer in China shall practise in a law firm. When a lawyer undertakes business, the law firm shall centrally accept authorisation, sign written authorisation contracts with the clients and, according to state regulations, collect fees from the parties and truthfully enter them in its accounts (Article 25).

71. In criminal cases, for the purposes of legal defence, the defendant may entrust citizens other than lawyers recommended by a people's organisation or the entity to which the defendant belongs (such as the company where he works or the school where he studies), or other citizens permitted by the people's court. These citizens are called 'defenders'. However, it is the lawyers' privilege to consult the file record of the current case, to acquaint themselves with the circumstances of the case, to meet and to correspond with the defendant in custody. Other defenders shall not enjoy this convenience unless they get a permit from the people's court.

72. Chinese lawyers have a national lawyers' association, but there is no special association for criminal lawyers. There is a national journal especially for lawyers, 'The Chinese Lawyer', published since 20 July 1988. In addition, there are some local lawyers' journals, such as 'Lawyers in Beijing'. Between 1 January 1994 and December 1999, there was also a national newspaper called the 'Daily Chinese Lawyer'. Unfortunately, that newspaper does not exist anymore. By the end of 2012 (according to the latest available statistics), there were 232,300 lawyers in China.

G. *Statistical Overview*

73. In what follows we will give a rough statistical picture of the Chinese criminal justice system, according to the most recently available statistics. The data comes from the Law Yearbook of China and the Working Report of the SPC submitted by the Chief Judge to the NPC.

In 2011, there were 1,690,000 policemen who had passed the examination of qualification for enforcement and about 40,000 policemen who had not (yet) passed this examination. In 2010, there were 190,000 judges at various levels of the people's courts.

In 2014, there were 245,918 personnel working at various levels of the people's procuratorates.

In 2011, there were 215,000 lawyers in China, of which 89.6% were full-time lawyers, 4.5% were part-time and others were in-house, legal aid or military lawyers.

In 2013, the Chinese people's courts at all levels received about 14,228,000 cases and completed about 12,947,000 cases, of which 954,000 cases were the criminal cases at the first instance, with 1,158,000 convicted criminals. In the same year, the Chinese people's procuratorate at all levels granted approval of arrest for 879,817 suspected criminals and initiated prosecution against 1,324,404 persons.

By the end of 2012, there were 681 prisons in China with 1,640,000 inmates. Of them, 30 prisons were specifically allocated to female inmates, totalling 93,051 persons in 2011. Besides that, the places for Education through Labour of 351 were closed or transformed to the rehabilitation centres for drug addicts, prostitutes or whoremasters.

V. Trends Within Criminal Law

74. Scientific research in the Chinese criminal justice field has been flourishing since 1979 when China survived the disaster of the Cultural Revolution. In light of the requirements of the rule of law and the needs of legal practice, a series of new research subjects have been developed: criminal law (substantive law), comparative criminal law, criminology, penology, criminal psychology, victimology, juvenile delinquency, criminal sociology, jurisprudence of labour reform, as well as criminal procedure, criminalistics and evidence. In addition, legal research continued in criminal philosophy, criminal policy and international criminal law, fields that were already studied before.

75. Among these subjects, the research in the field of substantive criminal law has been very productive, mainly because there were new issues to be resolved which were not covered by the Chinese Criminal Code of 1979 and because of the need for criminal law reform. However, this research is more theoretical than empirical due to the need for funds and data to conduct significant empirical research. Scholars and legislators have been very interested in the experiences of foreign countries, as they can push forward the comparative research of criminal law.

The research on criminal procedure has been very important too: not only did it support the revision of the Chinese Criminal Procedure in 1996 and 2012, but it also reinforces the rule of law at large.

76. Furthermore, criminology has been greatly developed as an independent discipline since its establishment at the end of the 1970s in China. Quite a lot of academic achievements have been made. In many law schools and colleges, courses of criminology, juvenile delinquency, criminal psychology and many others are offered. What is more, the criminological research is part of the state's research plan. Other indications of a lively criminological research community are the establishment of Associations of Criminology and Juvenile Delinquency, and the publication of yearbooks and journals. Many special institutions such as the Criminal Research Centre at Peking University and the Institution of Criminal Prevention and Reform through Labour at the Ministry of Justice have been set up.

§4. Sources of Criminal Law

77. The sources of criminal law in China are composed of international treaties and national legislation.

I. International Sources

78. As a member of the United Nations and a signatory state of many international treaties and conventions, the PRC has an increasing number of international obligations in the field of criminal law. On 23 June 1987, the Standing Committee of the NPC decided that the PRC shall, within the scope of its treaty obligations, exercise criminal jurisdiction over crimes prescribed in the international treaties to which the PRC is a party. Article 9 of the Criminal Code of 1997 sets that the CCC shall be applicable to crimes which are defined in international treaties signed and ratified by the PRC and over which the PRC exercises criminal jurisdiction in accordance with its international obligations.

However, international treaties and conventions are not directly applied in the internal legal order. The Chinese legislature adapts all the international obligations and implements them in the CCC. For instance, the CCC includes criminal offences in the area of anti-terrorism, anti-hijacking, drug offences, crimes of genocide, the crimes against the physical protection of nuclear material, the crime of taking hostages, which are all based on international treaties and conventions.

II. National Sources

A. The Constitution

79. At the domestic level, the Constitution is the primary source of criminal law and the Chinese Criminal Code explicitly refers to the Constitution in Article 1 of the CCC. The Constitution of the PRC of 1982, which is the current Constitution, contains many provisions relating to criminal law. For instance, it contains the principle of legality (Article 5 of the Const.), the inviolability of the socialist system (Article 1 of the Const.), the liability of the state to maintain public order and to suppress treasonable and other criminal activities that endanger national security, public security and the socialist economy, as well as other criminal activities (Article 28 of the Const.), the protection of the publicly owned property (Article 12 of the Const.) and the lawful private property (Article 13 of the Const.), the principle of equality before the law (Article 33 of the Const.), the inviolability of the fundamental rights of citizens (Chapter 2 of the Const.), the principle of checks and balances between the people's court, the people's procuratorate and the public security organ (Article 135 of the Const.).

Actually, the Chinese Constitution only contains principles of criminal law and criminal procedure. The provisions of the Constitution are, however, never been directly applied in Chinese legal practice and have never been quoted in any judicial judgments or orders. Moreover, there is no a constitutional court in China. The constitutional issues cannot be resolved in the people's court. According to the Chinese Constitution, the Standing Committee of the NPC and not the SPC holds the power to explain the meaning of the Constitution.

B. *Statutory Legislation*

80. In addition to the Constitution, the sources of statutory criminal law include the Criminal Code (for a further analysis of its contents, *see infra*, paragraphs 67 et seq.), separate criminal regulations and various economic and administrative laws and regulations which contain criminal provisions (*supra*, paragraph 32). The latter does not play a significant role in legal practice because of their incompleteness in providing criminal elements and punishment. These laws or regulations do not constitute a self-standing legal basis for a criminal prosecution; hence Chinese prosecutors and judges need to invoke other legal bases for their prosecution or judgments.

In accordance with the Legislation Law promulgated on 15 March 2000, criminal law is the basic law of the country. It is so fundamental that it can only be enacted by the NPC. Any other decrees, regulations or orders, no matter whether they are made by any level of the government or any other organisation will not be effective, as these bodies do not have the authority to enact criminal provisions. The Standing Committee of the NPC may supplement or amend the criminal law partially, but the amendment or the supplement cannot contradict the basic principle of the basic law (Article 7).

81. The term 'legislative illustration' refers to the explanation given by the representative of the working committee to the NPC which is in charge of drafting a law and preparing it for the congressional debate. It used to be considered as a part of that statute concerned. However, with the improvement of the Chinese legislative skill, legislative illustration has lost its significance in defining certain terms in a law and in being a part of the law.

It should be noted that the term 'legislative explanation' is different from the above notion of 'legislative illustration'. According to the Legislation Law, legislative explanations and amendments are kinds of Chinese law adopted by the Standing Committee of the NPC. Legislative explanation is used for redefining certain terms in the law, whereas amendments are used to change or supplement the legal aspects of an offence. By now, there are in the area of criminal law eight amendments and sixteen legislative explanations (including three for criminal procedure) (*supra*, paragraph 32).

C. *Judicial Explanations and Court Decisions*

82. Officially and academically, the term of 'case law' (in the strict meaning of 'judge-made law') is not recognised in China: Chinese judges do not have the power to create law. Neither does the doctrine of binding precedent apply to judicial decisions. That being said, judicial decisions do illustrate how judges understand and interpret certain terms, definitions and requirements laid down in the law. Considering the role courts play in the Chinese legal system, the term 'judicial explanations' is preferred to the term 'case law', even though, roughly speaking, the Chinese judicial explanations are comparable to 'case law' or 'jurisprudence' in Western countries. Chinese scholars do not consider judicial explanations as a source of criminal law, because they strongly adhere to the principle of legality in criminal law. In order to clarify the understanding of the meanings of laws and to safeguard their correct enforcement, the Standing Committee of the NPC adopted a Resolution Providing for an Improved Interpretation of the Law in 1981, which states that the SPC and the Supreme People's Procuratorate possess the authority to make judicial explanations for questions concerning the specific application of laws in practice. In light of this Resolution, the SPC and the Supreme People's Procuratorate have the power to enact judicial explanations. But their judicial explanations only have binding power within their own organisation, meaning that judges have to follow the guidance of the judicial explanations issued by the SPC but not those made by the Supreme People's Procuratorate, and that conversely, prosecutors do not necessarily have to follow the explanations given by the SPC, although the case will be finally tried in a court. To this date, both of the SPC and the Supreme People's Procuratorate have adopted regulations on enacting judicial explanation.

It should be noted that judicial explanations can actually take various forms, including 'explanations', 'regulations', 'replies' or 'decisions'. An explanation (in the strict sense) is to address the issues of the specific application of a certain law in the trial work or the application of law in the trial of the cases of a certain category or a certain kind of problems. A regulation consists in the formulation of norms or opinions which are necessary for the trial work on the basis of legislative spirit. A reply is an answer to a request for instructions on the specific application of law in the trial work by the higher people's courts or the Military Court of the PLA. Finally, a decision is an amendment or abolishment of judicial interpretations. In addition, the Supreme People's Procuratorate may also take the form of 'opinion' to issue its procuratorial explanation.

Despite the fact that judicial explanations are not considered a source of criminal law, they play an important role in legal practice in the Chinese criminal justice system, because they indicate how to correctly understand the meaning of the law and how to explain the issues of the law. Moreover, some judicial explanations also indicate the concrete standard of sentencing within the statutory punishment. All judges have to follow the judicial explanation, since they know that otherwise their decisions are likely to be reversed on appeal.

83. As explained in the previous paragraph, both the SPC and the Supreme People's Procuratorate have the power to issue judicial explanations. In order to avoid conflict of judicial explanations, both supreme institutions will typically issue an explanation jointly. As a final solution, each of the supreme institutions may bring the issue to the Chinese legislature's attention and ask for a legislative explanation.

84. The system of judicial explanation is good for China to develop its system of rule of law quickly and smoothly. However, it works out not quickly enough for the daily legal practice. From the date of promulgation, a judicial explanation may not be issued for months afterwards. This system also potentially threatens the authority of the legislation and so China has begun to create its own system of guiding cases. It is true that these guiding cases are playing an equivalent role to judicial explanation.

These guiding cases refer to those cases whose judgments have come into force and which satisfy the following conditions: (1) it attracts wide attention from society; (2) it is based upon the legal provisions which are, to a greater degree, on the principles of law; (3) it is representative in nature; (4) it is difficult, complicated or novel; and (5) it has a guiding function. The SPC shall be responsible for determining and uniformly publishing the guiding cases.

The selection of the guiding cases may be upon recommendation by a people's congress deputy, a member of the Chinese People's Political Consultative Conference, expert, scholar, lawyer, or any other person from the general public concerned about trial or enforcement by the people's court. When the guiding cases were issued by the SPC, people's courts at all levels shall use them as a reference when trying similar cases.

By early 2012, local people's court and local people's procuratorate could no longer validly issue legal documents of judicial explanations. They had to clear up their former documents of this nature. When they think certain issues are not clear enough in a law, they can submit a suggestion to the 'Supremes' and ask for an explanation.

§5. Classifications and Technique of Criminal Law

85. Besides the distinction between substantive criminal law and criminal procedure (*supra*, paragraph 29), one can make a distinction within substantive criminal law between general and special criminal law, core or unitary criminal law and accessory criminal law.

86. General criminal law refers to the Criminal Code of 1997 in China. It is the law which systematically and rather completely provides criminal offences and punishments. It succeeds all prior laws, some of which have been replaced and some of which, when contrary to the Code, shall be invalidated. Therefore, the Criminal Code contains the general rules of criminal law, which govern all criminal statutes.

The Criminal Code of 1997 consists of a General Part, a Specific Part and Supplementary Provisions.

The General Part of the Criminal Code of 1997 consists of five chapters with 101 articles, which contain the principles and rules common to criminal offences or in any case to the greater part of them. Briefly, they are: the tasks, basic principles and scope of application of the criminal law; the concept of crime and criminal liability, criminal preparation, attempt and abandonment, the accomplice liability, and 'unit' or corporate crime; the system of criminal punishment; the concrete application of punishment, including sentencing, recidivists, voluntary surrender, combined punishment for several crimes, suspension of sentence, commutation of punishment, parole, and limitation; and other provisions such as the definitions of the terms used within the Code. According to Article 101, the provisions in the General Part of the CCC are applicable to other laws and decrees with provisions containing criminal offences and penalties, but other laws may contain special provisions, which derogate from the rules of the CCC.

The Specific Part of the CCC consists of 350 articles (Article 102–452) and is subdivided into ten chapters as follows: Crimes Endangering National Security, Crimes Endangering Public Security, Crimes Disrupting the Order of the Socialist Market Economy, Crimes Infringing upon Citizens' Civil Rights and Democratic Rights, Crimes of Property, Crimes Obstructing the Administration of Public Order, Crimes Impairing the Interests of National Defence, Crimes of Embezzlement and Bribery, Crimes of Dereliction of Duty, and Crimes concerning Servicemen's Transgression of Duties.

Finally, the Supplementary Provisions provide the date when the Code becomes effective and the lists of laws which shall be invalidated after the Code is implemented.

87. Special criminal law is a body of criminal statutes which are not integrated into the Criminal Code and which supplements and revise of the Criminal Code. Special criminal law consists of specific provisions, which apply to specific criminal offences, specific persons or at a specific time. Theoretically, special criminal law may also have a limited territorial scope of application. However, so far that has not happened in Chinese criminal law. Occasionally, special criminal laws also contain general provisions such as provisions on the statute of limitations period and on sentencing.

It should be noted that there are no special criminal law codes such as the economic, social, environmental or traffic criminal law in China, though some countries may have.

Examples of special criminal law are the Decision Regarding the Punishment of the Crimes of Buying Foreign Currency by Cheating, Illegally Keeping or Transferring Foreign Currency outside the Territory and Illegally Buying or Selling Foreign Currency of 29 December 1998, the Amendment of the Criminal Code, and the Explanation Regarding Article 93, paragraph 2 of the CCC.

88. General criminal law and special criminal law are regarded as so-called core or 'unitary criminal law,' because they only define criminal offences and provide criminal penalties for those offences. Put differently, almost every article defines a punishable act and indicates the punishment.

By contrast, accessory criminal law refers to the criminal provisions outside of the Criminal Code which are accessory to economic and administrative regulations and laws. They begin with a serious compelling or prohibiting regulation and end with a principle provision looking like this: any violation of the law 'shall be punished according to the law' or 'shall bear the criminal responsibility it deserves'; or 'whoever, in violation of this law, is directly responsible for a serious accident caused by his act shall be investigated for criminal liability in the light of the circumstances and pursuant to certain articles of the Criminal Code'; or 'a violation of the law shall be investigated by applying a certain article of the Criminal Code'. Obviously, accessory criminal law in China cannot be directly and independently applied without the guidance of the Criminal Code.

On a final note, it is worth mentioning that there were numerous accessory criminal laws in the economic and administrative regulations which preceded the Criminal Code. The Resolution of the Standing Committee of the NPC on the Validity of the Laws and Decrees Enacted since the Founding of the PRC of 29 November 1979 provides that the laws and decrees enacted or approved by the Central People's Governments and the NPCs and their Standing Committees before the Fifth NPC shall remain in force as long as they do not contravene the current Constitution and laws. However, as a fact, the regulations with criminal provisions before that time have all been replaced by new laws and new regulations. Therefore, all significant accessory criminal laws are supposed to be subject to the Criminal Code and its supplements and revisions.

Part I. Substantive Criminal Law

Chapter 1. General Principles

§1. The Principles of Legality

I. The Maxim of Legality

89. The principle of legality in China is usually expressed by the maxim: 'there must be laws for people to follow, these laws must be observed, their enforcement must be strict and law breakers must be dealt with'. This principle is the general principle of the Chinese legal system and also the basic principle of Chinese criminal law. It is true that the meaning of legality in the general context of law is broader than that in criminal law.

However, the content of the modern ideology of the principle of legality can also be found in the Chinese laws. For instance, Article 5 of the Chinese Constitution provides that the PRC practices ruling the country in accordance with the law and building a socialist country of law. In the Chinese Criminal Procedure, there are many detailed regulations for public trial, presumption of innocence, right of defence, native language (more in *infra* after 362). It is a legal task of the Chinese Criminal Procedure to respect and protect human rights (Article 2 of the Chinese Criminal Procedure of 2012). So, the contents of the principle of legality cannot be seen only in the Chinese criminal law. Rather, this principle is reflected throughout the whole Chinese legal system.

90. The principle of legality is laid down in many legal texts. Article 5 of the Constitution of the PRC provides that all state organs, the armed forces, all political parties and public organisations and all enterprises and institutions must abide by the Constitution and the law. All Acts in violation of the Constitution or the law must be investigated. Article 28 of the Constitution provides that the state maintains public order and suppresses treasonable and other criminal activities endangering national security; it penalises criminal activities that endanger public security and disrupt the socialist economy as well as other criminal activities; and it punishes and reforms criminals. Article 126 of the Constitution and Article 4 of the OLPC provide that the people's court shall administer justice independently, subject only to the law. Article 13 of the Criminal Code gives an explicit definition of a criminal offence (*supra*, paragraph 27). Article 6 of the Criminal Procedure provides that in conducting criminal proceedings, the people's courts, the people's procuratorates and the public security organs must rely on the masses, base themselves on facts and take the law as the criterion. Article 399 of the Criminal Code provides that:

> any judicial officer who, bending the law for selfish ends or twisting the law for a favor, subjects to investigation for criminal responsibility a person he knows to be innocent or intentionally protects from investigation for criminal responsibility a person he knows to be guilty or, intentionally running counter to the facts and law, twists the law when rendering judgments or orders in criminal proceedings shall be sentenced to.

The Constitution and Criminal Procedure both explicitly provide that the law applies equally to all citizens and no privilege whatsoever is permissible.

II. The Maxim of Nullum Crimen, Nulla Poena Sine Lege

91. In the context of criminal law, the meaning of legality in China only refers to the maxim of *nullum crimen, nulla poena sine lege*, i.e., no criminal law, no crime and no punishment.

The Criminal Code of 1979 did basically follow the requirement of the maxim of *nullum crimen, nulla poena sine lege*, i.e., no criminal law, no crime and no punishment. However, as Chinese scholars have critiqued, it was not thoroughly carried out in that Code, since the 1979 CCC did not explicitly provide this maxim in its text and even permitted analogy, which allowed a judge to determine and punish a 'crime' which was not expressly defined in the Specific Part of the Criminal Code, according to whichever article in the Specific Part of the Criminal Code covered the most closely analogous crime. The judgment was then to be submitted to the SPC for approval as a strict control method.

The Criminal Code of 1997 provides that for acts which are explicitly defined as criminal acts in law, the offenders shall be convicted and punished in accordance with the law, otherwise, they shall not be convicted or punished (Article 3). In addition, the Code of 1997 abolished the provision of analogy. So, the maxim of *nullum crimen, nulla poena sine lege* became a statutory provision in the Chinese criminal law.

§2. The Principle of Equality

92. Article 4 of the Criminal Code of 1997 provides that, 'the law shall be equally applied to anyone who commits a crime. No one shall have the privilege of transcending the law.'

This is a principle which has been recently added to the CCC and reflects the requirement of the constitutional principle of legality. In accordance with this principle, anyone who committed a crime, regardless of his nationality, race, profession, family background, sex, religious belief, educational degree, property circumstance, official position, and meritorious service, shall undertake the criminal responsibility he deserves and cannot have any exception.

§3. The Principle of Proportionality

93. Article 5 of the 1997 CCC provides that, 'The degree of punishment shall be commensurate with the crime committed and the criminal responsibility to be borne by the offender.'

The principle of proportionality has also been explicitly added into the Code. In accordance with this principle, the punishment shall be proportionate to the severity of the offence and to the degree of responsibility and culpability of the offender, and punishment shall not exceed the proportion the crime deserved.

There are many articles within the code which reflect this principle. Article 61 provides that when sentencing a criminal, punishment shall be imposed based on the facts, nature and circumstances of the crime, the degree of harm done to society and the relevant provision of the Code. Articles 62 and 63 provide that the criminal shall be sentenced to a punishment within the limits of the prescribed punishment in cases where the circumstances of a crime call for a heavier or a lighter punishment under the provisions of the Code, or be sentenced to a punishment less than the prescribed punishment in cases where the circumstances call for a mitigated punishment.

Article 63 also provides that even if the circumstances of a crime do not warrant a mitigated punishment under the provisions of the Code, the criminal may, upon the verification of the SPC, be sentenced to a punishment less than the prescribed punishment if, according to the concrete circumstances of the case, even the minimum prescribed punishment would be too severe. In order to prevent this provision from being misused, the Standing Committee of the NPC provides the 8th Amendment to the CCC in 2011, which requires that the penalty shall be given within the range immediately below the statutory range, if there are two or more ranges of sentencing under the CCC.

There are still no general sentencing guidelines in China. However, there seems to be a tendency that either for both criminal statutes and judicial explanations to create more defined levels in the prescribed punishment for sentencing convenience.

§4. The Principle of Correspondence Between Subjective and Objective

94. Unlike the principle mentioned above, this principle is not statutory but is theoretical.

This principle requires that to constitute a crime, a person should have fulfilled both the objective and subjective requirements; they should have acted or omitted objectively but also have a guilty mind subjectively. When either requirement is not fulfilled, there shall not be a crime. The strict criminal liability in the Common Law System is so far unknown in Chinese criminal statutes.

In the CCC, Article 14 provides that the intentional crime requires the guilty mind of intention. Article 15 provides that the negligent crime requires the guilty mind of negligence. In addition, Article 16 provides that if an act in fact results in harmful consequences due to unavoidable or unforeseeable causes rather than intent or negligence, it shall not be deemed a crime.

§5. The Principle of Being Responsible for One's Own Crime

95. This principle is also theoretical rather than statutory.

This principle requires that the criminal responsibility shall be borne by the criminal who has committed the crime and an innocent is not to be implicated in a criminal case.

Unfortunately, it was an evil practice of ancient Chinese criminal law to involve innocents in criminal cases and make them undertake the criminal liability. This practice was rampant in the so-called Cultural Revolution (*supra*, paragraph 24) and Chinese people suffered greatly from it. Therefore, this principle appears to have originated from the historical experience of the Chinese people.

This principle has been incorporated into many provisions of the CCC. For example, we can see it in the concept of crime (Article 13), in the provisions of the criminal constitution, in the provisions of joint crime (Articles 25–29), etc.

Specifically, Article 59 provides that:

> confiscation of property refers to the confiscation of part or all of the property personally owned by a criminal. Where confiscation of all the property of a criminal is imposed, the amount necessary for the daily expenses of the criminal himself and the family members supported by him shall be taken out. When a sentence of confiscation of property is imposed, property that the criminal's family members own or should own shall not be subject to confiscation.

The Criminal Code of 1997 defines corporate (or 'unit') crime (*see also infra*, paragraphs 156). Article 30 provides that:

> any company, enterprise, institution, state organ, or organisation that commits an act that endangers society, which is prescribed by law as a crime committed by a unit, shall bear criminal responsibility.

However, the Code strictly limits the criminal liability for a 'unit' crime to the unit itself and the persons who are directly responsible for it. Article 31 provides sets that:

> where a unit commits a crime, it shall be fined, and the persons who are directly in charge and the other persons who are directly responsible for the crime shall be given criminal punishment. Where it is otherwise provided for in the Specific Part of the Code or in other laws, those provisions shall prevail.

§6. The Principle of Humanitarianism

96. The principle of humanitarianism is also a theoretical principle in Chinese criminal law. This principle requires that a criminal shall be humanely treated and forbids the use of corporal and humiliating punishment.

Although the death penalty is still in the CCC, it is under strict control. The death penalty shall not be imposed upon persons who have not reached the age of 18 at the time the crime was committed or upon women who are pregnant at the time of trial (Article 49). The provision that persons who had reached the age of 16 but not 18 could be sentenced to death with a two-year suspension of execution, if the crime committed was particularly serious, was in the 1979 CCC but abolished in the 1997 CCC. In the 8th Amendment to the CCC in 2011, the death penalty was not allowed to be imposed upon any person who has reached the age of 75 at the time of trial, unless he has caused the death of another person by especially cruel means. In addition, the attitude towards the creation of further capital offences appears to have changed. No new capital offences were added into the CCC during the 8th Amendment of 2011 but more were abolished. In the 8th Amendment of 2011, the death penalty was abolished for the crimes of smuggling cultural relics, precious metals, rare animals or their products or ordinary goods (Articles 151, 153), the crimes of fraud in terms of banking bills such as checks, drafts and letter of credit (Articles 194, 195), the crimes involving invoices for tax refunds (Articles 205, 206, 264) and the crimes of robbing and stealing ancient cultural ruins and ancient tomb burial objects or ancient human fossils and ancient vertebrate fossils (Article 328) or ordinary goods (Article 264). Furthermore, the 9th Amendment of 2015 abolished the death penalty for the crimes of smuggling weapons, ammunition, nuclear materials or counterfeit currencies (Article 151), the crime of counterfeiting currencies (Article 170), the crime of illegal fund raising (Articles 199 and 192), the crime of organising or forcing anyone else into prostitution (Article 358), the crime of obstructing any military personnel on duty from performing (Article 426), and the crime of fabricating rumours to shake people's confidence in army during wartime (Article 433). Chinese criminal law is progressing towards abolishing the death penalty.

The systems of suspension of sentence, commutation of punishment and parole are to encourage the criminals to truly recognise their guilt, to show repentance and to speed up their correction and reform. Article 247 even provides that it shall be strictly forbidden to extort a confession by torture. Any judicial officer who extorts a confession by torture shall be given a punishment and whoever causes injury or disability to a person through corporal punishment shall be charged with the crime of injury and given a heavier punishment.

In the execution of punishment, this humane treatment makes criminals' correction and reform very successful.

§7. The Purpose and the Tasks of the Criminal Code and the Basic Criminal Policy

97. Article 1 of the CCC provides that the purpose of the Criminal Code is to punish crimes and to protect the people. Article 2 provides that:

> the tasks of the Criminal Code of the People's Republic of China is to use criminal punishment to fight against all criminal acts in order to safeguard security of the state, to defend the state power of the people's democratic dictatorship and the socialist system, to protect property owned by the state, and property collectively owned by the working people and property privately owned by citizens, to protect citizens' civil (or 'personal'), democratic and other rights, to maintain public and economic order, and to ensure the smooth progress of socialist construction.

98. The concept of criminal policy is a topic under debate. Generally, it can be understood in two ways: within the framework of criminal law or within the wider political context. Within the criminal law, the concept of criminal policy is similar to the concept of the purpose of criminal punishment. Within the political context, the concept of criminal policy refers to the general guidance of the ruling party, i.e., the CCP, for the criminal law. In the academic circle of the Chinese criminal law, the criminal policy is commonly understood as that to combine punishment with leniency which used to be explicitly stipulated in the Criminal Code of 1979. However, in the 1997 CCC, this depiction is omitted; nevertheless, the CCP still requires it to be stressed in legal practice. Therefore, some scholars still hold that it is also a principle of the Chinese criminal law.

This policy requires that criminal offences and criminal circumstances shall be treated carefully and differently based upon the facts of the case and the detailed provisions of the law. The heinous criminals should be severely punished and the criminals who really want to abandon evil and show good behaviour should be leniently treated. Accordingly, for example, the Criminal Code provides heavier punishment for the intentional crimes, the principal criminals and recidivists while lighter punishment is to be administered for the negligent crimes, the accomplices and those who make a voluntary surrender.

Practically, this principle is proven to be very helpful in breaking up criminal groups and providing them with a possible basis for correction and reform.

Chapter 2. Scope of Application of Criminal Statutes

§1. Principles Concerning the Applicability of Criminal Statutes with Respect to Time

99. The principles concerning the applicability of Chinese criminal statutes with respect to time have three aspects: the entry into force of criminal law, the invalid time, and the retroactivity of criminal law.

I. Entry into Force of Criminal Law

100. Article 452 of the Criminal Code of 1997 provides that this Code shall go into effect as of 1 October 1997.

Actually, the CCC of 1997 was adopted at the Second Session of the Fifth NPC on 1 July 1979 and revised at the Fifth Session of the Eighth NPC on 14 March 1997. The NPC purposely reserved about half a year for the Code to come into force because the Criminal Code is one of the important basic laws, and so it is necessary to provide some time before the effective date for all citizens to be familiar with the Code and for the executive organs and judicial organs to get ready to implement it.

II. Invalidity of Criminal Statutes

101. According to a statistic in the Report of the Legislative Affairs Committee of the Standing Committee Concerning the Re-arrangement and Suggestions of the Laws Enacted before the End of 1979, there were 134 pieces of law enacted by the First Session of the Chinese People's Political Consultative Conference, the Central People's Government and the NPCs. Of them, 111 pieces have ceased to be effective. The laws became invalid in the following manner:

- 11 pieces were rendered ineffective by new laws;
- 41 pieces were replaced by new laws;
- 29 pieces ceased to be effective for the reason that the applicable objects and situations had changed;
- 30 pieces ceased to be effective because they were out of date.

On 24 November 1984, the Standing Committee approved this Report and explicitly announced these laws ineffective. Among the list of this report, there were some criminal laws and regulations, for example, the Regulation Concerning the Punishment of Counter-revolution and the Regulation Concerning the Punishment of Embezzlement.

So, the time during which these criminal laws and regulations were invalid before the Criminal Code of 1979, was resolved.

102. Article 452 of the Criminal Code of 1997 provides that the regulations, supplementary provisions and decisions enacted by the Standing Committee of the NPC, as listed in Appendix I of this Code, which have been incorporated into this Code or are no longer applicable, shall be invalidated as of the date this Code goes into effect.

The separate criminal laws listed in Appendix I of the Criminal Code are as follows:

(1) Interim Regulations on Punishment of Servicemen Who Commit Crimes Contrary to Their Duties.
(2) Decision Regarding the Severe Punishment of Criminals Who Seriously Sabotage the Economy.
(3) Decision Regarding the Severe Punishment of Criminals Who Seriously Endanger Public Security.
(4) Supplementary Provisions Concerning the Punishment of Crimes of Smuggling.
(5) Supplementary Provisions Concerning the Punishment of Crimes of Embezzlement and Bribery.
(6) Supplementary Provisions Concerning the Punishment of Crimes of Divulging State Secrets.
(7) Supplementary Provisions Concerning the Punishment of Crimes of Catching or Killing Precious and Endangered Species of Wildlife under Special State Protection.
(8) Decision Regarding the Punishment of Crimes of Insulting the National Flag and the National Emblem of the PRC.
(9) Supplementary Provisions Concerning the Punishment of Crimes of Unlawfully Excavating the Sites of Ancient Culture or Ancient Tombs.
(10) Decision Regarding the Punishment of Criminals Who Hijack Aircrafts.
(11) Supplementary Provisions Concerning the Punishment of Crimes of Counterfeiting the Registered Trademark.
(12) Decision Regarding the Punishment of Crimes of Manufacturing and Trading in Counterfeit and Inferior Goods.
(13) Decision Regarding the Punishment of Crimes of Infringement of Copyright.
(14) Decision Regarding the Punishment of Crimes of Against the Company Law.
(15) Decision Regarding the Handling of Criminals Undergoing Reform Through Labour and Persons Undergoing Rehabilitation Through Labour Who Escape or Commit New Crimes.

Article 452 of the Criminal Code of 1997 also provides that the regulations, supplementary provisions and decisions enacted by the Standing Committee of the NPC, as listed in Appendix II of this Code, shall be retained. Among them, the provisions on administrative penalty and administrative measures shall remain in force; however, since the provisions on criminal responsibility have been incorporated into this Code, the relevant provisions of this Code shall prevail as of the date this Code goes into effect.

The separate criminal laws listed in Appendix II of the Criminal Code are as follows:

(1) Decision Regarding Prohibiting Drugs;

(2) Decision Regarding the Severe Punishment of Criminals Who Smuggle, Manufacture, Sell and Disseminate Obscene Articles;
(3) Decision Regarding the Severe Punishment of Prostitution and Visiting Prostitution;
(4) Decision Regarding the Severe Punishment of Criminals Who Abduct, Sell and Kidnap Women and Children;
(5) Supplementary Provisions Concerning the Punishment of Crimes of Tax Evasion and Refusal to Pay Taxes;
(6) Supplementary Provisions on the Severe Punishment of Crimes of Organising or Transporting Other Person(s) to Illegally Cross the National Border (Frontier);
(7) Decision Regarding the Punishment of Crimes of Disrupting Financial Order;
(8) Decision Regarding the Punishment of Crimes of Falsely Making or Forging or Illegally Selling Special Invoices for Value-added Tax.

III. Retroactivity of Chinese Criminal Law

103. The retroactivity of criminal law refers to whether a criminal law can be applied for acts committed before it becomes effective. If yes, the law has a retroactive force. If not, the law has no retroactive force.

The Retroactivity of criminal law is provided in Article 12 of the Criminal Code of 1997 as follows:

> If an act committed after the founding of the PRC and before the implementation of this Code was not deemed a crime under the laws at the time, those laws shall apply. If the act was deemed a crime under the laws in force at the time and is subject to prosecution under the provisions of Section 8, Chapter IV of the General Part of this Code, criminal responsibility shall be investigated in accordance with those laws. However, if this Code does not deem it a crime or impose a lighter punishment, this Code shall apply.

104. In order to clarify how to deal with the judgments which were made according to the old law and which have become effective, Article 12 also provides that, 'any judgment that has been made and has become effective according to the laws at the time before the implementation of this Code, shall remain valid.'

105. There is no special provision on Retroactivity in the separate criminal regulations made after the Criminal Code of 1997.

The special regulations on Retroactivity in the separate criminal regulations made before the Criminal Code of 1997 are no longer effective, since those laws were invalidated (*supra*, paragraph 84).

§2. Principles Concerning the Applicability of Criminal Statutes with Respect to Space

106. The territorial jurisdiction is stipulated in Article 6 through Article 10 of the Criminal Code of 1997.

When dealing with the applicability of criminal statutes with respect to space, the Chinese criminal law recognises several principles; the territorial principle, the principle of nationality, the protective principle and the universal principle.

I. Territorial Jurisdiction

107. In accordance with Article 6 of the Criminal Code of 1997, anyone who commits a crime within the territory of the PRC shall be punishable according to the Chinese criminal law.

Article 6 provides an exception for this regulation: 'except as otherwise specifically provided by law'. This exception includes the following circumstances:

- Article 11 provides that the criminal responsibility of foreigners who enjoy diplomatic privileges and immunities shall be resolved through diplomatic channels.
- Article 90 provides that where the provisions of this Code cannot be completely applied in national autonomous areas, the people's congresses of those autonomous regions or the provinces concerned may formulate adoptive or supplementary provisions based on the political, economic and cultural characteristics of the local nationalities and the basic principles stipulated in this Code, and these provisions shall go into effect after they have been submitted to and approved by the Standing Committee of the NPC. In reality however, there are no such provisions in the national autonomous areas, most likely because the criminal law provides the basic living standards for people of all nationalities already.
- Article 8 of the Basic Law of the Hong Kong and Macau Special Administrative Regions of the PRC provides that the laws previously in force in Hong Kong and Macau, i.e., the common law, rules of equity, ordinances, subordinate legislation and customary law, shall be maintained, save for any that contravene the Basic Law and are subject to any amendment by the Hong Kong and Macau Special Administrative Region's legislature. Therefore, Hong Kong and Macau do enjoy a high degree of autonomy with their independent judicial power, including that of final adjudication. In the Annex III of the Basic Law, i.e., National Laws to Be Applied in the Hong Kong and Macau Special Administrative Regions, the Criminal Law is not listed.

108. The territorial principle is based upon state sovereignty. Article 6 of the Criminal Code of 1997 provides that the Code is applicable to anyone who commits a crime on board a ship or an aircraft of the PRC. In addition, as China has acknowledged, according to the Vienna Convention on Diplomatic Relations of 18 April 1961, foreign embassies, consulates and their diplomatic representatives are not subject to native criminal jurisdiction. Therefore, the Chinese criminal law shall be applicable to the offences committed within Chinese embassies and consulates.

This state sovereignty has complete power and authority on its territory. Article 6 even provides that if the criminal act or its consequence takes place within the territory of the PRC, the crime shall be deemed to have been committed within the territory of the PRC.

109. The state applies its criminal law to every offence committed on its territory, whatever the offender's nationality may be. Article 3 of the Exit-Entry Administration Law, effective as of 30 June 2012, provides that 'the lawful rights and interests of foreign nationals within the territory of China shall be protected by law. Foreign nationals within the territory of China shall abide by the laws of China and shall not compromise the national security, injure the public interest, or disrupt the public order of China.' Article 88 of that law provides that 'whoever is suspected of a crime for any violation of this Law shall be subject to criminal liability.'

110. The country's territory mentioned in Article 6 refers to land territory, territorial water, i.e., internal water and territorial sea, and space.

The land territory refers to all land within the boundary line.

In accordance with the Law of Territorial Sea and the Contiguous Zone of 25 February 1992, the Chinese territorial sea is limited to twelve nautical miles, measured from the basic line of territorial sea. The basic line of the territorial sea adopts the principle of a straight line based on the neighbouring basic points. The water areas towards the land are the internal waters of the PRC. According to the Law of Territorial Sea and the Contiguous Zone, the Chinese government made a declaration which announced the exact points of the basic line of the territorial sea around the Diaoyu Islands on 10 September 2012 and submitted the legal document to the General Secretary of the United Nation on 13 September 2012.

From the outer fringes of the Chinese territorial sea, there is a water area called the contiguous zone with a size of twelve nautical miles.

The sovereignty of the state also extends to the airspace over the land territory and over the territorial waters as well as to the bed of the territorial waters and to the subsoil of the land and the territorial waters.

Within the contiguous zone, the state shall exercise its jurisdiction in order to prevent and punish any violation of the laws concerning security, customs, finance, hygiene, the management of entry and exit on its land territory, internal waters and the territorial sea.

II. Extraterritorial Jurisdiction

111. The applicability of criminal statutes to offences committed outside China is a supplement to the basic territorial principle. In accordance with Articles 7 through 10 of the Criminal Code of 1997, punishment of offences committed by a Chinese person or by a foreigner outside the territory of the PRC shall only take place in cases specifically mentioned by Chinese criminal law.

112. Article 7 provides that this Code is applicable to the citizens of the PRC who commit a crime prescribed in this Code outside the territory and territorial waters and space of the PRC. However, if the maximum punishment to be imposed on this person is fixed-term imprisonment of not more than three years as stipulated in this Code, he may be exempted from investigation for criminal responsibility. This Code shall be applicable to any state functionary or serviceman who commits a crime prescribed in this Code outside the territory and territorial waters and space of the PRC.

Theoretically, Article 7 is reflective of the principle of nationality.

113. Article 8 provides that this Code may be applicable to any foreigner who commits a crime outside the territory of the PRC, against the state of the PRC or against its citizens, if for that crime, this Code prescribes a minimum punishment or fixed-term imprisonment of not less than three years; however, this does not apply to a crime that is not punishable according to the law of the place where it was committed.

Theoretically, Article 8 is reflective of the protective principle.

III. Jurisdiction Based upon International Duties

114. As mentioned above (*supra*, paragraph 56), China has been a signatory to many international treaties and shall exercise criminal jurisdiction over crimes prescribed in those international treaties to which the PRC is a party or has acceded. On 23 June 1987, the NPC adopted the Decision on Exercising Criminal Jurisdiction over the Crimes Prescribed in the International Treaties to Which the PRC Is a Party or Has Acceded.

Article 9 of the Criminal Code of 1997 provides that this Code shall be applicable to crimes which are stipulated in international treaties, concluded or acceded to by the PRC and over which the PRC exercises criminal jurisdiction within the scope of obligations, prescribed in these treaties, it has agreed to perform.

Theoretically, Article 9 is reflective of the universal principle.

IV. The Effect of Foreign Adjudication and Execution

115. Article 10 of the Criminal Code of 1997 provides that anyone who commits a crime outside the territory of the PRC, for which according to this Code he should bear criminal responsibility, may still be investigated for his criminal responsibility according to this Code, even if he has already been tried in a foreign country. However, if he has already received criminal punishment in the foreign country, he may be exempted from punishment or given a mitigated punishment.

§3. Principles Concerning the Applicability of Criminal Statutes with Respect to Persons

116. Chinese criminal law is applicable to all persons according to the above-mentioned principles of the applicability of criminal law with respect to time and space, however, certain persons may be granted immunities from criminal proceedings or privileges under certain circumstances.

In terms of the system of amnesty, there is only the special amnesty in the Chinese legal system. According to item 17 of Article 67 of the Chinese Constitution, the power to grant a special amnesty is invested in the Standing Committee of the NPC and the

President of the PRC has the power to promulgate this decision. There is no system of grand-amnesty in China.

In the history of the PRC, special amnesty has been granted seven times, during the period of 1959–1975. This special amnesty was principally applied to war criminals who were convicted for crimes committed before 1949, when the PRC was founded, but who were able to show that they would abandon evil and do good.

On 29 August 2015, a special amnesty was granted to a limited group of criminals in order to mark the seventeenth anniversary of the victory of the Chinese People's War of Resistance against Japanese Aggression as well as the World Anti-Fascist War and to reflect the concept of the rule of law and the humanitarian spirit. The groups who were granted this special amnesty included the following four types of criminals:

- Prisoners who fought in the Chinese People's War of Resistance against Japanese Aggression or the Chinese People's War of Liberation.
- Prisoners who fought in wars against foreign invaders to protect national sovereignty, security and territorial integrity after the founding of PRC. However, those convicted of embezzlement or bribery, violent crimes such as intentional homicide, rape, robbery, kidnapping, arson, explosion, poisoning with dangerous substances, or organised violent crimes, organised gang crimes, the crime of endangering national security, or terror offences and those who were principal criminals in organised crimes or repeat offenders were not to be included.
- Prisoners who had reached the age of 75 with serious physical disabilities and could not live on their own.
- Prisoners who committed crimes while under the age of 18 and were sentenced to prison for not more than three years or had remaining terms to be served of not more than one year. However, those convicted of serious violent crimes such as intentional homicide or rape, terror offences, or drug trafficking were not included.

I. Immunities and Privileges Based on the Deputyship of the People's Congresses at Various Levels

117. In the Chinese Constitution of 1982, Article 75 provides that deputies to the NPC may not be held legally liable for their speeches or votes at its meetings; Article 74 provides that no deputy to the NPC may be arrested or placed on criminal trial without the consent of the Presidium of the current session of the NPC or, when the NPC is not in session, without the consent of its Standing Committee.

In the Law of the Deputies to the NPC and the Local People's Congresses at Various Levels of 3 April 1992, Article 29 restates Article 75 of the previous Constitution but extends the scope to deputies of the local people's congresses at various levels. In addition, Article 30 provides that no deputy to a local people's congress at or above the county level may be arrested or put on trial without the consent of the Presidium of the current session of the people's congress or, when the people's congress is not in session, without the consent of its Standing Committee.

If a deputy of a people's congress at or above the county level is caught committing a crime and is detained, the organ executing the detention must immediately report the matter to the standing committee of that people's congress. However, no other compulsory measures prescribed by law can be applied to the deputy of a people's congress at or above the county level without the approval of the Presidium or the standing committee of that people's congress.

The executing organ shall report it immediately to the people's congress at the level of the township, nationality (ethnic) township and town when it has a deputy of that people's congress under arrest, criminal trial, or other lawful compulsory measures.

II. Immunities Based on Age

118. According to Article 17 of the Criminal Code of 1997, a person who has committed an offence may not be held criminally responsible because of his age:

> Anyone who has not reached the age of 14 shall not bear criminal responsibility. Anyone who has reached the age of 14 but not the age of 16 shall bear criminal responsibility for committing intentional homicide, intentionally inflicting injury upon another person so as to cause serious injury or death of the person, or commits rape, robbery, drug-trafficking, arson, explosion or poisoning. Anyone who has reached the age of 16 and commits a crime shall bear criminal responsibility.

The offences listed for those who have reached the age of 14 but not 16 to undertake criminal responsibility are not limited only to crimes as a whole. They may also refer to an act. When a younger person commits a kidnap, a crime which is not in the list, and causes the intentional death, a crime which is in the list, for instance, he shall still be convicted as a criminal for intentional homicide though he will never be convicted for the crime of kidnap.

However, if a person who has reached the age of 14 but not the age of 18 commits a crime, he shall be given a lighter or mitigated punishment. When a person is not given criminal punishment because he has not reached the age of 16, the head of his family or his guardian shall be ordered to discipline him. When necessary, he may be taken in by the government for rehabilitation.

In 2008, a supplement was added to Article 17 as follows: 'a person who reached the age of 75 may be given a lighter or mitigated punishment, if he commits an intentional crime, or shall be given a lighter or mitigated penalty, if he commits a negligent crime'.

III. Immunities Based on Personality

119. Traditionally, Chinese criminal law adopted the view of the Continental Law that only human beings could bear criminal responsibility and corporations could not.

However, a great change took place in 1987. The Customs Law of the PRC was the first law in the Chinese history making a corporation subject to criminal punishment. Article 47 of the Customs Law provides that where an enterprise, an institution, a state organ or a public organisation is guilty of smuggling, the judicial organ shall investigate and determine the criminal responsibility of the person or persons in charge and the person or persons directly answerable for the offence. The judicial organ shall then issue an order to impose a fine on the unit and confiscate the smuggled goods or articles, the means of transport used for smuggling and the illegal proceeds obtained therefrom. After this development, other separate criminal regulations have made 'units' or corporate bodies punishable for the crimes of smuggling, speculation, bribery, trademark violations, tax evasion and others. In the Criminal Code of 1997, Articles 30 and 31 set out the criminal liability of a unit. Article 30 provides that any company, enterprise, institution, state organ, or organisation that commits an act that endangers society, which is prescribed by law as a crime committed by a unit, shall bear criminal responsibility. Article 31 provides that where a unit commits a crime, it shall be fined, and the persons who are directly in charge and the other persons who are directly responsible for the crime shall be subject to criminal punishment. Where it is otherwise provided for in the Specific Part of the Code or in other laws, those provisions shall prevail. Therefore, corporate criminal liability has not yet become a general principle of the Chinese criminal law, though it is provided for in the General Part of the Criminal Code (*see infra*, paragraph 156).

IV. Immunities Based on International Public Law

120. Foreign sovereigns, diplomatic missions and international organisations, as well as their representatives, will enjoy immunity from criminal proceedings in China in accordance with international conventions and treaties, namely the Vienna Convention on Diplomatic Relations of 18 April 1961 and the Vienna Convention on Consular Relations of 24 April 1961.

Chapter 3. General Principles of Criminal Liability

§1. Introduction

I. Criminal Liability

121. Criminal liability means a kind of legal liability for a criminal offence, or a legal result, i.e., penal sanctions for committing certain acts or omissions prohibited by criminal law.

122. Since criminal liability implies a criminal offence, the question arises as to what the basic requirements of a criminal offence are. Generally, the basic elements of a criminal offence in the criminal constitution are the basis of criminal liability in China.

II. Criminal Constitution and the Basic Elements of Criminal Offences

123. At present, the Chinese criminal law circle still generally believe that the criminal constitution refers to the totality of the subjective and objective elements necessary for constituting a crime prescribed by the criminal law. China's criminal constitution has the same meaning and the same function as the criminal elements in the common law system or the criminal definition (Tatbestand) in the German criminal law. Today, the Chinese criminal law theory no longer maintains that the fulfilment of the criminal constitution alone is enough to have a person convicted. A conviction can only be possible when the facts of a case have fulfilled the requirement of the criminal constitution and when there are also no reasonable defences. In a case where a reasonable defence is recognised, e.g., when there is a justified self-defence, the fulfilment of the criminal constitution will not lead to the accused person's conviction.

124. Though the criminal constitution is closely linked with the notion of crime, they are separate concepts. Considering the concept of crime to be both a legislative and judicial concept (*supra* paragraph 28), people can easily say that the criminal constitution is linked with the judicial concept of crime, while the definition of crime shows what a crime is and what its basic characteristics are. The general concept of the criminal constitution is the induction and abstraction of the specific criminal elements of various specific offences.

The criminal constitution consists of the detailed requirements of the elements which will constitute a crime. It is the concrete standard for inculpating a criminal offence.

125. Chinese criminal law theory largely studies the phenomenon of the criminal constitution in two ways: general criminal constitution and specific criminal constitution.

General criminal constitution is the core study of the general aspects of the criminal law. It includes, for example, the jeopardised social relations, the harmful conduct and its consequence, the criminally liable age and capacity, and criminal mental states, which are usually provided in the General Part of the Criminal Code.

Specific criminal constitution refers to the specific constitution of various crimes, which is usually provided in the specific provisions s of criminal law, either in the Criminal Code or not.

In determining whether a criminal should be convicted of an offence, the facts should conform to not only the general requirements prescribed in the General Part of the Criminal Code, but also to the specific requirements of the specific crime.

126. As reflected in many other countries, setting out the basic elements that make up a criminal offence is one of the major problems of the general Chinese substantive criminal law.

Although there are many arguments among Chinese criminal law scholars on how many basic elements should be needed to constitute a criminal offence and how to express them, the most common and influential argument is the following:

> There are four basic elements in the criminal constitution, i.e., (1) criminal object, (2) criminal objective aspect, (3) criminal subject, and (4) criminal subjective aspect.

127. In this chapter, we shall mostly deal with the general criminal constitution. The specific criminal constitution shall be dealt with in Chapter 6.

§2. The Theory of Criminal Constitution

I. Criminal Object

128. Chinese criminal law theory holds that the criminal object refers to the Chinese social relations protected by criminal law and jeopardised by criminal offence.

129. Actually, the social relations protected by Chinese criminal law are very broadly provided in Article 2 (*supra*, paragraph 26) and Article 13 (*supra*, paragraph 27), as well as in the Specific Part of the Criminal Code and other criminal provisions, appearing as national security, property, individual person's rights and various social orders, etc.

However, the social relations cannot be the criminal object until they are jeopardised by a criminal offence. The harmful consequence can be physical or material as well as non-physical or immaterial. Under certain circumstances when the law is so provided, it can even be a kind of danger or threat, for example, the danger sufficient to overturn or destroy a means of transport in the crime of sabotaging (Article 116 of the Criminal Code of 1997). When causing serious consequences, the crime shall be punished according to Article 119.

130. Theoretically, the criminal object can be divided into three categories: general criminal object, kindred criminal object and direct criminal object.

General criminal object refers to the object commonly jeopardised by all crimes, i.e., the overall socialist social relations protected by Chinese criminal law and violated by any crime. The significance of general criminal object is to disclose the common nature of a crime and the social-political significance of the struggle against crime. When the concept of crime was divided into both legislative and judicial (*supra* paragraph 28), the concept of general criminal object was replaced by the legislative concept of crime and is fading its significance.

Kindred criminal object refers to the object which is commonly jeopardised by certain categories of crime, i.e., certain aspects of the socialist social relations. The theory of kindred criminal object is the theoretical basis for the system of the Specific Part of the Criminal Code. In arranging the order of the chapters in the Specific Part of the CCC, the Chinese legislature takes the principle that the severity of the social harmfulness comes first and the criminal subject appears afterwards. Therefore, chapters one through six shall protect the kindred criminal objects sequentially as national security, public security, market order, personal rights, property and social administrative order. Social administrative order is a term for miscellaneous objects which could not be covered by other chapters. From chapters seven through ten, the criminal objects shall be listed as national defence, anti-corruption, dereliction of governmental duties and military interests, whose order is arranged according to the criminal subject in a specific area, e.g., governmental officials or military servicemen.

Direct criminal object refers to the concrete social relations directly jeopardised by the crime. The direct criminal object is one of the basic elements of various concrete criminal constitutions.

131. In Chinese criminal law theory, the criminal object is different from the criminal target. The criminal target is the concrete thing or person, which appears as the physical expression of the direct criminal object. For example, in theft, the property stolen is the criminal target while the ownership of the property is the criminal object. Another example, in murder, the person killed is the criminal target, but the criminal object is the right of life. In many cases, the criminal target may remain unimpaired, e.g., the stolen property may not be damaged when returned to the victim. However, the criminal object, e.g., in the former example, the ownership of the property shall be definitely violated.

Accordingly, the major differences between criminal object and criminal target are the following:

- Criminal object determines the nature of the crime but criminal target does not.
- Criminal object is the absolute element of any crime. But for some crimes such as escape from custody, it is hard to say what the criminal target is.
- All crimes will definitely violate certain types of criminal object, i.e., the specific social relation, but will not necessarily impair the criminal target.

II. Criminal Objective Aspect

A. General Description

132. The criminal objective aspect or criminal objective elements consist of all objective characteristics prescribed by criminal law.

The criminal objective aspect is closely linked with the criminal object. Criminal object shows what kind of social relation has been violated and criminal objective aspect explains how it was violated and what kind of harmful consequence it causes.

Criminal objective aspect is one of the absolute basic criminal elements in criminal constitution. Chinese criminal law shall not be applicable to mere ideas which have not put into practice and shall not be concerned with people's thoughts and emotions which are not converted into action.

133. According to the necessity for establishing a criminal offence, the criminal objective aspect can be divided into two types: Absolutely necessary elements and selective elements. Absolutely necessary elements refer to those necessary for constituting every crime, i.e., external harmful conduct (acts or omissions) and the harmful consequences it causes. Selective elements refer to those only necessary for certain crimes which criminal law specially require, i.e., the time, the place, the method, and the target of a crime.

134. In Chinese criminal law, the descriptions of the criminal objective aspect are usually very clear. A typical example is perjury in Article 305 of the CCC: 'if, during an investigation or trial, any witness, expert witness, recorder or interpreter intentionally gives false evidence or makes a false expert evaluation, record or translation concerning circumstances that bear an important relation to a case, in order to frame another person or conceal criminal evidence, he is guilty of perjury.' Article 305 of the CCC is deemed as the most complete criminal offence in the Chinese criminal code, since it provides a complete set of elements: time of place (during an investigation or trial), criminal subject (expert witness, recorder or interpreter), criminal subjective aspect, i.e., the intent (intentionally) and even the criminal purpose (in order to frame another person or conceal criminal evidence), criminal objective aspect, i.e., the criminal conduct (gives false evidence or makes a false expert evaluation, record or translation concerning circumstances that bear an important relation to a case).

B. Harmful Conduct (Acts and Omissions)

135. Harmful conduct refers to the conduct which displays a human being's consciousness and will, and is objectively harmful to society and prohibited by criminal law.

Only human behaviour or conduct can become the harmful conduct in the sense of criminal law. There is no human conduct and no criminal offence, if an event is only the result of force majeure such as natural forces, the action of an animal or any other person who is not under the actor's direction.

136. In criminal law, harmful conduct varies from offence to offence. In Chinese criminal law theory, the concepts of conduct crime and consequence crime have been commonly used since the end of the last century. The conduct crime refers to those criminal offences in which the criminal object will be violated when there is a conduct defined by the criminal law. The consequence crime refers to those in which the criminal object will not be deemed as violated until a consequence appears (*infra* paragraph 117ff.).

However, any harmful conduct can be defined by law in terms of acts or omission to act.

137. Most of the criminal articles define the offences in such a way that they aim at affirmative acts or conduct. The element of the criminal act exists in doing something which should not have been done, e.g., robbery and murder (Articles 263 and 232) where the violation always concerns a prohibition. The act or the conduct may consist of a physical movement such as the destruction of property, or, according to certain articles, it may consist of verbal acts such as a false charge (Article 242), defamation or verbal insults (Article 246).

138. Some criminal articles define offences in terms of omissions. The criminal element of the omission exists in a failure to act, in omitting to do what should have been done.

In Chinese criminal law theory, an omission has three characteristics or requirements:

- The actor has a certain duty to act. The traditional duty derives from three sources, i.e., the legal duty laid down by law, the professional duty, and the duty arising from one's former act. The traditional duty is still applicable today, but new development has begun. Some scholars talk about the contractual duty which, however, leads to the difficulties in distinguishing the duty in criminal law and in civil law. Now, the theory of guarantor is becoming popular. Accordingly, the duty which will trigger the criminal liability of an omission shall depend upon the position of the actor and whether they have undertaken the responsibility of a guarantor to prevent the damages from happening, either against other legal interests or against the legal interests he shall protect.
- There is an actual possibility to perform the duty. When it is impossible for a person to perform his duty, no matter whether this is due to their capacity or a difficult situation, the person who has the duty but did not perform it, shall not be liable for the omission.
- There is a harmful consequence arising from the failure of performing the duty. Criminal liability shall never be imposed without a harmful consequence in accordance with the Chinese criminal law.

In Chinese criminal law, offences of omission are rare. In the criminal law theory, there are two types of omission. The pure omission offences refer to those whose constitutions require only omission by the criminal law. The typical one is the crime of refusing his proper duty to support an aged person, minor, sick person or any other person who cannot live independently (Article 261). The impure omission offences refer to those which can be constituted either by an omission or by an act, such as intentional killing (Article 232).

C. *Harmful Consequences*

139. The notion of harmful consequence refers to the violation of a criminal object. However, the harmful consequence has been in theory understood as the violation of a criminal target, too (*supra* paragraph 131), especially in the context of criminal attempt.

140. But in the context of the general criminal constitution, the harmful consequence shall be linked with the criminal object, so that it displays the extent and the degree of the violation of the criminal object. In order to see it clearly, we can in theory divide the harmful consequence into different categories:

- direct and indirect harmful consequences, e.g., in the offence of violating traffic regulations and causing serious accidents, those damages involving severe injuries, deaths, or great losses of public and private properties are direct harmful consequences, but those damages in the victims' family or are the so-called indirect harmful consequences.
- physical and non-physical harmful consequences, e.g., physical harmful consequences can be commonly seen in the offences of injury or theft but non-physical harmful consequences are typically existing in the offences such as insult and defamation;
- unitary and compound harmful consequences. The former consequences are typically in the offence of killing or theft, since people will typically only loose life or property. The latter are in the offence of robbery, since the consequences relate to not only life or health, but also property.

141. In the CCC, the significances of harmful consequences are as follows:

- to make a physical or material harmful consequence the prerequisite of a crime; for example, the crime of negligent injury (Article 234) requires the harmful consequence of severe bodily injury and the crime of theft and fraud should seize a relatively large amount of property;
- to make certain danger, though no severe material harmful consequence has occurred, the prerequisite of certain specific crimes; for example, Article 118 provides that whoever sabotages electric power or gas facilities or other inflammable or explosive equipments and thereby endangers public security, if serious consequences have not yet resulted, shall be sentenced;
- to make the physical or material harmful consequence the basis for another article with a heavier punishment; for example, if serious consequences have resulted, the crime of sabotaging electric power shall be punished according to Articles 119 instead of 118.

142. It is true that there are some articles in the Criminal Code which literally have no requirement of a harmful consequence, such as false charge and defamation (*supra*, paragraph 137). However, the law does usually require 'the serious circumstances' for convicting persons of these crimes, which include the requirement of harmful consequence, whether a physical or non-physical one. But in recent years, the Chinese legislature has started to stipulate certain offences without the requirement of any 'serious circumstances', e.g., drunken driving (Article 133A). There are debates on how to implement these laws. In practice, the SPC is required to observe the general conditions in the concept of crime (*supra* paragraph 27).

D. Causation

143. Causation means the relation of between the harmful conduct as cause and harmful consequence as result.

Only when the harmful consequence was really caused by one's own harmful conduct can he be held responsible for the criminal offence. It is obvious that one cannot be responsible for what he did not cause.

There are still some academic debates as to whether causation is one of the absolutely necessary elements (*supra* paragraph 133) of the criminal law theory. It seems that the conduct crimes (*supra* paragraph 136) do not need a causation to be established. However, when people understand the criminal consequence as a violation of criminal object (*supra* paragraph 139) and when, in the case of a conduct crime, there is a need to evaluate the damages for the purpose of sentencing, causation is absolutely necessary or at least shall be helpful.

144. In the Chinese theory of criminal law, it is still hard to say which kind of theory of causation is dominant today. People do not openly accept the 'but for' principle from the common law system or the theories of 'Aequivalenztheory' or 'condicio sine qua non' from the civil law, nor do they openly abandon the so-called 'absolute causation theory' from the former Soviet legal system. All are still within the field of vision of the Chinese scholars of criminal law. Causation is not so much of a practical issue than it is theoretical one. Regardless, the research into causation has begun to distinguish the imputable relation from causation in Chinese criminal law theory. Accordingly, causation is understood as the natural ensuing relations between an act and a result, while the imputable relation refers to only that which conforms to the legal regulations between the harmful conduct and the consequence which shall be imputed to it.

145. Traditionally, the so-called absolute causation had been dominant. But the more modern trend shows high interest in the 'theory of objective imputation', which was developed by the German scholar Prof. Dr Claus Roxin.

146. The so-called absolute causation is composed of three steps of examination. It requires the fulfilment of three basic characteristics: objectivity, relativity, and inevitability.

Objectivity means that causation shall be an objective reality independent of one's will and cannot rely on one's own subjective inference. Relativity means that the concepts of the harmful conduct and the harmful consequence have only a relative meaning, and so are dependent on the particular circumstances. Causation shall be successive in time and shall, in criminal law, focus upon the criminal liability of the actor. Inevitability means that causation in criminal law shall be an inevitable one. Only the intrinsic and inevitable relation which will, in conformity with the law, cause the harmful result, can be deemed as the criminal causation.

147. The so-called theory of objective imputation is based upon such a rule: one shall be the wrongdoer in the context of criminal law, if he created an unallowable risk to the legal interests protected by the criminal law without any justifiable ground and if the risk has already been realised in a prohibited consequence.

On this basis, people can talk about the exceptions, i.e., the situation which shall not be attributable. Now, the commonly accepted situations are as follows:

(1) Acts which reduce the risk shall be excluded, since the actor did not create the risk to the protected legal interests rather, his acts were to help improve the bad situation.
(2) Acts which do not create the risk shall be excluded, which means that any accidental event cannot be imputed to the people.
(3) Acts which are within the allowable risk in fields such as traffic, industry and sports shall be excluded. The common liability is only a negligent one when people exceeded the allowable limits.
(4) Acts which do not coincide with the purpose of the prohibition against the risk shall be excluded. For instance, causing a person to have a myocardial infarction (heart attack) by scaring him when overtaking his car in a dangerous manner shall not be imputed as a bodily injury to that guy, because the purpose of the rule against overtaking is to avoid cars colliding with one another and not to prevent the occurrence of myocardial infarctions.
(5) Acts shall be excluded when the victim jointly and deliberately gives plays to that act which cause self-harm. For instance, A sells drugs to B and B injects himself with the knowledge of the risk. A shall only be punished for selling drugs but not for killing B, neither intentionally nor negligently.

148. Causation is sometimes very complicated. One reason can often cause many results and equally, one result may be caused by many reasons. In reality, causation can appear more complicated: for example if more than one offender commits more than one criminal offence and causes more than one harmful consequence. It is within the scope of causation to analyse the principal reason and the secondary reason in order to correctly determine the criminal liabilities of each offender.

It is true that the studies of causation mainly refer to those crimes committed by an act. For those crimes committed by omission, causation cannot be understood from the perspective of 'causing' but from 'preventing' the result.

149. Causation provides only the objective basis for criminal responsibility. In order to convict the criminal, other elements of the criminal constitution need to be satisfied, such as the subject and subjective aspect.

E. The Time, the Place, and the Method of Committing a Crime

150. The time, the place and the method for committing a crime are the selective elements in criminal objective aspects (*supra*, paragraph 133).

All crimes are committed at a certain time, at a certain place and by a certain method. However, most crimes in Chinese criminal law do not consider time, place and method as their constitutive elements. For these crimes, the offender will be convicted, no matter when, where and how he committed the criminal offence. In these cases, the selective elements might affect the degree of harmfulness of the crime and therefore the severity of the criminal punishment because a different time, place and criminal method will lead to a different impact upon society.

It is true that in the Chinese Criminal Code, there are certain articles which explicitly prescribe a required time, place or method. For example, Article 340 provides that:

> whoever, in violation of the law or regulations on protection of aquatic resources, catches aquatic products in an area or during a season closed to fishing, or uses prohibited fishing gear or methods for the purpose, if the circumstances are serious, shall be sentenced to.

In these crimes, the time, place and method shall be the prerequisite for constituting them.

With regards to those crimes for which the criminal law does not require a specific time, place or method, such as intentional killing, these factors shall still be considered given that different times, places or methods may have a different impact upon the society. The Prosecutors and judges will definitely consider a murder in the central part of a city to be more serious than the same scale murder in a remote village.

III. Criminal Subject

151. Criminal subject refers to the person who committed the criminal offence and shall therefore bear criminal responsibility.

Though Chinese criminal law does not define person, in theory, a person can be considered to mean both a human being (or 'natural person') and a 'unit' (i.e., a corporate body) such as an enterprise, an institution, a state organ, or a public organisation.

A. Natural Persons as Criminal Subjects

152. According to the Chinese Criminal Code, a natural person cannot become a criminal subject until he meets the following criteria:

- He has committed some harmful conduct.
- He has reached the age to undertake criminal responsibility.
- He has the capacity for criminal responsibility.

153. The requirement of the age to undertake criminal responsibility is provided in Article 17 of the Criminal Code of 1997 (*supra*, paragraph 118). Briefly speaking, the age to undertake criminal responsibility is divided into four stages. The first stage applies to any person below aged 14, who will be exempted from criminal responsibility, though minors who have done what otherwise would be prosecuted, shall be under the strict discipline of the head of their family or, when necessary, subject to rehabilitation by the state. The second stage applies to a person above 14 and below 16, where criminal responsibility is only possible for eight types of offence, i.e., intentionally killing, intentionally injuring another and causing serious injury or death, rape, robbery, drug trafficking, arson, explosion and poisoning. The third stage applies to those above 16, where an actor shall undertake full criminal responsibility. The fourth stage is for those above 14 and below 18, where an actor shall be given a lighter or even mitigated punishment.

154. The capacity for criminal responsibility is provided in Articles 18 and 19 of the Criminal Code of 1997.

Article 18 provides that a mental patient who causes harmful consequences at a time when he is unable to recognise or control his own conduct, upon verification and confirmation through legal procedure, shall not bear criminal responsibility; any person whose mental illness is of an intermittent nature shall bear criminal responsibility if he commits a crime when he is in a normal mental state; any intoxicated person who commits a crime shall bear criminal responsibility.

For those who shall not bear criminal responsibility because of mental illness, his family members or guardian shall be ordered to keep him under strict watch and control and arrange for his medical treatment. When necessary, the government may compel him to receive medical treatment.

Article 19 provides that any deaf-mute or blind person who commits a crime may be given a lighter or mitigated punishment or be exempted from punishment.

155. The conditions mentioned above (*supra*, paragraph 152) are the common requirements for every criminal offender. However, there are some crimes, e.g., embezzlement and malpractice, in Chinese criminal law requiring a certain additional personal status, such as state functionary or judicial functionary. In these crimes, the one without the legal prescribed status cannot become the criminal subject.

The status of state functionary is linked with the state function and not its position. According to the legislative explanation of 2,000, the members of a villagers' committee or of any other village grass-roots organisation shall be regarded as 'state functionaries who perform public services according to law' as mentioned in Article 93 of the CCC, when they assist the people's government to exercise the administration tasks related to the funds and materials, land and house sites, taxes, and family planning or permanent residence, etc. Therefore, when they illegally embezzle any public money or property by taking advantage of their position during the course of performing these public services, the crimes such as embezzlement, misappropriation of public money and bribery shall apply to them. This is so even though they are not officially state functionaries and the crimes do explicitly need criminal subjects to have a status of 'state functionaries who perform public services according to law' (*infra* paragraph 289).

B. Corporate Bodies ('Units') as Criminal Subjects

156. As mentioned above (*supra*, paragraph 119), a 'unit' – which is the term used in China largely coincides with the terms 'corporate bodies' or 'legal entities' (*see infra*) – could not traditionally become a criminal subject until the promulgation of the Customs Law in 1987 when change occurred. A unit can be part of a corporation or company and can be a criminal subject as long as it is prescribed as such in the law. One of the social reasons why China adopts the term of 'unit' and not the term of corporation or corporate body is due to the large size of the state-owned enterprises.

For instance, the Bank of China and the Industrial and Commercial Bank of China (ICBC) are such large enterprises, which consist of some 10,000 branches and departments, that it would be inconceivable to hold such an enterprise criminally liable for every breach of law, even those committed by local directors.

According to the Criminal Code of 1997, the judicial explanations of the SPC and other regulations, a unit shall be deemed as a criminal subject, if the following conditions are fulfilled:

- The unit has committed an act that endangers society, which is prescribed by law as a crime committed by a unit. It is true that a unit cannot be held criminal liable for some offences, e.g., theft (Article 264) and forgery of money (Article 170).
- The units which are subjects of criminal law are companies, enterprises, institutions, state organs, or organisations. They are lawful units and usually incorporated according to the civil law, governmental organic law and other laws of the PRC, including the foreign-Sino joint venture and co-operative enterprises, as well as the wholly foreign owned and the privately owned companies. However, if a company, enterprise and institution, which is incorporated by a person for the purpose to commit the illegal or criminal activities, commits a crime, or if the company, enterprise and institution takes it as their main business to commit crimes, it shall not be deemed as a crime of the entity. Enterprises and institutions are usually legal persons, however, the status of legal person is not necessary for the unit to become a criminal subject. The branches and inner-departments of a company might be qualified as a unit and commit a unit crime, if they commit the wrongdoing in the name of their units and the illegal enrichments go to the units themselves. But the villagers' committee cannot be a unit under the criminal law, since the Organic Law of the Villagers' Committees provides in its Article 2 that these committees are the mass organisation of self-government at the grass-roots level, in which villagers administer their own affairs, educate themselves, serve their own needs and in which election is conducted, decision adopted, administration maintained and supervision exercised by democratic means. So, the villagers' committees do not fall within the scope of unit crime listed in Article 30 of the CCC.
- The crime shall be committed for the unlawful interests of a unit and not for an individual person. If the crime was committed in the name of the unit but for a certain individual person's own interest, that will not be a unit crime. The crime shall be convicted as a crime committed by a natural person.

According to the opinion of the SPC, the criminal responsibility of a unit can be triggered not only by the decision made collectively or individually by the head of the unit, but also by the acts of the employees of that unit who played a major role in committing that crime. As far as the scope of a governmental unit is concerned, it is commonly agreed that a governmental unit can be deemed as committing a crime only when it did so within the scope of its operation or business, though this debate is ongoing.

In accordance with the Criminal Code, the punishments for a unit crime are a fine for the unit and punishment for the persons who are directly in charge and the other persons who are directly responsible for the crime, unless where it is otherwise provided for in the Specific Part of the Code or in other laws. In addition, a unit which is found guilty of a crime might be also subject to an administrative sanction, such as withdrawal of business licence.

IV. Mens Rea ('Subjective Aspect of Criminal Liability')

A. General Description

157. The term *mens rea* (or translated literally from Chinese: 'subjective aspect of criminal liability') (i.e., the criminal subjective element, criminal mental state, guilty mind or culpability) refers to the mental state, intent or negligence the criminal offender possesses for his own harmful conduct and the harmful consequences therefore caused. But the concept of the 'criminal subjective aspect' is not the same as the concept of blameworthiness. Usually, the question as to whether an act is blameworthy shall be considered later when the criminal constitution is completely fulfilled.

In Chinese criminal law, no conduct can lead to a criminal punishment without a legally prohibited state of mind. The criminal subjective aspect is therefore one of the constitutive elements.

Logically, the contents of the criminal subjective element shall include the facts concerning the criminal object and the criminal objective aspect. Whether the criminal subjective element shall contain the recognition of social harmfulness is still unclear. General tendency is as follows: it shall exclude the criminal responsibility if the actor was not aware of the social harmfulness.

158. Intent and negligence are the two types of the criminal mental state prescribed in the Criminal Code. Strict liability is so far not recognised in the Chinese criminal law.

However, the criminal subjective aspect also includes the criminal purpose and criminal motive. Besides that, the problems of ignorance and mistake are also issues to be considered, which will be discussed in Chapter 4.

159. Intent or negligence is the vital element to be satisfied to constitute a criminal offence. Either of these elements can independently and completely express the mental state of a criminal perpetrator.

The criminal purpose exists only in the intentional crimes and is not a requirement to fulfil every criminal offence. It is the selective element for constituting certain crimes.

The criminal motive is not a constitutive element at all. It cannot affect the satisfaction of the constitutional elements of a crime but will affect the determination of the subjective malignancy of the criminal perpetrator and consequently the severity of the sentence issued.

160. It is very important to identify whether a criminal offence has been committed intentionally or negligently. The Criminal Code provides criminal responsibility generally for intentional crimes and criminal responsibility for negligent crime is only possible when the law so provides. It is obvious that an intentional crime is very often more dangerous than a negligent crime and shall be subject to a more serious punishment.

B. Intent

161. In accordance with Article 14 of the Criminal Code of 1997, intent is the mental state of intentional crime. Intent refers to the mental state where a person clearly knows that his act will produce socially dangerous consequences but who wishes or allows such consequences to occur.

162. There are two characteristics of intent.

Concerning consciousness, the person clearly knows that his act will, inevitably or possibly, produce socially dangerous consequences.

Concerning will, the person wishes or allows such consequences to occur.

163. According to the characteristics, intent can be theoretically divided into two types: direct intent and indirect intent.

Direct intent refers to the mental state of clearly knowing that one's act will inevitably or possibly produce socially dangerous consequences and that one wishes such to occur.

Indirect intent refers to the mental state of clearly knowing that one's act will possibly produce socially dangerous consequences and allowing such to occur.

C. Negligence

164. In accordance with Article 15 of the Criminal Code of 1997, negligence is the mental state of a negligent crime. It refers to the mental state in which a person who should have foreseen that his act would possibly produce socially dangerous consequences but who fails to prevent them from happening through negligence or, having foreseen the consequences, readily believes that they can be avoided, the result being that these consequences do occur.

165. To constitute a negligent crime, there must be a certain objective harmful consequence prescribed in law that has occurred.

166. Based upon the characteristics in terms of consciousness and will, negligence can theoretically be divided into two types: careless negligence and negligence with undue assumption.

167. Careless negligence exists when a person does not realise the harmful consequences of his conduct, though he should and would have avoided it if he had foreseen the danger.

The standard to determine if the person should foresee the risk has long been a topic of discussion. Now, the academic debate on this issue will no longer focus upon whether a subjective standard or if an objective standard shall be adopted, i.e., if a person's obligation to foresee shall be based upon his own intellectual ability and professional capacity or upon the average level of ordinary people. Today's issue is more about which standard shall go first. The more influential opinion is to take the objective standard as the basis and the subjective standard as supplement. It means that the perpetrator whose personal capacity is below the average level will still be deemed as negligent, but he shall be excused because a person cannot undertake the liability which is not in line with his capacity. For those whose personal capacity is above the average level, the obligation of foreseeing the risk shall be determined only according to his real level of standard of capacity.

168. Negligence with undue assumption exists when a person has foreseen the harmful consequences of his conduct but believes, recklessly, that the harmful result will not occur. Although his mental state is close to intent (indirect intent), it is different from intent, because the perpetrator would not have acted if he had known the actual consequence. The key points for distinguishing negligence with undue assumption from indirect intent are as follows: First, negligence with undue assumption does absolutely negate the harmful result while the indirect intent just tolerates the result: when the result does not occur, it is fine; when it does occur, it is also fine for the perpetrator. Second, negligence with undue assumption heavily relies upon certain conditions which would have prevented the occurrence of the harmful result, while the indirect intent relies upon nothing because the expectation is that nothing will happen.

D. Criminal Purpose

169. Criminal purpose refers to the result which a criminal offender wishes to obtain through his harmful conduct.

Criminal purpose directly indicates the target of the criminal offender. Though a criminal purpose does not mean the total content of a mental state, it usually displays the nature of the criminal object the crime jeopardised and therefore shows the characteristic of a mental state.

Because criminal purpose involves the seeking of a particular result, it is natural that criminal purpose can exist only in criminal intent.

170. In the Specific Part of the Chinese Criminal Code, there are many crimes requiring a certain criminal purpose, such as the purpose of profit (e.g., Articles 217 and 228), the purpose of illegal possession (Articles 192 and 193), and the purpose to frame another or conceal criminal evidence (Article 305), as its constitutive element. Without the purpose prescribed by law, the requirements for the crime cannot have been fulfilled.

In the Chinese criminal law, the requirement of criminal purpose may be referred to in another way. For instance, the offence of false accusation (Article 243) must be 'in an attempt to subject others to criminal investigation' and the robbery stipulated in Article 269 must be 'in order to conceal booty, resist arrest or destroy criminal evidence'. In addition, there are some special offences such as theft (Article 264) and fraud (Article 266) which do not contain a literal requirement of purpose in the text of the law, though academically, scholars usually believed that they shall be committed with criminal purpose, because the words of theft and fraud in Chinese include the meaning of the purpose already!

171. For those offences for which criminal law does not explicitly require a criminal purpose, the criminal purpose is not a constitutive element. However, the type of actual purpose in a criminal case will affect the sentence and, sometimes, will be helpful to determine the type of crime. For example, the difference between murder and intentional injury depends upon whether there was a purpose to kill the victim.

E. Criminal Motive

172. Criminal motive refers to the inner motivation to commit the crime. It is not a constitutive element because there is no crime in Chinese criminal law requiring criminal motive.

The difference between purpose and motivation might be very complicated in the sense of psychology. However, it is only necessary to check whether there is any special requirement of criminal purpose for a certain offence. All other elements of mental state will be considered in a similar way to a person's motivation, which shall only affect sentencing.

173. Criminal motive can show the degree of subjective malignancy. When criminal law requires the serious circumstance or the flagrant circumstance, criminal motive is undoubtedly one of the elements which can display it.

In legal practice, criminal motive is one of the main elements affecting the severity of a sentence.

Chapter 4. Justification, Excuse and Other Grounds of Impunity

§1. General Principles

174. Justification and excuse are gradually becoming an independent topic in the theory of Chinese criminal law. However, the issues under these topics might have previously been discussed in the fields of self-defence or mistakes.

Strictly speaking, the concepts of justification and excuse are not yet completely accepted in China. In Chinese criminal law and criminal law theory, the statements 'shall not be considered as a crime', 'shall not deemed as a crime', 'shall not bear criminal responsibility' mean that the person is innocent. The stipulation of 'exemption from punishment' means the person is guilty but need not be punished. These provisions appear to express a meaning similar to that of justification or excuse.

175. Like criminal law in western countries, Chinese criminal law deals with the issues of justification and excuse in order to negate, exclude or exempt an accused person from criminal responsibility. In the theoretical structure of Chinese criminal law, the issues of justification or excuse always follow the positive description of criminal constitution under which one should bear a criminal responsibility. The main function of justification and excuse is to make an exception to the general rule.

176. When reading this chapter, one should keep in mind that the concept of social harmfulness is of great importance in the theoretical system of Chinese criminal law (*supra*, paragraphs 26 and 27). The basic reason for justifying or excusing harmful conduct is to exclude social harmfulness (e.g., self-defence or necessity), or because it results in so little harm that criminal punishment is unnecessary (e.g., discontinuation, duress or coercion).

§2. Self-Defence

I. General Description

177. In accordance with Article 20 of the Criminal Code of 1997, self-defence refers to an act that a person commits in order to stop an unlawful infringement of an aggressor and to prevent the interests of the state and the public, or his own or other person's right of the person, property or other rights from being infringed upon, resulting in harm to the aggressor.

Self-defence shall not bear criminal responsibility as long as the person's act of justifiable defence does not obviously exceed the limits of necessity and does not cause undue harm. However, if a person acts in defence against an ongoing assault, murder, robbery, rape, kidnap or any other crime of violence that seriously endangers his personal safety, thus causing injury or death to the aggressor of the unlawful act, it is not undue defence, and he shall not bear criminal responsibility.

However, a defender shall bear criminal responsibility in the case where his legitimate defence noticeably exceeds the necessary limits and causes great harm. But he shall receive a mitigated punishment or even be exempted from punishment.

178. As far as the basic characteristics of self-defence are concerned, there is not a commonly accepted ideology in Chinese criminal law theory. However, Chinese criminal law is gradually adopting the concept of social correction. A justified defence is when an individual does the right thing by excluding the social harmfulness of an unlawful attack and is an expression of what society believes is the correct course of action.

179. In addition to the universally accepted rule that a person cannot be expected to remain passive when in immediate danger of unlawful physical harm from an aggressor, and that one has the right to use such force as is necessary to avoid this danger, Chinese criminal law theory holds that self-defence is necessary to stop an unlawful attack and is supportive of people to struggle against crime.

In China, self-defence is deemed as a lawful right for Chinese citizens. It is very often believed as a kind of moral obligation. When one is able to defend oneself at the moment of the crime but cowardly does not do so and let the public and private interest suffer great losses, he will be given serious moral condemnation, or even disciplinary sanction. However, for those such as the police who bear the duty to fight against crime, self-defence is even a legal obligation. A policeman shall undertake criminal responsibility when he should defend a crime but abandons his professional duty and therefore leaves the lawful interests greatly suffered as a result.

II. Conditions

180. Self-defence is a right provided by law to Chinese citizens. However, if the right is incorrectly performed and exceeds the limits of necessity and causes undue harm, the act will change from a beneficial one to a harmful one and criminal responsibility will therefore arise.

In the Chinese criminal law, there are two types of legal result for self-defence (*supra* paragraph 177). The justified defence shall bear no criminal liability, and shall be deemed as 'justification'. The defence exceeding necessary limits and causing great harm might be exempted from criminal liability, and should be called an excuse.

181. Ascertaining a justified defence is always an issue in legal practice and for academic debate. However, the following points are commonly required.

A. An Unlawful Conduct by Another Person

182. First of all, a justified self-defence shall be against an unlawful conduct by another person. An unlawful conduct is an attack threatening the lawful interest. The unlawful conduct usually refers to a criminal offence. However, it can also be a tortious act. At the moment when facing the offender, a person will usually find it very difficult to tell whether the act they are being subject to is criminal or torturous in nature.

Obviously, self-defence cannot be used against the lawful act such as the lawful detention or arrest. Anyone who forcibly resists while police are carrying out a lawful detention or arrest shall be guilty of a new crime (Article 277) or other crimes if injury or death was therefore caused.

183. In cases involving harmful conduct committed by a minor or insane person, the defence shall be in principle justified only if the actor knows nothing about the fact of infancy or insanity or if the actor is unable to escape from the unwanted situation at that moment.

184. When the harmful conduct is triggered by the victim's previous intentional provocation, the victim's conduct cannot be justified as self-defence. This is the so-called provocative defence in criminal law theory.

B. *An Ongoing Unlawful Conduct*

185. The unlawful conduct shall be an ongoing one.

Logically, self-defence shall not be applied to the unlawful attack which has not yet begun or has already stopped. The beginning point when self-defence may be taken will be similar to the point when an act was deemed as execution in attempt. But they shall not be the same, because certain acts in the stage of criminal preparation, which has not yet begun to directly commit the conduct, might be doubtfully qualified the target of self-defence. Some of these acts might not be, such as a shop-lifter standing closely behind a customer in front of a cashier without stretching out his hand. Some might be, such as a fury man reaching his hand on the pistol in the pocket but not yet pulling it out.

As far as the stopping point is concerned, self-defence will not take the completion of a crime as its standard.

186. That the unlawful conduct is actually happening means that a lawful interest is under the direct and urgent threat of the unlawful conduct, so a basis for justifying the defence is created.

To defend an attack not really existing, no matter whether it is by imagination or by subjective inference, is an imaginary defence.

To defend an attack not yet happening or having already ended is an untimely defence. Neither imaginary nor untimely defence can be justified as self-defence.

C. *Protection of Lawful Interests*

187. A justified self-defence shall only protect lawful interests which the defender has a right to protect. The Chinese criminal law provides a broad scope to protect of 'the state's and public interest or the rights of the person, property or other rights'. However, whether all people, at any given time have the right to protect any type of interest listed in the law, is still under research. The general understanding seems to be so: any individual person has the right to protect his own interests in life, health, freedom and property, as well as others' when in a situation of urgency. For the state's interest and the wider public interest, however, an individual person shall consider the availability of policeman or other official enforcements before he starts his own defence, only when the public security forces are unavailable will the protection of the interests be allowed.

188. The conduct against the third person, no matter whether the third person is the close relative of the attacker or not, cannot be deemed as a justified defence. The rationale of this rule is that defence is designed to stop the unlawful conduct and to protect the lawful conduct. However, cases of Joint crime will be exceptions to this rule, and in those circumstances, the defence might be directed against any of the accomplices, even though they may not be the one who is directly carrying out the attack.

D. Situation of Justification

189. A justified defence shall be possible only when the defender realised the situation of justification and a purpose of defence is not necessary.

190. In the cases of casual defence, a justified defence shall be possible only when the examinations on both of the act and the result are legitimate. For instance, A dislikes B's style on a bicycle and intentionally knocked him down. But A's action unexpectedly saved C from being robbed by B, whose real plan, A had known absolutely nothing. A is not able to use any defence, because his act is an unlawful attack.

E. Necessity

191. The method and strength of a justified defence can be as strong as it is necessary to defend the unlawful attack. The self-defence shall not exceed the limits of necessity. The Chinese criminal law commonly agreed that the defence should stop as soon as the attacker is under control or has lost the ability to continue the attack. The conduct that exceeds the limits of necessity and causes undue harm is called an excessive defence and should bear criminal responsibility.

The necessity of the method will not depend upon the proportionality between an unlawful attack and the defending act, however, it shall be subject to the restriction of social ethics.

In the Criminal Code of 1997, two standards apply to this issue:

> Firstly, the code provides that if a person's act of justifiable defence obviously exceeds the limits of necessity and causes serious damage, that shall constitute an excessive defence and the person shall bear criminal responsibility.

> Secondly, it provides that for the defence against an on-going assault, murder, robbery, rape, kidnap or any other crime of violence that seriously endangers his personal safety, there shall not be undue defence, even if the defence causes injury or death to the perpetrator of the unlawful act.

192. All of these conditions must simultaneously exist. If any of them is absent, the defence shall not be effective.

III. Legal Liability

193. In accordance with Article 20 of the Criminal Code, consideration shall be given as to whether to offer a mitigated punishment or exemption from punishment if the defence obviously exceeds the limits of necessity and causes undue harm. In defending the crime of violence that seriously endangers one's personal safety, such as murder, rape and robbery, it is not undue defence, even if the aggressor of the unlawful act was injured or killed, the defender shall not bear criminal responsibility.

194. In General Principle of Civil Law, Article 128 provides that a person who causes harm in exercising justifiable defence shall not bear civil liability. If justifiable defence exceeds the limits of necessity and undue harm is caused, an appropriate amount of civil liability shall be borne. In Chinese Torts Law, Article 30 provides the similar regulations.

§3. Necessity

I. General Description

195. In accordance with Article 21 of the Criminal Code of 1997, necessity refers to an act that a person is compelled to commit in an emergency to avert an immediate danger to the interests of the state or the public, or his own or another person's property or other rights.

In the Chinese criminal law, there are also two types of legal result for necessity. If a necessity is justified, which means it does not exceed the limits of necessity and does not cause undue harm, the actor who commits the necessity shall bear no criminal liability. This is considered to be a justification. However, if a necessity exceeds necessary limits and causes great harm, it shall be deemed as excuse when using it to claim exemption from criminal liability.

196. The basic characteristic of necessity is the sacrifice of the minor over the major, or the smaller over the larger when conflict arises between these two types of lawful interests.

Obviously, necessity will cause damage to some lawful interests, but it has consequently saved the greater lawful interests. Looking at the subjective aspect, the actor is to protect the greater lawful interest and has no alternative but to sacrifice the minor. Therefore, necessity is an act which is conducive to a better society and is not guided by the guilty mind.

II. Conditions

197. In order to be able to consider necessity as a justification, rather than an excuse, the two following conditions are commonly required.

A. An Immediate Threat of Danger

198. Necessity must be carried out for the sake of protecting certain lawful interests from the threat of danger.

The danger may stem from a natural calamity such as flood, earthquake or typhoon or from an animal's invasion, or from another's unlawful attack. However, the unlawful attack by the other person cannot be one which is defendable. In addition, an actor can also not use the excuse of necessity to resist a lawful act, e.g., a lawful arrest by a policeman.

199. In accordance with Article 21, necessity shall not apply to a person who has been given a specific responsibility in his post or profession. For example, a fireman in front of a fire or a captain faced with a sinking boat cannot escape, regardless of his duties, by the excuse of necessity.

200. Necessity must avert an immediate danger to lawful interests. The danger must be a reality and cannot be an imaginary one. The danger must be an immediate and urgent one. Any untimely danger cannot become the prerequisite of necessity.

201. Necessity must be the only way to avoid the danger. Both the interest which is to be protected and the interest which is to be sacrificed are lawful interests. Therefore, it should only be in a situation without any alternative solution, that necessity can be used as a justification or excuse. If there is another way to protect the lawful interests under threat, one cannot claim that their actions should amount to necessity.

B. Superior Interests to Be Protected

202. It is the legitimate purpose of necessity to protect the superior interests over the interests of comparatively minor importance one. Only in these circumstances can we say that the necessity is conducive to an improved society rather than harmful to society.

203. The Chinese Criminal Code says nothing about how to evaluate the big or small, major or minor. But the superiority can be evaluated by interests or by act.

As far as the interests to be protected are concerned, necessity shall observe the hierarchy of the value in the interests, i.e., the personal interests of life and health shall be in the supreme position, and the personal interests shall be more important than the property interests. Property interests can be measured by the value of the property. One cannot sacrifice a person's life for another person's health or one person's life for another person's life. Exception is possible but shall be subject to the strict examination on a case-by-case basis. For instance, one refuge's life in the hand of terrorists might not be more important than the mass interests of a state.

In the process of balancing the acts to decipher when necessity should be used, people should give consideration to the nature of different types of necessity. For the aggressive necessity, where the victim is the person who has nothing to do with the danger which was threatening the actor, the interests to be protected shall be so large or so important that they are disproportionate to the sacrificed ones. However, in the defensive necessity, where the victim is the source of the danger to the actor, the requirement of disproportionate might not be so obvious. The Chinese criminal law circle does not clearly agree to the life-for-life necessity, though it is commonly acceptable to sacrifice an infant's life in order to save his mother.

204. The two conditions set out above must simultaneously exist. If either of them is absent, the defence of necessity shall not be available.

III. Legal Liability

205. In accordance with Article 21 of the Criminal Code of 1997, consideration shall be given as to whether a mitigated punishment or exemption from punishment should be offered when the necessity has exceeded the limits of necessity or caused undue harm.

206. In General Principles of Civil Law, Article 129 provides that if harm occurs because of the necessity, the person who gave rise to the danger shall bear civil liability. If the danger arose from natural causes, the person claiming necessity may either be exempt from civil liability or bear civil liability to an appropriate extent. If the necessity taken is improper or exceeds the limits of necessity and undue harm is caused, the person who took the necessity shall bear civil liability to an appropriate extent. In Chinese Torts Law, Article 31 provides the similar regulations.

§4. Other Grounds for Impunity

I. Consent of the Victim

207. Consent of the victim has become a topic in the Chinese criminal law theory, principally as a ground of defence. In the Chinese criminal law, consent of the victim as a defence is impliedly expressed in the procedure requirement of 'upon complaint' for certain offences. For instance, to prosecute insult is only possible when the victim raised his complaint, according to Article 246 of the Chinese Criminal Code.

There are still debates about the nature and scope of consent of the victim. However, it is commonly agreed that consent shall be made in the ex-ante, valid and not unlimited situation. Consent of the victim when the situation involves public interests, life and violation of social ethics shall be invalid.

208. In the Specific Part of the Chinese Criminal Code, there are four provisions requiring that the prosecution need to be based upon complaint of the victim. They are as follows:

- Article 246 provides that whoever, by violence or other methods, publicly humiliates another person or invents stories to defame him, if the circumstances are serious, shall be guilty. However, the offence shall be handled only upon complaint, except where serious harm is done to public order or to the interests of the state.

- Article 257 provides that whoever uses violence to interfere with another person's freedom of marriage shall be guilty. However, the offence shall be handled only upon complaint.
- Article 260 provides that whoever maltreats a member of his family, if the circumstances are flagrant, shall be guilty. However, the offence shall be handled only upon complaint, if no serious injury or death to the victim was caused.
- Article 270 provides that whoever unlawfully takes possession of another person's money or property under his custody and refuses to return it, or whoever unlawfully takes possession of an object, which another person has forgotten about or buried, and refuses to hand it over, shall be guilty when the amount is relatively large. However, the offence shall be handled only upon complaint.

In the General Part of the Criminal Code of 1997, Article 98 provides that 'to be handled only upon complaint' as mentioned in this Code means that a case shall only be handled if the victim brings a complaint. However, if the victim is unable to bring a complaint because of coercion or intimidation, a people's procuratorate or a close relative of the victim may bring a complaint for him.

209. Obviously, if the victims of the offences mentioned above do not raise a complaint, their cases would usually not be brought into the courts. For these cases, only by private prosecution can the offences be tried.

In accordance with Article 206 of the Criminal Procedure, a people's court may conduct mediation in a case of private prosecution; the private complainant may arrange a settlement with the defendant or withdraw his prosecution before a judgment is made.

Article 15 of the Criminal Procedure provides that in any of the following circumstances, no criminal responsibility shall be investigated; if investigation has already been undertaken, the case shall be dismissed, or prosecution shall not be initiated, or innocence shall be declared: '(4) if the crime is to be handled only upon complaint according to the Criminal Code, but there has been no complaint or the complaint has been withdrawn.'

Thus, for the crimes for which the Criminal Code requires the victim's complaint, the victim can change his mind during the proceedings. Logically, the consent of the victim is a definite defence in these cases.

210. For certain offences other than those mentioned above, however, the lack of the victim's consent is an explicit or implicit element of the crime. The offence of rape is a typical example; whether the intercourse is against the will of the woman is a key factor in determining whether the conduct shall be considered a crime or not.

211. Consent of the victim may be a defence for offences involving private property, reputation and, to certain degree, physical integrity and sexual freedom.

Whether the consent of a victim can be acceptable in a case involving another person's life, typically in the case of euthanasia, is under a heated debate. However, the leading principle is so far still that euthanasia is unacceptable.

II. Minority

212. Criminal responsibility needs sufficient maturity of personality so that one can be capable of adjusting his conduct and reforming himself according to laws. Only after a certain age can a person be qualified in the sense of criminal law to undertake criminal responsibility. The Chinese Criminal Code has provided the requirement for the different levels of age to undertake certain criminal responsibility (*supra*, paragraph 118).

213. Children under the age of 14 are totally incapable of criminal responsibility (*supra*, paragraph 153). Thus, the fact that the defendant has not reached the age of 14 can be a definite defence for any criminal prosecution.

Children above the age of 14, but under 16, are deemed partially incapable of criminal responsibility. The fact that the defendant is under 16 can become a defence for those offences which are not mentioned by criminal law or which do not have the characteristic of seriously undermining social order, as the listed crimes may have (*supra*, paragraph 153).

III. Insanity and Intoxication

214. In accordance with Article 18 of the Criminal Code (*supra*, paragraph 154), insanity can be a definite defence but intoxication cannot.

215. When evidence sufficiently shows that the offender was insane at the time he committed the prohibited act, he will not be held accountable.

In legal practice, whether a person is insane shall be verified and confirmed through legal procedure. In accordance with Article 145 of the Criminal Procedure, an identification or evaluation expert shall prepare a written expert opinion and sign it after completion of an identification or evaluation. An identification or evaluation expert who intentionally conducts false identification or evaluation shall be subject to legal liability. According to the Decision on the Administration of Judicial Authentication of 2005 promulgated by the Standing Committee of the NPC, any individual, legal person or any other organisation may apply to engage in judicial authentication. If they pass the examination of the judicial administrative department of the provincial people's government, they shall be registered, listed and shall be announced.

So, whether a person is insane cannot be judged only by the opinions of the judges.

216. Since the Criminal Code explicitly provides that any intoxicated person who commits a crime shall bear criminal responsibility, intoxication can then not be used as a defence to prove innocence. In the 8th Amendment to the CCC in 2011, drunk driving became a new type of offence in China.

IV. Force Majeure

217. In accordance with Article 16 of the Criminal Code of 1997 (*supra*, paragraph 94), force majeure can be a defence. Whenever the harmful consequence occurs in the unavoidable or unforeseeable situation, no crime can therefrom be found, because there cannot be any blameworthy conduct if the defendant lost his freedom of choice and had no criminal mental state or culpability.

V. Duress and Inducement

218. In the 1979 CCC, inducement was still a circumstance which could exempt the accused person from criminal punishment. However, this circumstance was deleted in the 1997 CCC. Inducement is now only a circumstance which can be used to a judge's discretion for sentencing purposes.

Strictly speaking, duress is not an independent ground of justification or excuse in Chinese criminal law. It is, at most, a circumstance which might exempt the defendant from criminal punishment. In a situation where the accused person is coerced into participating in a crime, he may be exempted from criminal law punishment, though a mitigated punishment is also possible. It shall not be disputed that duress is a ground of excuse. However, whether duress is a ground for justification, e.g., in the case of necessity, is still unclear.

Article 28 of the Criminal Code of 1997 provides that anyone who is compelled to participate in a crime shall be given a mitigated punishment or be exempted from punishment in the light of the circumstances of the crime he commits.

Chinese criminal law theory generally agrees that the conditions for exempting the compelled criminals from punishment are as follows:

- regarding the objective aspect, he participated in a crime occasionally and passively, committed only some secondary conduct, played a supplementary role in a crime;
- regarding the subjective aspect, he involuntarily or not really voluntarily committed the criminal offence, though he knows or knows something about what he is doing.

219. The person who is coerced into participating in a crime is different from the person who has totally lost his freedom of choice or knew nothing about what he himself was doing and what would really happen. The latter can raise the defence of force majeure but the former cannot.

The coerced criminals are also different from the person who voluntarily participate in a crime, but certainly, the former's culpability is much weaker than the latter's.

VI. Ignorance or Mistake

220. There is no regulation about ignorance or mistake of fact or law in the text of Chinese criminal law. However, ignorance or mistake may greatly affect the criminal subjective aspect. In Chinese criminal law theory, the topic of ignorance and mistake has been included in the criminal subjective aspect, and so the criminal responsibility should be considered in conjunction with the circumstances of ignorance or mistake.

However, when ignorance or mistake can exclude criminal responsibility entirely, it shall definitely become the ground of justification or excuse.

The classical theory about the issue of ignorance or mistake is according to the law and fact. This theory is still influential in Chinese criminal law. However, the current studies and theories on ignorance or mistake have been expansive. New division has been worked out according to the facts and circumstances of a case which shall influence the constitution or exclusion of a crime.

A. Ignorance or Mistake of Law or Fact

221. Ignorance or mistake of law or ignorance of fact is the topic of classical theory in defence. The rules in dealing with the ignorance or mistake are rather simple: ignorance or mistake of law shall have no influence upon the accused person's criminal responsibility but ignorance or mistake of fact will.

222. In the case of ignorance or mistake of law, the accused person knows clearly what he was doing, but was not aware of or mistook the significance of his act in law or the nature of social harmfulness of his conduct.

There are three circumstances relevant to this aspect as follows:

> The first circumstance is that the conduct is not a criminal offence prohibited by criminal law, but the person mistakenly thinks that it is a criminal offence. For example, a person mistakes his self-defence for an illegal attack.

> The second circumstance is that the conduct is a criminal offence in criminal law, however, the person believes that it is not a crime. For example, a husband wrongfully thinks that he can mistreat his wife without bearing any criminal responsibility.

> The third circumstance is the misunderstanding of the legal significance of one's own conduct. For example, a person steals an electric wire which is in use. He shall be charged for the crime of sabotaging electric power and might be sentenced to more than ten years imprisonment, but he just thinks that only the crime of ordinary theft with the maximum punishment of five years imprisonment is applicable.

In all these cases, the person's misunderstanding will not affect the actual criminal liability. The judgment shall be made according to law. When the law says no criminal liability, he will not be convicted. When the law states that there should be criminal liability, he will be convicted according to law, according to the type of crime and to the degree stipulated in those laws. No more and no less.

The problems might appear in the cases where the crimes take a certain economic or administrative prohibition as a prerequisite, however, the accused persons have reasonable causes for not being aware of it. In this circumstance, the classical theory has to make an exception. This type of ignorance or mistake will negate the criminal liability of intentional crime and might be a ground for impunity.

223. In the case of ignorance or mistake of fact, the general principle is: if what the defendant mistakes is the fact necessary for a criminal constitution, this ignorance or mistake will affect his criminal responsibility; if what he mistakes is the fact outside the requirements of a criminal constitution, it will not affect the criminal responsibility.

Since the recognition of the facts concerning the criminal object and the criminal objective aspect (*supra* paragraph 157) are the important contents of criminal mental state, the ignorance or mistake of these facts will affect the criminal responsibility significantly.

Generally, there are the following circumstances to be discussed according to this theory.

The first circumstance is about the ignorance or mistake of the facts concerning the target at which one's conduct is aimed. If the person did not realise the harmfulness of his conduct, e.g., he mistook a farmer who was mowing for a wild bear, shot and killed him, he will according to the concrete circumstance be guilty of a negligent crime or be acquitted because of force majeure. If, however, what the person ignored or misinterpreted is only the criminal target and has nothing to do with criminal object, his criminal responsibility will remain unaltered. For example, the person mistakes A for B and kills him. He will be guilty of intentional homicide because the life of either A or B is the criminal object protected by criminal law. No matter who he was killing, he will commit the crime.

The second circumstance is about the ignorance or mistake of the fact concerning the criminal method. In this case, the person has a misunderstanding of the nature of the criminal method he chose. For example, he mistook grains of sugar for the poison, white arsenic, and wanted to use it to kill others. Because the consequence of death did not occur, the person will bear the criminal liability of attempt only.

The third circumstance is about the ignorance or mistake of the causation, i.e., the person has a misunderstanding of the actual development between the harmful conduct and the harmful consequence. For example, the person just wanted to lightly injure another person, however, the injured person died because of not being able to get proper treatment. The person should only bear the criminal liability of intentional injury with the result of death.

B. Ignorance or Mistake of Facts and Circumstances Concerning Constitution or Exclusion of Crime

224. Ignorance or mistake of facts and circumstances concerning constitution or exclusion of crime is a new theory, which makes a different division of ignorance or mistake.

225. Ignorance or mistake of facts and circumstances concerning constitution of crime includes ignorance or mistake of target, at which a crime aims, and causation. This type of ignorance or mistake is nothing to do with the issue of the nature of a crime or social harmfulness.

The ignorance or mistake of facts and circumstances concerning the criminal target concerns only the natural attribute of the object one's conduct aims at. When the value of the object in the actor's mind is the same as that in reality, the intent shall not be excluded. For instance, A is going to kill B but mistakenly deems C as B and kills C. A still has intent of murder, since the value of the life of B is the same as A's. However, when the value of the object in an actor's mind is not identical with that in reality, the intent shall be excluded. The standard of identity is whether the consideration of a new criminal constitution shall be necessary. For instance, A thinks what he was trying to do by throwing a piece of stone is to drive away a troublesome cat in his garden but actually hit the head of B who was hiding there, with the intention of trying to steal later. For B's injury or death, A shall only be held responsible for negligence.

The ignorance or mistake of facts and circumstances concerning causation refers to the situation where the actual process of a case deviated what the actor had thought. This type of ignorance or mistake concerns only the cases of intentional crime. Negligent crime is the typical example of this type of ignorance or mistake but there are special regulations in the criminal law for these types of crimes. In the case of deviation, the intent can only be excluded when the deviation of causation is important. This standard of importance has two key aspects to be considered: First, whether the deviation can be expected to go to such a scope out of ordinary living experience? Second, whether an additional evaluation of criminal law is necessary for the situation after the deviation? Usually, the first criterion is enough for the one-act case. For instance, A throws B from a bridge into a river and thought B would drown. However, B was killed by hitting on the pier of the bridge. This deviation of causation is unimportant and shall not exclude the intent of A. In the multi-act cases, the second criterion shall also be applied. For instance, A tried to kill B and B passed out. As A thought that B was already dead, he drove B to a secluded place to bury the body. However, he got into a traffic accident and B really died. Here, it is necessary to make an additional legal evaluation for B's death. So, A shall have intent for that attempted killing and be negligent for his death.

226. Ignorance or mistake of facts and circumstances concerning exclusion of crime principally refers to the ignorance or mistake of prohibition and the ignorance or mistake of allowable acts. Both of them will make the actor believe that he is allowed to commit an act, though that act actually conforms to the provision in the criminal law.

227. The ignorance or mistake of prohibition usually refers to the circumstance where the actor realised all of the facts of a conduct but still believed what he was doing was not wrong. In the former theory (*supra* paragraphs 199 et seq.), this type of ignorance or mistake would be deemed as the ignorance or mistake of criminal object or of social harmfulness. For instance, a foreign tourist was trying to bring a palaeontologist fossil home because he believed he was allowed to do so and did not think it could amount to a cultural relic. However, there is a provision in the Law on Cultural Relic Protection stipulating fossils of palaeo vertebrates and palaeo anthropoids of scientific value shall be protected by the state in the same way as cultural relics (Article 2 of the Law). The theory of the ignorance or mistake of prohibition in China is very much influenced by German theory. The rule in dealing with the ignorance or mistake of prohibition is to see if this ignorance or mistake is avoidable or unavoidable. Only the unavoidable ignorance or mistake of a prohibition can affect criminal liability.

The ignorance or mistake of allowable acts has very similar rules to the former situation but goes in another direction. It is not about the ignorance or mistake of prohibition but of allowableness. For instance, a governmental official accepts a valuable gift in an international event because he thought that was allowed according to the customs, which is a ground of impunity. But actually, his understanding is wrong.

The standard for ascertaining unavoidableness is to see if the actor has had any opportunity to find out the truth and if he has done his best.

228. The theory is still under development. The old theory and the new theory are both used in practice.

C. Special Case

229. It is common in the Chinese theory of ignorance or mistake of fact to study the problem of mistake of conduct, i.e., when the person committed some harmful conduct, where what resulted was not the result he expected because of the limit of objective conditions. For example, A wants to kill B. He shot, but failed because of his poor skill. In this case, A should still bear the criminal responsibility of attempt of intentional homicide.

Strictly speaking, mistake of conduct is not a problem of ignorance or mistake of fact. However this concept is still very similar with each in many respects and so the Chinese criminal law theory links them together.

VII. Family Relationship

230. The family relationship between the offender and his victim to a certain degree may become a personal ground of impunity for a limited category of criminal offences, typically for crimes against property.

Chinese judicial explanations issued by the SPC and the Supreme People's Procuratorate, always require a distinction to be made between the theft in the family or between the near relatives with the ordinary type of theft in society. Recently, the two Supremes stress that anyone who steals the property of a family member or close relative and has been forgiven thereafter may generally not be deemed as a criminal or he shall be given a more lenient punishment according to the circumstances of the case, if criminal liability is investigated (found in the Explanation of the Supreme People's Court (Expl. of SPC) and the Supreme People's Procuratorate on Several Issues concerning the Application of Law in the Handling of Criminal Cases of Theft in 3 April 2013).

231. In Chinese criminal law, a family relationship cannot be an absolute ground for impunity. For instance, with regards to the offence of providing forbidden assistance to offender, family relationship shall not be an excuse. Articles 310–312, for instance, provides that whoever knowingly provides a hiding place, money or property to a criminal, helps the criminal escape or gives false testimony to protect the criminal, refuses to provide testimony for espionage investigation, or helps in hiding illegal spoils, shall be guilty. When the helper conspires to commit the offence before it was committed, he shall be treated as a conspirator to the crime. In these offences, the

Chinese criminal law theory provides no exception for the criminal responsibility on the basis of the family relationship.

VIII. Other Grounds of Impunity Provided in the Criminal Code

232. In addition to the circumstances mentioned above, there are some provisions in the Chinese Criminal Code of 1997 providing grounds for impunity.

233. Article 24 provides that an offender who voluntarily discontinues a crime or voluntarily and effectively prevents the consequences of the crime from occurring in the course of committing a crime shall be exempted from punishment.

234. Article 27 provides that an accomplice who plays a secondary or auxiliary role in a joint crime might be exempted from punishment. Article 28 provides that a coerced person might be exempted from punishment.

235. Article 10 provides that if any person commits a crime outside the territory of the PRC, for which according to this Code he would bear criminal responsibility, he may still be investigated for his criminal responsibility according to this Code, even if he has already been tried in a foreign country. However, if he has already received criminal punishment in the foreign country, he may be exempted from punishment.

236. Article 19 provides that any deaf-mute or blind person who commits a crime may be exempted from punishment.

237. Article 22 provides that an offender who prepares the instruments or creates the conditions for a crime may, in comparison with the one who completes the crime, be exempted from punishment.

238. Article 37 provides that if the criminal circumstances are so minor that a criminal punishment is not necessary, he may be exempted from it; however, he may, depending on the different circumstances of the case, be reprimanded or ordered to make a statement of repentance, offer an apology or pay compensation for the losses, or be subjected to administrative penalty or administrative sanctions by the competent department. Article 37 of the 1997 CCC has become the general legal basis for excuse.

239. Article 67 provides that anyone who voluntarily delivers himself up to justice and truthfully confesses his crime after he committed the crime may be given a lighter or mitigated punishment. The ones whose crimes are relatively minor may be exempted from punishment. If a criminal suspect or a defendant under compulsory measures or a criminal serving a sentence truthfully confesses his other crimes that the judicial organ does not know, his act shall be regarded as voluntary surrender.

Article 68 provides that any criminal who performs such meritorious services as exposing an offence committed by another, which is verified through investigation, or produces important clues for solving other cases may be given a lighter or mitigated punishment. Any criminal who performs major meritorious services may be given a mitigated punishment or be exempted from punishment. Any criminal who not only voluntarily surrenders after committing the crime but also performs major meritorious services shall be given a mitigated punishment or be exempted from punishment.

240. Article 53 provides that when a fine has been ordered, if a person has true difficulties in paying because of an irresistible disaster, the fine may be reduced or remitted according to the circumstances.

Superior order is no longer an absolute defence. In the Chinese Civil Servant law of 2005, Article 54 provides that a civil servant shall be subject to the corresponding liabilities according to law, if he carries out any decision or order that is obviously unlawful.

Chapter 5. Incomplete Criminal Offences and Joint Crime

§1. Criminal Preparation, Criminal Attempt and Abandonment

241. Criminal preparation, criminal attempt and abandonment (or 'criminal discontinuation') exist only in intentional crime. Chinese criminal law theory commonly agrees that it is impossible to have such a problem in negligent crimes, because the wrongdoer pursued no harmful result by his conduct and no physical harmful consequence required by negligent crime appeared before it was constituted.

242. In order to realise a criminal desire, a criminal usually does some preparation, thoroughly or casually, and then begins to commit the crime. When he fulfils it, the crime is complete.

Sometimes, the criminal will begin to commit the crime as soon as he has an evil idea, without preparation. For example, A sees a new bicycle unlocked in front of a building and steals it immediately.

Sometimes, it may happen that a criminal offence falls short of completion for reasons independent of his will, such as the victim's resistance or the interruption of another's force. The conduct can only constitute a criminal attempt.

Sometimes, a criminal may even voluntarily abandon his evil idea, stop his conduct or effectively prevent the harmful consequence from occurring in the proceeding of the criminal preparation or after beginning to commit the crime. The conduct will form a criminal discontinuation.

In the Chinese criminal law theory, the issues of incomplete offence will be discussed in five stages: determination, preparation, execution, consummation and completion.

243. Chinese criminal law punishes criminal preparation, criminal attempt and criminal discontinuation, because the person possesses a criminal mental state in the criminal subjective aspect, and has in the criminal objective aspect committed the harmful conduct and jeopardised the criminal object, i.e., violated certain social relations protected by criminal law. However, these types of conduct may only be subjected to relatively light punishment because the harmful consequence has not been reached. In the stage of determination, only those acts can be offences when they are so stipulated by the criminal law. In the stage of consummation, people may argue if it is still an attempt. For instance, A steals B's TV set but was arrested just out of the door of B's house.

I. Criminal Preparation

244. Article 22 of the Criminal Code of 1997 provides that criminal preparation refers to the preparation of the instruments or the creation of the conditions for a crime.

245. Criminal preparation has two characteristics.

One is the act to prepare for a crime. Anything involving the preparation of the instrument or the creation of the condition for a crime will be included in this term. This characteristic displays that the criminal desire is no longer only in the mind of the actor but has begun to be realised and threatens society. It is this characteristic that distinguishes criminal preparation from the simple indication of a criminal mind, which is not a crime and cannot be criminally punished.

The other is that the preparation has not reached the point of beginning to commit the harmful conduct required as a constitutive element of the crime. This characteristic draws a line between criminal preparation and criminal attempt.

246. Since criminal preparation has not begun to commit the crime and has not aroused the physical harmful consequence, the Criminal Code of 1997 provides a lighter punishment or exemption from punishment for it (cf. *supra*, paragraph 237).

II. Criminal Attempt

247. Article 23 of the Criminal Code of 1997 provides a legal definition for criminal attempt. Accordingly, criminal attempt refers to a case where an offender has already begun to commit a crime but is prevented from completing it for reasons independent of his will.

Theoretically, criminal attempt has two categories.

According to whether the harmful conduct has been completed or not, the criminal attempt can be divided into the completed criminal attempt and the incomplete criminal attempt. A puts poison into B's food but is discovered before it is eaten. A commits a completed criminal attempt. In the other case, a criminal who is tearing a woman's clothing and about to rape her when he is arrested shall only be guilty of an incomplete criminal attempt.

According to whether the harmful conduct can be actually completed or not, the criminal attempt can be divided into the possible criminal attempt and the impossible criminal attempt. The impossible criminal attempt may be formed due to the criminal method or the criminal target. To use a gun without a bullet to shoot another is the impossible criminal attempt because of the criminal method. However, to steal an empty strongbox is the impossible criminal attempt because of the criminal target.

248. Criminal attempt has three conditions which should simultaneously exist. There will be no criminal attempt if any of them are missing.

249. The first one is that the actor has begun to commit the crime. He has gone beyond the stage of criminal preparation and has begun to execute the concrete harmful conduct, pursuing the criminal result. If it is not prevented by an interruption independent of his will, the crime will be completed.

Whether the actor has begun to commit the crime is an important distinction between the preparatory act and the act of execution. As in many other countries, the issue of where the line should be drawn between these two types of acts shall be dealt with upon the basis of fact. In Chinese legal practice, some tests have been developed:

- whether the act has been so close to the criminal object that the object has been under the direct threat of the crime;

- whether the act can possibly cause the criminal consequence directly;
- whether the act has displayed the criminal mind.

Generally, if the actor's criminal will has in a subjective aspect directed the act and has committed the harmful conduct as required by the criminal constitution of that crime, the commencement of the execution will be realised. Obviously, it will rely on a case-by-case examination.

250. The second condition is that the crime is prevented from being completed. This is the distinction between criminal attempt and criminal completion.

Since the criminal consequence has various forms (*supra*, paragraphs 118 and 119), whether the crime has been completed should fully consider the concrete requirement of the criminal constitutions. It is indeed that the criminal attempt is common in the crimes requiring physical criminal consequence.

It is important to notice that, when a crime is prevented from being completed, it does not mean that nothing harmful occurs after the commencement of the execution. Rather, it is often that an actor did not realise the criminal result he had expected but caused other harms. For example, A shot B, intending to kill B. However, B only lost one of his legs because he was saved by other people. A should be guilty of intentional homicide (attempt), though only serious bodily injury occurred.

251. The third one is that the crime is prevented from being completed for reasons independent of the actor's will. This is the distinction between criminal attempt and criminal discontinuation.

There are no restrictions on what a reason independent of the actor's will might be in Chinese criminal law. The reason may include the actor's personal reasons such as sudden illness, poor skill or knowledge to commit the crime, the actor's subjective reasons such as ignorance or false idea of the existence of the criminal target, or of the objective conditions to fulfil the crime, and other reasons such as the resistance of the victim, the interruption of natural force, other people or even the prevention by the public authorities.

252. Although a criminal attempt has directly threatened the criminal object, its social harmfulness may still be less serious than the criminal completion. So, in Article 23, it provides that an offender who attempts to commit a crime may, in comparison with one who completed the crime, be given a lighter or mitigated punishment. Actually, exemption from criminal punishment is still possible in the case of criminal attempt in legal practice. But it shall not take Article 23 as legal basis, rather, it will take Article 13 (*supra* paragraph 27) for the reason that the act is clearly of minor importance and little harm.

III. Abandonment (Criminal Discontinuation)

253. Article 24 of the Criminal Code of 1997 provides that abandonment (or 'criminal discontinuation') refers to cases where, in the course of committing a crime, the offender voluntarily discontinues the crime or voluntarily and effectively prevents the consequences of the crime from occurring.

According to Chinese criminal law theory, criminal discontinuation may occur at the stage of criminal preparation and after the commencement of its execution. However, it cannot occur with criminal attempt at the same time, because they have different characteristics. This is different from many countries. The reason is the legislative regulation. In Chinese criminal law, there is a specific provision on criminal discontinuation besides criminal attempt. So, criminal discontinuation is a statutory circumstance and not a circumstance which exists only in the criminal law theory.

254. A criminal discontinuation has three inseparable characteristics.

255. The first one is that a criminal discontinuation shall occur before the criminal completion.

Sometimes, cases will be complicated. When the harmful conduct has been completed but the harmful consequence has not appeared yet, the actor is required to effectively prevent the consequence from occurring. For example, the victim ate the poison provided by the actor. The actor should try his best to save the victim's life. If he fails, there will be no criminal discontinuation.

However, if the actor voluntarily retrieves the loss or compensates the victim for the loss, e.g., the thief returns intact what he has stolen, there will still be no criminal discontinuation.

256. The second one is that the actor should voluntarily discontinue his conduct. This characteristic makes the distinction from criminal attempt. In criminal attempt, the actor stops because of a reason independent of his will; in criminal discontinuation, the actor stops because of his will.

The reasons for voluntary discontinuance can be various. Sincere repentance, other's admonition or rebuke, sympathy or compassion for the victim, fear of the heavy punishment, and so on, are the most common reasons for the criminal discontinuation in Chinese legal practice.

The special cases are the following two circumstances:

- the case that the actor still believes that he is capable of furthering his conduct, while it is actually impossible, should be dealt with as a criminal discontinuation;
- the case that the actor quits his conduct because he misinterprets the possible situation for impossible conditions should be dealt with as a criminal attempt.

In legal practice, the criterion in distinguishing criminal discontinuation and criminal attempt is still the formulation: 'I can but I don't want' means criminal discontinuation, 'I want but I can't' means criminal attempt. However, this psychological criterion is under challenge, and the normative criterion is under development. According to the normative criterion, only when a wrongdoer shows that he has returned to the lawfulness can he be deemed as voluntary discontinuation.

257. The third one is that the criminal discontinuation should be a thorough and effective one.

The actor cannot temporarily abandon or suspend his criminal desire. However, this condition does not mean that the actor shall be required not to commit a crime of the same type anymore.

Although an effective discontinuation usually requires an active act to prevent the harmful result from occurring, an inactive act in certain cases will do, as long as the criminal completion will not be reached.

258. Because criminal discontinuation shows that the actor voluntarily quits the criminal desire and prevents the society from serious harm, the Criminal Code provides an exemption from punishment for the actor who does not cause damage and a mitigated punishment for the actor who causes any damage (*supra*, paragraph 233). The damage here usually refers only to the material damage. For the immaterial damage, for instance, a guy steals a fire weapon but finally returns them all safely, he will be exempted.

§2. Accomplice Liability ('Joint Crime' or Complicity)

I. General Remarks

259. The term 'joint crime' in Chinese criminal law is about the same as accomplice liability or complicity in other countries. Article 25 of the Criminal Code of 1997 provides that a joint crime refers to an intentional crime committed by two or more persons jointly.

According to the Chinese criminal law, joint crime can only be formed by intentional crime. In recent years, studies on the topic of negligent joint crime begin but not yet become an important area for research.

Obviously, a crime can be committed not only by one person but also by more than one person jointly. In the latter case, the crime usually causes more serious harm to the society.

260. In order to constitute a joint crime, it should theoretically have the following conditions.

261. The criminal subject should have two or more persons who possess the criminal capacity to commit the crime. The person without criminal capacity, e.g., under the prescribed criminal age or having a mental illness, cannot become a joint criminal, but rather only a 'tool' used by the real criminal. But a unit can be the criminal subject for joint crime with other unit or a natural person in other unit.

262. The joint criminals should in criminal subjective respects have a joint criminal intent, which means that every criminal has an intentional mental state for what they are doing and what their conduct will produce, and that every criminal knows that he is not committing the harmful conduct alone.

The case where more than two persons negligently commit a crime shall not be deemed as a joint crime, because of the requirement of criminal subjective aspect (*supra* paragraph 259) and because of the specific regulation of the criminal law (*infra* paragraph 264).

263. The joint criminals should commit a joint criminal offence. Though they may in many cases divide their work among themselves, e.g., in the case of theft, one may be on the lookout while the other may commit the crime, what they commit is to aim at the same criminal object or even the same criminal target. However, the joint criminal offenders do not need to have exactly same criminal intent. In their contents of knowledge, the organiser, instigator and helper might have different characteristics. The joint criminal offence does not require that every offender in a criminal case shall know exactly what his conspirator has done or will do. A typical example is the so-called one-sided conspirator, who provides assistance while the main actor does not know.

264. The following situations are not deemed a joint crime in Chinese criminal law:

- two or more persons intentionally violate the same criminal object but they have no joint criminal intent;
- one person commits the criminal offence by intent, the other by negligence, though their conducts jointly cause the same criminal result;
- joint negligent crime. In accordance with Article 25 of the Criminal Code of 1997, a negligent crime committed by two or more persons jointly shall not be punished as joint crime; however, those who should bear criminal responsibility shall be individually punished according to the crimes they have committed.

II. Forms of Joint Crime

265. In the Chinese criminal law theory and the Chinese criminal law, a joint crime has the following forms:

- According to whether there is a division among the criminals, a joint crime can be divided into simple joint crime and complicated joint crime. The former has no clear division among criminals but the latter has.
- According to the condition to form a joint crime, a joint crime can be divided into an arbitrary joint crime and a necessary joint crime. The former can be committed either by one person or more but the latter can be committed only by two or more persons.
- According to the time forming the joint criminal intent, a joint crime can be divided into the joint crime with conspiracy and without conspiracy. The former means that the joint criminal intent was formed before the commencement of the execution but the latter was after.
- According to whether the joint crime has a relatively fixed leadership, a joint crime can be divided into the common joint crime and special joint crime. The former is the joint crime without fixed leadership. The latter is the criminal organisation and criminal group.

266. Criminal organisation is the most dangerous joint crime. In the Criminal Code of 1979, there were some provisions involving this term in Chinese criminal law. For example, in the Criminal Code of 1979, there were criminal organisations of smuggling (Article 118), speculation (Article 119) and hooligans (Article 160). In the separate criminal regulations, there was the criminal organisation of embezzlement.

The SPC, the Supreme People's Procuratorate and the Ministry of Public Security jointly issued the Explanation Concerning the Currently Concrete Application of Laws in Dealing with the Cases of Criminal Organisations on 15 June 1984, which explained the characteristics of a criminal organisation as follows:

- three or more persons were involved, and the important members were relatively fixed;
- relatively fixed organisation and division of works;
- relatively strict internal discipline;
- secret criminal scheme of one or more types;
- usually having been formed for a substantial period of time or even making crime its regular business.

After summarising these experiences, the Criminal Code of 1997 provides in Article 26 that a criminal organisation refers to a relatively stable criminal organisation formed by three or more persons for the purpose of committing crimes jointly.

267. In the Specific Part of the 1997 CCC, the law may provide more detailed conditions for certain criminal organisations. For instance, Article 294 of the 8th Amendment provides that an organisation with the nature of an underground society shall have following characteristics: (1) a criminal organisation is quite stable in formation with a rather large number of members, especially with clear organisers or leaders and regular members; (2) economic interests are gained by their organised illegal or criminal activities or other means, and the organisation's financial strength is strong enough to support its activities; (3) its illegal or criminal activities were organised and committed many times by violence, threat or other means and people were bullied, cruelly injured, killed or suffered by other evil activities; (4) it dominates a certain area by committing illegal or criminal activities or taking advantage of the harbouring or connivance by the state functionaries, forming an illegal control or significant influence in a certain area or sector, which seriously disrupts the economic and social order.

III. Parties to Criminal Offences

268. Many countries' criminal laws classify the joint criminals by either the division of the criminal work or the function of the criminals. However, Chinese criminal law has adopted the standard that the function of the criminal works and the division of criminal work helps, so that the joint criminals can be classified as principal criminals, accomplices, people coerced to participate in a crime and criminal instigators.

A. Principal Perpetrator

269. Article 26 of the Criminal Code of 1997 provides that a principal criminal refers to any person who organises and leads a criminal group in carrying out criminal activities or plays a principal role in a joint crime.

There are two types of principal criminal in the Chinese criminal law: ringleader and other principal criminals.

Article 97 of the Code provides that 'ringleader' refers to any criminal who plays the role of organising, plotting or directing in a crime committed by a criminal organisation or a crowd. Article 26 of the Code provides that any ringleader who organises or leads a criminal organisation shall be punished on the basis of all the crimes that the criminal organisation has committed.

With respect to other principal criminals, they shall be punished on the basis of all the crimes that he participates in, that he organises or directs (Article 26 of the Criminal Code of 1997).

270. There are many provisions in the Specific Part of the Criminal Code providing heavier punishment for the principal criminals. For example, Article 103 provides that:

> among those who organise, plot or carry out the scheme of splitting the state or undermining unity of the country, the ringleaders and the others who commit major crimes shall be sentenced to life imprisonment or fixed-term imprisonment of not less than 10 years; the ones who take an active part in it shall be sentenced to fixed-term imprisonment of not less than three years but not more than 10 years; and the other participants shall be sentenced to fixed-term imprisonment of not more than three years, criminal detention, public surveillance or deprivation of political rights.

For certain crimes, only the principal criminal shall be convicted. For example, Article 292 of the Criminal Code of 1997 provides that where people are gathered to engage in affrays, the ringleaders and the active participants shall be punished.

B. Accomplice

271. Article 27 of the Criminal Code of 1997 provides that an accomplice refers to any person who plays a secondary or auxiliary role in a joint crime.

An accomplice shall yield to the principal criminal in committing a crime. He only assists or forwards the execution of the crime and usually cannot directly cause the harmful, especially the seriously harmful, consequences.

It is important to understand that an accomplice in the Chinese criminal law cannot possess the main power or capacity to control the crime, which shall start or stop the commission of the crime. In Chinese criminal law, the term of 'helper' or 'aider' is not officially used. A helper can be a principal criminal, if his help is of vital importance in that crime. In the Specific Part of the 1997 CCC, the offences of smuggling (Article 156) and insurance fraud (Article 198), drug offences (Articles 349 and 350) and the offence of embezzlement (Article 382) only say that the participants shall be punished as a joint crime but will not be punished only as an accomplice.

272. Article 27 also provides that an accomplice shall be given a lighter or mitigated punishment or be exempted from punishment. That is because an accomplice does not play a principal role in a crime and the social harmfulness he causes is less serious than that which is caused by the principal criminal.

C. The Person Who Is Coerced to Participate in a Crime

273. This topic is closely linked with the topic of duress and inducement, which we have discussed above in paragraphs 196 and 197.

D. Instigators

274. In accordance with Article 29 of the Criminal Code of 1997, an instigator is a person who instigates others to commit a crime.

The basic characteristic of an instigator is that he does not commit the crime himself, rather, he instigates others to do it. The conditions to constitute an instigator are as follows:

- In the objective aspect, one shall have the conduct to instigate others to commit a crime to constitute an instigator. The conduct may be anything active such as advice, request, incite, induce, even a threat. It may be not only in the oral or written form such as in a dialogue or in a letter, but also in the bodily movement such as a gesture or an expression in his eye, in certain cases.
- In essence, to be an instigator one shall have the intent to instigate. The instigator wishes or allows the harmful consequence he instigates to occur.

275. Article 29 of the Criminal Code of 1997 provides that an instigator shall be punished according to the role he has played in the joint crime. That means if the instigator plays the principal role in the joint crime, he shall be punished as a principal criminal; if, however, the instigator plays only the secondary or auxiliary role in the crime, he shall be punished as an accomplice. It is impossible for an instigator to be a person coerced to participate in a crime.

To punish an instigator, it is important to distinguish the instigator from the crime committed in the way of instigation, e.g., the crime of instigating state functionaries or armed forces, the people's police or the people's militia to commit armed rebellion or armed riot (Article 104 of the Criminal Code of 1997).

In order to protect the minor people, Article 29 provides that anyone who instigates a person under the age of 18 to commit a crime shall be given a heavier punishment. However, anyone who instigates a person under the age of 14 or without criminal capacity to commit a crime shall be deemed the one who committed the crime himself.

In the case that the instigated person has not committed the instigated crime, Article 29 provides that the instigator may be given a lighter or mitigated punishment, adopting the same principle as for the criminal attempt. It is obvious that a person shall not be an instigator anymore if he commits the crime himself personally after he instigates others to do so. He shall then be punished directly as a perpetrator.

Chapter 6. Classification and Survey of Criminal Offences

§1. General Classification of Criminal Offences

276. It is true that criminal offences in a criminal code may be classified in different ways. Besides the classification of intentional and negligent crime in the General Part of the Criminal Code of 1997, the criminal offences are in the Specific Part classified into ten categories according to the theory of kindred criminal object (*supra*, paragraphs 62 and 108).

Actually, there is a further classification under the kindred criminal object in the Specific Part of the Criminal Code of 1997, i.e., under Chapter III 'Crimes of Disrupting the Order of the Socialist Market Economy' and Chapter VI 'Crimes of Obstructing the Administration of Public Order' (for details *see infra*, paragraphs 260 and 265). The reason for this further classification is the consideration on the systematical arrangement of the various types of offences in these areas. By inserting the 'Section' under 'Chapter', the Chinese legislature has made numerous and disorderly offences into a system.

277. The term of political crime is unknown in the Chinese criminal law. It is a misunderstanding to think that the crime of counter-revolution in Chapter I of the Specific Part of the Criminal Code of 1979 is a political crime. The term of the crime of counter-revolution was given because of historical reasons. Actually, the crime is against the national security. Now, the name of Chapter I of the Specific Part is changed to 'Crimes of endangering National Security' in the Criminal Code of 1997.

278. Chinese criminal law does not adopt the classification of crime (felony), misdemeanour and contravention (petty misdemeanour or violation), which somewhat depends on the severity of the punishment.

The Chinese classification is largely based upon the degree and extent of the social harmfulness or the size of the criminal object. Obviously, national security is the largest criminal object and violating it has the most serious social damage. Second to it is the public security and so on and so forth.

Exceptions can be seen in Chapter VII 'Crimes of Impairing the Interests of National Defence', Chapter VIII 'Crimes of Embezzlement and Bribery', Chapter IX 'Crimes of Dereliction of Duty', and Chapter X 'Crimes of Servicemen's Transgression of Duties'. These chapters are classified according to the criminal subject, which is supplementary to the main rule of classification by criminal object (*supra* paragraph 130).

§2. Survey of Criminal Offences

279. Obviously, it is not possible to present in a few pages an exhaustive survey of all the criminal offences in Chinese criminal law. Therefore, our explanation will be limited to a concise representation of the structure and the contents of the Specific

Part of the Criminal Code. The important contents of supplements and revisions in the separate criminal regulations will be mentioned in this context when necessary.

The latest development of the Chinese criminal law can only be mentioned at the legislative level. However, there are many important developments at the level of judicial explanation (*supra* paragraph 60), the most important of which can be mentioned.

I. Crimes Endangering National Security

280. As mentioned above (*supra*, paragraph 277), the Crimes of Counter-revolution were changed into the Crimes Endangering National Security.

The Explanation concerning the CCC (Draft), explains the reason why the name was changed as follows:

> in consideration of that this country has moved from the period of revolution into the new historical era to concentrate ourselves on the socialist modernization construction and the Constitution has fixed the leadership of the Chinese Communist Party on the national affairs, it is believed from the viewpoint of national system and the interests to safeguard the country as a whole as well as from the view of law that it is more appropriate to provide the Crimes of Endangering National Security for the criminal conducts endangering the People's Republic of China than the Crimes of Counter-Revolution. This is also for the protection of the criminal justice system of our country.

The crimes of treason, espionage, defection to the enemy and armed rebellion are the typical crimes of endangering national security.

New development after 1997 has attempted to make the requirements for these offences clearer. For instance, the offence of defecting by governmental officials no longer requires the endangerment of the PRC national security. It shall be sufficient for this offence that a governmental official leaves his post without authorization during the time of performing his public functions and defects from the country.

II. Crimes Endangering Public Security

281. Crimes endangering public security refer to any acts that are intentionally or negligently committed to harm the safety of life, health or significant public and private property of the indefinite majority of the people.

In this chapter, the crimes can be roughly classified as the following categories:

- The crimes committed by dangerous methods, e.g., arson, dike breaching, explosion, and poisoning; In recent developments, the term of poisoning was more clearly defined as spreading the pathogen of infectious diseases, poisonous or radioactive substances (Articles 114, 115).
- The crimes committed to harm the specific criminal targets which will easily cause great losses to the society, e.g., transportation vehicles, transportation

facilities, electric power or gas facilities, inflammable or explosive equipment, communication equipment. The crime of hijacking an aircraft is also included in this chapter.

- The crimes involving illegal manufacturing, trafficking, transporting or stealing and forcibly seizing guns or ammunition.
- The crimes involving serious accidents such as traffic accidents, accidents in the work place and accidents by violating the regulations on the control of the dangerous items such as explosives and inflammable things. The accidents caused by violating the state regulations on building safety and fire prevention shall also accordingly bear criminal responsibility; the new offences of drunk driving and dangerous driving were stipulated in the 8th Amendment of 2011 and supplemented in the 9th Amendment of 2015 (Article 133A).
- The crime of forming, leading or actively participating in a terrorist organisation (Article 120). The new offence of financing terrorist activities was added into the 1997 CCC (Article 120A). In the 9th Amendment of 2015, Article 120 was added which implements a fine as a supplementary punishment. In addition, the anti-terror criminal law was strengthened by expanding and specifying the conducts of preparation or advocating in Articles 120A through 120F.

III. Crimes Disrupting the Order of the Socialist Market Economy

282. Crimes of disrupting the order of the socialist market economy refer to any acts that are committed by violating national economic regulations and sabotaging the national economic regulatory activities, which disturbs the social economic order, undermines the national economy and the people's livelihood and makes the national economy suffer great losses. Alongside the construction of the Chinese market economy, the legislation in this area has been improved.

Unlike other chapters, this chapter is composed of eight sections, such as:

- Crimes of producing and marketing fake or substandard commodities. The revision and supplements after 1997 were focused on improving protection of pharmacy (Article 141), food safety (Articles 143, 144), and medical instrument (Article 145).
- Crimes of smuggling. The new criminal legislations (the 8th and 9th Amendments) are involved in abolishing death penalty for all crimes of smuggling (Articles 151, 153), improving protection of rare plants and their products from smuggling out of the country (Article 151), prohibiting transportation of the solid, liquid or gaseous waste into China by evading supervision and control of the Customs (Article 152), and adjusting the criminal penalties for the offences of smuggling.
- Crimes disrupting the order of administration of companies and enterprises. The legislative improvements are related to improving the protection of the corporate obligations to reveal the accounting report of finance to the shareholders and the public (Article 161). The protection for financial vouchers, financial accounting books or financial statements (Article 162A) was strengthened. The offence of false bankruptcy was stipulated (Article 162B). The offence of bribery committed

by non-governmental officials has been expanded from including only companies and enterprises to also recognise 'other institutions' (Articles 163, 164). This shall cover arbitrators and referees in sport games, especially football games, and the foreign or international officials (Article 164). The conduct defined in Article 164 will also be subject to a fine, as an accessory penalty, added by the 9th Amendment. The protections of foreign currency, state-owned companies, and listed companies (Articles 167, 168, 169A) have also been strengthened.

- Crimes disrupting the order of financial administration. The new criminal legislation is focused on abolishing the death penalty for the crime of counterfeiting currencies and removing the limits which had prevented sentencing fines above a certain amount, improving the protection on establishment of a financial institution (Article 174), on obtaining any loan, acceptance of any instrument, letter of credit, letter of guarantee, etc. from any bank or any other financial institution (Article 175A), on administration of credit cards (Article 177A). In addition, the prohibition of insider trading and the protection of the information and operation in security and commodity future markets have been improved (Articles 180, 181, 182). The protection of assets and operations in the financial companies, institutions and enterprises has improved, this protection covers; commercial banks, stock exchanges, futures exchanges, securities companies, futures brokering companies, insurance companies, social security fund management institutions, housing accumulation fund management institutions, insurance companies, insurance asset management companies, securities investment fund management companies and other financial companies (Articles 185, 185A, 186, 187, 188, 190, 190A). The legislation on money laundering has been improved according to the international convention (Article 191).
- Crimes of financial fraud. The new criminal legislation provides for the offence of credit card fraud (Article 196). In addition, the death penalty for the offences of fraud of financial bill, bank document and letters of credit and the offence of illegal fund raising (Articles 192, 194, 195) were abolished in the 8th Amendment of 2011 (for Articles 194, 195) and totally in the 9th Amendment of 2015 (Articles 199, 192). This group of crimes no longer contains any capital crime. However, the scope of corporate crime in this section was expanded.
- Crimes jeopardising the administration of tax collection. The new criminal legislation attempts to improve the criminal constitutions for the offences of tax evasion (Article 201), abolish the death penalty for tax-related offences (Articles 205, 206) and strengthen the protection given to invoices (Articles 205A, 209, 210A).
- Crimes against intellectual property rights. Although there are not new criminal legislation in this section, the intellectual property protection has been strengthened in legal practice by some new judicial explanations (*supra* paragraph 60) of the SPC.
- Crimes disrupting market order. The new criminal legislation introduces the offences of progressively recruiting others to participate in a selling system (Article 224A), of illegal business without special licence (Article 225), coercive trading (Article 226), as well as the illegally trading the land use right (Article 228).

283. It is true that the Crimes of Disrupting the Order of the Socialist Market Economy are some of the most active fields in the Chinese criminal law. Ten out of the twenty-three separate criminal regulations made between 1979 and 1997 were in this field and two out of the three supplementary regulations were made after 1997, i.e., the Decision Regarding the Punishment of the Crimes of Buying Foreign Currency by Cheating, Illegally Keeping or Transferring Foreign Currency outside the Territory and Illegally Buying or Selling Foreign Currency and the Amendment of the Criminal Code, are included in this chapter (*supra*, paragraph 32).

284. The crimes of disrupting the order of the socialist market economy are not the same as the economic crimes. Economic crime is a term with a broader meaning, which generally includes the crimes in this chapter, the crimes in the chapter of Crimes of Property Violation (*infra*, paragraph 286) and some crimes in other chapters and separate criminal regulations.

IV. Crimes Infringing upon Citizens' Civil and Democratic Rights

285. This chapter gives an overview of the crimes infringing upon the civil (or 'personal') rights and democratic rights of citizens and the crimes disrupting marriage and the family, as well as the contents of some separate criminal regulations. It includes the following types of crimes:

- crimes against a person's life, i.e., intentional homicide and negligent killing;
- crimes against a person's health, i.e., intentional injury and negligent injury;
- crimes infringing a person's freedom, e.g., unlawful detention, unlawful search, trespassing, abducting, kidnapping and trafficking in human beings;
- crimes against a person's reputation and personality, e.g., insult and defamation;
- crimes infringing a person's democratic rights, e.g., violation of the electoral law, violation of a citizen's legitimate freedom of religious belief, infringing upon the customs and habits of minority nationalities and infringing upon the citizen's freedom of correspondence;
- false charge and crimes of extorting confession or testimony by torture and related crimes;
- crimes against marriage, e.g., interfering with another person's freedom of marriage by force or bigamy;
- crimes against the family, e.g., mistreating a member of the family, abandonment, and abduction of children under the age of 14.

The new developments of the criminal legislation in the 8th and 9th Amendments in this area are focused on the following points:

- New offences were added on the protection of people's livelihood. The new offences in the 8th Amendment include illegal trafficking of human organs (Article 234A), illegal employment of minors under the age of 16 to conduct dangerous and heavy works (Article 244A), illegal obtainment and provision of private information (Article 253A), organising disabled persons or minors below the age of 14 by force or coercion to beg (Article 262A), organising minors to commit illegal conducts such as theft, fraud, blackmail (Article 262B). In the 9th Amendment, protection offered by criminal law was strengthened in the areas of private information (Articles 246, 253A) and domestic violence (Articles 260, 260A).

– The criminal constitutions were more clearly written and the severity of punishments was adjusted. The adjustments led to some increase in punishment. For instance, the criminal constitution for the offences of forcing another person to work by violence, threat or restriction of personal freedom, was better clarified and the punishment was increased from maximum three years to ten years (Article 244). New circumstances were also added, where a lighter punishment would be possible for lighter cases. For instance, the minimum punishment for the offence of kidnap was ten years imprisonment but new legislation provides that the punishment above five years imprisonment shall be applied when the circumstances involve a minor and that the capital offence shall only be treated as such when the perpetrator intentionally causes serious injury or the death of the victim (Article 239). The offence of indecency (Article 237) was expanded from application only to females, to all kinds of persons. The offence of only buying an abducted woman or child lost the opportunity of not being prosecuted in the 9th Amendment of 2015. However, in circumstances where there has been no maltreatment of the abducted child or no obstructing the rescue of the woman or child, it is still possible to get only a lighter punishment.

V. Property Crimes

286. Property crimes refer to the intentional illegal possession of the property of another person and any acts which intend to destroy the property of another person.

The crimes in this chapter include; robbery, theft, fraud, forcibly seizing another's property, extortion, misappropriation of private or corporate property, misappropriation of the state funds allocated for disaster relief, emergencies, flood control, care to disabled servicemen and families of revolutionary martyrs and servicemen, and social relief.

The new developments of the criminal legislation in this area are focused on the following points:

– The criminal constitutions were more clearly revised and the severity of punishment were adjusted. The offence of theft will now include the new types of burglary, carrying a lethal weapon for the purpose of stealing and picking pockets, while the death penalty has been abolished (Article 264). Other offences are extortion (Article 274); a new offence of refusal to pay labour remunerations though capable of doing so (Article 176A) was added and the offence of illegally seizing was supplemented by a new constitutional circumstance of committing the offence more than twice, if the amount involved was small or minor (Article 267).

VI. Crimes Obstructing the Administration of Public Order

287. Crimes obstructing the administration of public order refer to any acts that intentionally obstruct the administration of the state organ and disturb public order.

Like the crimes of disrupting the order of the socialist market economy, this chapter is classified into nine sections as follows:

- Crimes disturbing public order. The new criminal legislation added a stronger protection for the policemen in enforcement (paragraph 5 of Article 277), expanded and enhanced the protection over any official document, certificate or seal of a state authority, a seal of any company, enterprise, public institution or people's organisation, any citizen's identification card, passport, social security card, driver's licence or any other certificate that may be used to prove identity in accordance with the law (Article 280). The control over special espionage devices, eavesdropping or secret photographing devices was strengthened (Article 283). A new offence of test cheating was added (Article 284A). The offences of illegally obtaining or controlling the data of a computer information system and any assistance given in the aforementioned crimes were added into the offence of intruding into computer information system (Article 285). The acts of producing and distributing computer viruses were clarified as the offence of destroying computer information systems (Article 286). Cybercrime and radio broadcasting were more carefully regulated (Articles 286A, 287A, 287B, 288). The protection of public order has been explicitly extended to medical service (Article 290). New offences have been added involving the spreading of mendacious dangerous substances such as pathogens of infectious diseases, explosives, poisonous or radioactive substances or other substances, or fabricating terrorist information on threats of explosion, biochemical threats or radioactive threats, or, while clearly knowing that the terrorist information is fabricated, intentionally disseminating such information, thus seriously disrupting public order (Article 291A). The punishment for the offence of undermining public order by a person through their provocative and disturbing behaviours has been enhanced from a maximum of five years imprisonment to ten years (Article 293). The criminal constitution and punishment for the offences of underground societies have been improved (Article 294, *see supra* paragraph 267). The death penalty for the offence of teaching criminal methods has been abolished (Article 295). The prevention of superstitious sects, secret societies, and evil religious organisations has been improved (Article 300) and the offence of gambling is now under better controlled (Article 303).
- Crimes impairing judicial administration. The new criminal legislation for the offence of harbouring a criminal has been improved together with the regulation of money laundering (Article 312, *see supra* paragraph 282). A new offence of filing a civil lawsuit based on any fabricated facts was added (Article 307A). The offence of refusing to carry out a decision or order made by a people's court has seen further clarification (Article 313) and the offence of disrupting a judiciary's order has been improved (Articles 308A, 309, 311).
- Crimes against control of the national border (frontier). The conduct that illegally crosses China's frontier (border) for the purpose of joining a terrorist organisation,

receiving training on terrorist activities or conducting terrorist activities was regulated as a crime (Article 322).

- Crimes against control of cultural relics; New criminal legislation clarified that the regulations on cultural relics shall also be applied to ancient human fossils and ancient vertebrate fossils that have scientific value (*supra* paragraphs 74, 205). The death penalty for the offence of robbing ancient cultural ruins and ancient tomb burial objects that have historical, artistic, and scientific value has now been abolished (Article 328).
- Crimes impairing public health. The new criminal legislation has improved the criminal constitution for the offence of violating the regulations of the quarantine law on the entry and exit of animals and plants (Article 337).
- Crimes impairing the protection of environment and resources. The new criminal legislation is involved in improving the offences of major environmental pollution (Article 338), serious environmental pollution by illegally imported solid waste (Article 339), illegally using and damaging farmland (Article 342), illegally mining (Article 343), illegally logging, damaging and handling the valuable trees (Article 344) and illegally logging and trading forest or other trees in large quantity (Article 345).
- Crimes of smuggling, trafficking in, transporting and manufacturing narcotic drugs. The control over the raw materials or auxiliary materials for manufacturing drugs such as acetic anhydride, ethyl ether and chloroform were strengthened (Article 350).
- Crimes organising, forcing, luring, sheltering or procuring other persons to engage in prostitution. The new criminal legislation provides criminal liability also for the act of assistance to the organiser (Article 358). However, the death penalty was abolished for the crimes of organising or forcing anyone else into prostitution (Article 358). In addition, the provision of Article 360 (paragraph 2) was deleted, which means that the conduct of visiting young girl prostitutes under 14 years old shall be treated as the crime of rape ever after.
- Crimes of producing, selling or disseminating pornographic materials. The new criminal legislation expands the meaning of pornographic books, movies, pictures and videos to the internet and website (Articles 363, 367).

VII. Crimes Impairing the Interests of National Defence

288. Crimes of impairing the interests of national defence refer to any acts that impair the interests of national defence.

This is a new chapter in the Criminal Code of 1997 and is composed of the following crimes:

- Crimes impairing warfare and military activities, e.g., obstructing a serviceman from performing his legal duty by violence or threat and intentionally providing false information about the enemy to the armed forces during wartime;
- Crimes impairing construction of the national defence and the military forces, e.g., sabotaging weapons or equipment, military installations or military

telecommunications, knowingly providing substandard weapons or equipment or military installations to the armed forces. New criminal legislation expands the offence of sabotaging weapons and equipment, military facilities or military communications from only intentional actions being relevant to negligent conduct also able to meet the requirements of the crime.

- Crimes impairing the administrative order of national defence, e.g., gathering people to assault a military restricted zone or disturbing the order of the military administrative zone. New criminal legislation expands the protection for the armed forces of their specific characteristics such as uniform and vehicle licences to other documents, certificates and seals of armed units (Article 374).
- Crimes of refusing to perform the legal obligation for national defence, e.g., rejecting requisition for military purpose during wartime, refusing or escaping military service in wartime. New criminal legislation expands the act from rejecting requisition to rejecting expropriation (Article 381).

VIII. Crimes of Embezzlement and Bribery

289. Crimes of embezzlement and bribery refer to the acts of a state functionary where by taking advantage of his official position he illegally possess or uses public property, accepts bribes or obtains other illegal interests, so that his professional honesty is violated.

This is a new chapter in the Criminal Code of 1997. It is a chapter of crimes specially designed for combating the corruption of the state functionary. In accordance with Article 93 of the Criminal Code of 1997, the term of state functionary refers to persons who perform public service in state organs. Persons who perform public service in state-owned companies or, enterprises, institutions or people's organisations, persons who are assigned by state organs, state-owned companies, enterprises or institutions to companies, enterprises or institutions that are not owned by the state or people's organisations to perform public services and the other persons who perform public service according to law shall all be regarded as state functionary.

In accordance with the Explanation Regarding Article 93, paragraph 2 of the CCC (*supra*, paragraph 32), the personnel working in the basic organisations of villages, such as villager's committees, shall belong to 'the other persons who perform public service according to law', when they assist the people's government to do the following administrative works:

- administration of the money or goods allocated for disaster relief, emergency rescue, flood prevention and control, support to disabled servicemen and families of revolutionary martyrs and servicemen, aid to the poor, migration and social relief;
- administration of the money or goods which are donated by the society for public welfare;
- operation and administration of the state-owned land;
- administration of the compensation fees for requisition of land;
- collection or payment of taxes for others;

- works concerning family planning, census register and conscription;
- assist with other administrative management for a people's government.

Therefore, when the personnel working in the basic organisation of a village such as a villager's committee engages in the public service mentioned above, takes advantage of their position and illegally occupies or misappropriates the publicly owned money or goods or extorts or accepts bribes, they shall be punished as a criminal and shall be convicted of the crimes prescribed in this chapter.

The crimes in this chapter includes embezzlement, misappropriation of public funds, bribery and the related crimes, failing to declare one's bank savings outside the territory of China and failing to prove the source of one's property is legitimate when a person's property or expenditure obviously exceeds his lawful income and the difference is significant.

New criminal legislation attempts to address the following issues:

- To clarify the meaning of misappropriation. According to the legislative explanation to Article 384, misappropriation shall include the act of providing public funds for one's self, his relatives or friends or to other natural persons to use, of providing public funds in his own name for other units to use, and of deciding himself in the name of his unit to provide public funds for other units to use, in order to obtain personal benefits in return (Article 384); to stipulate the offence of trading in influence (Article 388A).
- To increase the punishment from maximum five years to ten years for the offence of a failure to explain by state functionaries, the legitimacy of their property clearly exceeding their legitimate income (Article 395).
- In the 9th Amendment of 2015, there is a significant provision: in a case where a person convicted of the crime of embezzlement shall be sentenced to death with two-years suspension, he may be given a condition that no commutation or parole is possible after his sentence is reduced to life imprisonment upon expiration of the two-year period. It is generally believed that the death penalty in the crime of embezzlement is de facto abolished.
- The offence of trading in influence and other anti-bribery criminal laws (Articles 390, 390A, 391, 392, 393) were significantly improved.

IX. Crimes of Dereliction of Duty

290. Crimes of dereliction of duty refer to any acts that are committed by a state functionary, by taking advantage of his office or because of neglect of duty, which disrupt the administration of a state organ and cause great losses of public or private interest.

The crimes in this chapter are composed of the following categories:

- Crimes committed by any functionary of a state organ, e.g., abusing his power or neglecting his duty and thus causing heavy losses to public money, property or the interests of the state and the people and intentionally or negligently divulging state secrets. New criminal legislation clarifies that these offences shall be applied to the state functionaries in the departments of Customs and foreign exchange control (Article 397).

- Crimes committed by a judicial functionary, e.g., bending the law for selfish ends or twisting the law as a favour to another person or releasing a criminal suspect, a defendant or a criminal held in custody without authorisation. New criminal legislation clarifies that these offences shall be applied to the judicial functionary in the department of enforcement (Article 399). In addition, a new offence has been created which is applicable to arbitrators which prohibits these people intentionally acting contrary to the facts or law and making wrongful ruling in the process of arbitration (Article 399A).
- Crimes committed by an administrative functionary, e.g., malpractice for personal gain, such as failing to transfer a person that should be transferred to a judicial organ according to law to be investigated for criminal responsibility or approving an application for the incorporation and registration of a company or an application for the issue and listing of shares or bonds submitted by a company that does not meet the conditions provided by law.
- Crimes committed by the state functionaries who work in the department of tax, forestry, environmental protection, public health, land administration, customs, commodity inspection, animal and plant quarantine organ, passports, visa or other exit and entry certificates. Also those state organs who are endowed with the functions and responsibilities of rescuing a woman or child who is abducted, sold or kidnapped but fail to do so on receiving a request for rescue. New criminal legislation adds an offence specifically for misconduct in the administration of food safety (Article 408A).

X. Crimes of Servicemen's Transgression of Duties

291. The crimes in this chapter were stipulated in the Interim Regulation on Punishment of Servicemen Who Commit Crimes Contrary to Their Duties (*supra*, paragraph 32) and incorporated in the Criminal Code in the criminal law reform of 1997.

292. In accordance with Article 420 of the Criminal Code of 1997, the Crimes of Servicemen's Transgression of Duties refer to any act of a serviceman in transgression of his duties that endangers the military interests of the state and which shall therefore be subjected to criminal punishment according to law.

The crimes stipulated in this chapter shall apply to officers, civilian staff, soldiers in active service and cadres with military status of the Chinese PLA, police officers, civilian staff and soldiers in active service, cadres with military status of the Chinese People's Armed Police, reservists and other persons performing military tasks (Article 450).

293. The crimes in this chapter can be committed during wartime as well as in normal time. In accordance with Article 451, the term of wartime means the time when the state declares the state of war, the armed forces receive tasks of operations or when the enemy launches a surprise attack. The time when the armed forces execute martial law tasks or cope with emergencies of violence shall be regarded as wartime.

294. The crimes in this chapter are roughly composed of three categories:

- crimes of endangering warfare, e.g., disobeying an order during wartime and thereby jeopardising a military operation, injuring himself in order to evade his military obligation during wartime or deserting the armed forces in violation of the military service law;
- crimes of sabotaging equipment or materials for warfare, e.g., causing an accident leading to the serious injury or death of another person due to the first person's neglect of duty, altering without authorisation the use of weapons and equipment allocated or abandoning weapons or equipment;
- crimes of violating serviceman, common people and war prisoner, e.g., abusing his power and maltreating a subordinate, deliberately abandoning a wounded or sick serviceman on a battlefield, cruelly injuring innocent residents in an area of military operation or plundering their money or property during wartime or maltreating a war prisoner.

The judicial explanation for the offences in this Chapter has been improved by the Supreme People's Procuratorate (*supra* paragraph 60). The new legislation of the 9th Amendment of 2015 provides for the abolition of the death penalty for the crime of obstructing any military personnel from performing their duties (Article 426) and the crime of fabricating rumours to shake people's confidence in the army during wartime (Article 433). This is the first time the death penalty has been removed for the Crimes of Servicemen's Transgression of Duties. In legal practice, there have not been many cases from this Chapter in recent years.

§3. Criminal Offences in Laws Other than the Criminal Code

295. Besides the criminal offences of the Criminal Code and the separate criminal regulations, there are many criminal provisions in the non-criminal laws, i.e., economic, administrative and civil laws and regulations (*supra*, paragraph 32). Indeed, these criminal provisions are increasingly used by the law-makers as an instrument of law enforcement. However, these provisions are principle provisions, equated provisions and accordant provisions (*supra*, paragraph 32), which cannot be directly and independently applied without the guidance of the Criminal Code.

Chapter 7. The Sanctioning System

§1. General Sanctioning System

296. In accordance with section 1, on types of punishment and Chapter 3 on penalties, of the General Part of the Criminal Code of 1997, criminal penalties are divided into principal penalties and accessory penalties (Article 32).

The principal penalty is the punishment which can only be independently imposed. The accessory penalty is the punishment which is usually imposed as an accompaniment. However, when there is a specific criminal provision in the Specific Part of the CCC, an accessory penalty may also be imposed independently.

Traditionally, Chinese theory of criminal law holds that there is only one principal penalty in one judgment which is to be executable, regardless of how many counts of crimes a person is found guilty of. However, this customary rule has been changed in the 9th Amendment of 2015. Accordingly, when a judgment for a case involves the conviction of a person for more than one count of offence, both the imprisonment and criminal detention shall be imposed but only the imprisonment shall be executed. However, if imprisonment and surveillance, or criminal detention and surveillance, shall be imposed in that judgment, surveillance shall still be executed after imprisonment or criminal detention has been executed.

297. In accordance with Article 33 of the Criminal Code of 1997, the principal penalties are as follows:

- public surveillance;
- criminal detention;
- fixed-term imprisonment;
- life imprisonment; and
- the death penalty.

298. In accordance with Article 34, the accessory penalties are as follows:

- fines;
- deprivation of political rights; and
- confiscation of property.

299. In addition to the principal and accessory penalties, deportation may be imposed independently or additionally to a foreigner who commits a crime (Article 35 of the Criminal Code of 1997).

300. In addition to receiving a criminal punishment according to law, the criminal shall be sentenced to compensate for the economic losses in the light of the circumstances, if a victim has suffered economic losses as a result of a crime. If a criminal who is liable for civil compensation is sentenced to a fine at the same time but his property is not sufficient to pay both the compensation and the fine, or if he is sentenced to confiscation of property at the same time, he shall, first of all, bear his liability for civil compensation to the victim (Article 36).

301. In accordance with Article 37 of the Criminal Code of 1997, if the circumstances of a person's crime are minor and do not require criminal punishment, he may be exempted from it; however, he may, depending on the different circumstances of the case, be reprimanded or ordered to make a statement of repentance, offer an apology, pay compensation for the losses, or be subjected to administrative penalty or administrative sanctions by the competent department.

In the 9th Amendment of 2015 a new article, Article 37A has been added in the CCC. Accordingly, the people's court may prohibit, in light of the circumstances of the crime committed and the need for preventing the commission of any other crime, those who are given a penalty due to a crime committed by taking advantage of his or her profession or a crime committed in violation of the specific obligations required by his or her profession, from engaging in the relevant profession for three to five years from the date when the penalty ends or the date when the person is released on parole. This type of prohibition will be supported by a criminal sanction. In case a person who is prohibited from engaging in the relevant profession violates the decision made by the people's court, he shall be punished by the public security authority. However, if the circumstances are serious, he shall be convicted and punished in accordance with Article 313 of the CCC for a kind of contempt of court. Of course, when there are other prohibitions in other laws or regulations on this kind of engagement in the profession, such provisions shall prevail, e.g., Article 7 of Lawyer's Law prohibited the disbarred lawyer from obtaining a practice licence again.

Briefly speaking, whether there are security measures in the Chinese criminal law has been a topic of academic discussion. Therefore, whether the sanction in Article 37A is a new kind of criminal punishment or actually acts as a kind of security measure, shall become a topic for academic debate in the future.

§2. Punishments

I. Principal Penalties

A. Public Surveillance

302. Although public surveillance shall be decided by the judgment of a people's court and executed by a public security organ (Article 38 of the Criminal Code of 1997), this is the only principal punishment in the Chinese criminal punishment system which is not executed in a prison.

Public surveillance refers to the punishment which restrains some of the criminal's freedoms but does not confine him to custody, rather, it puts him under the watch and supervision of a public security organ and the masses while his sentence is executed.

303. The term of public surveillance shall not be less than three months and not more than two years (Article 38). In the case of combined punishment for several crimes, it may not exceed three years (Article 69). The term's date of execution shall be counted from the date the judgment; if the criminal is held in custody before the execution of the judgment, one day in custody shall be considered two days of the term sentenced (Article 41). Upon the expiration of a term of public surveillance, the executing organ shall immediately announce the termination of public surveillance to the criminal sentenced to public surveillance and to the work unit or the people of the place where he resides (Article 40).

New criminal legislation provides the following supplements to Article 38 of the CCC: In light of the circumstances of the criminal case, a criminal sentenced to public surveillance may also be prohibited from engaging in certain activities, entering certain areas or places or contacting certain persons during the term of execution. In case that the criminal sentenced to public surveillance violates these prohibitions, he shall be punished according to the Law concerning Punishments against Public Security Administration. Criminals sentenced to public surveillance shall be subject to social correction, which shall be carried out by the specific state organ (i.e., organ of social correction according to Article 258 of Chinese Criminal Procedure) with the assistance of other state organs or social organs and volunteers to correct their guilty minds and the bad habits of their conduct (Article 38).

304. Although public surveillance is not enforced in custody, it does not mean that the sentenced criminal will go free completely. Article 39 of the Criminal Code provides the regulations which any criminal who is sentenced to public surveillance shall observe during the term in which his sentence is being executed as follows:

- observe laws and administrative rules and regulations, and submit to supervision;
- exercise no right of freedom of speech, of the press, of assembly, of association, of procession or of demonstration without the approval of the organ executing the public surveillance;
- report on his own activities as required by the organ executing the public surveillance;
- observe the regulations for receiving visitors stipulated by the organ executing the public surveillance; and
- report to obtain approval from the organ executing the public surveillance for any departure from the city or county he lives in or for any change in residence.

Criminals sentenced to public surveillance shall, while engaged in labour, receive equal pay for equal work.

305. Public surveillance is designed to punish criminals who have committed minor crimes. This punishment is conducive to reducing the population in custody, to bring the watch and supervision of the masses into full play, and to give appropriate consideration to the difficulties of the criminal's family.

B. Criminal Detention

306. Criminal detention is a principal punishment of short-term stays in custody. The term of criminal detention shall not be less than thirty days and not more than six months (Article 42). In the case of combined punishment for several crimes, it may not exceed one year (Article 69). The term of criminal detention shall be counted from the date on which the judgment begins to be executed. If the criminal is held in custody before the execution of the judgment, one day in custody shall be considered one day of the term sentenced (Article 44).

307. Criminal detention is also a kind of light punishment. Where a criminal is sentenced to criminal detention, his sentence shall be executed by the public security organ in the vicinity. During the period of execution, a criminal sentenced to criminal detention may go home for one to two days each month, and an appropriate remuneration may be given to those who participate in labour (Article 44).

C. Fixed-Term Imprisonment

308. The fixed-term imprisonment is the most often applied punishment in the Chinese punishment system, because there is a wide scope for setting the term of punishment and it may be suitable for various crimes.

The term of fixed-term imprisonment shall not be less than six months and not more than fifteen years (Article 45). In the case of combined punishment for several crimes, the term may be extended to not more than twenty years, if the sum of terms of fixed-term imprisonment is less than thirty-five years, or to not more than twenty-five years, if the sum of terms is thirty-five years or more (Article 69, *see infra* paragraph 349). When the death sentence with a suspension of execution is commuted to fixed-term imprisonment (Article 50, *see infra* paragraph 318), the term may be extended to twenty-five years.

The term of fixed-term imprisonment shall be counted from the date the judgment begins to be executed. If the criminal is held in custody before the execution of the judgment, one day in custody shall be considered one day of term sentenced (Article 47).

309. The criminal sentenced to fixed-term imprisonment or life imprisonment shall serve his sentence in prison or another place for the execution. Anyone who is able to work shall do so in order to gain education and reform (Article 46, also cf. *supra*, paragraphs 40 et seq.).

D. Life Imprisonment

310. Life imprisonment is a very tough punishment for criminals. It can only be imposed on those whose crimes are especially serious but do not necessarily involve a death sentence. This will apply to many types of criminal such as a murderer, rapist, arsonist, robber, smuggler, swindler, and so on.

311. The criminal sentenced to life imprisonment shall serve his sentence in prison or another place for the execution (Article 46). He shall be under strict supervision and heavy guard. When necessary, he may be separately imprisoned. Those who are able to work shall do so in order to gain education and reform (Article 46 and cf. *supra*, paragraph 41).

When the criminal reforms himself actively, shows true repentance or performs meritorious service, his sentence may be commuted or he may be granted parole according to the law, except for those who are recidivists or were sentenced for crimes of violence such as homicide, explosion, rape, robbery, kidnap, arson, dissemination of hazardous substances or organised violent crime (Article 81, *see infra* paragraph 377).

E. The Death Penalty

312. The death penalty is the most serious punishment in Chinese criminal law. It is a punishment which deprives a criminal of his life. The death penalty shall be executed by such means as shooting or injection (Article 252 of the Criminal Procedure of 2012).

Although the death penalty has a long history in criminal law, it is restricted in the Chinese legal practice in many ways, as follows.

313. The restriction of the applicable criminals:

> The death penalty shall only be applied to criminals who have committed extremely heinous crimes (Art. 48 of the Criminal Code of 1997). In Chinese criminal law and legal practice, only the most heinous criminals who commit the most serious crimes of endangering national security or public security, undermining economic order and causing great losses of life and property can be sentenced to death.

314. The restriction of the applicable criminal subject:

> Persons who have not reached the age of 18 at the time the crime was committed or women who are pregnant at the time of trial shall not be sentenced to the death penalty (Art. 49 of the Criminal Code of 1997). The regulation that a person who has reached the age of 16 but not the age of 18 may be sentenced to death with a two-year suspension of execution if the crime committed was particularly serious, was abolished in the Criminal Code of 1997. Therefore, the death penalty can absolutely not be applied to minors in accordance with the Chinese criminal law.

New criminal legislation adds that death penalty shall not be given to a person who has reached the age of 75 at the time of trial, unless he has caused the death of another person by especially cruel means (Article 49). The death penalty for 13 non-violent crimes was also abolished, which is found in Articles 151, 153, 194, 195, 205, 206, 264, 295, 328 (*supra* paragraphs 260, 263, 264, 265).

315. The restriction of the procedure for review of the death penalty:

> In accordance with Art. 48 of the Criminal Code of 1997, all death penalty, except for those that, according to law, should be decided by the Supreme People's Court, shall be submitted to the Supreme People's Court for verification and approval. Death sentences with a suspension of execution may be decided or verified and approved by a higher people's court.

On 2 September 1983, the Standing Committee of the NPC put an amendment in its Decision Regarding the Revision of the Organic Law of the People's Court, which provides that cases involving sentences of death, except for those cases where the sentences have been imposed by the SPC, shall be submitted to the SPC for approval. The SPC may, when it deems it necessary, authorise higher people's courts of provinces, autonomous regions, and municipalities directly under the Central Government to exercise their power to approve cases involving the imposition of death sentences on cases involving homicide, rape, robbery, causing explosions and other crimes gravely endangering public security and disrupting social order. According to this amendment, the SPC was given this power on 9 September 1983. However, the Chinese legislature enacted an amendment, effective as of 1 January 2007, announcing that all death penalties, except for those that should be adjudicated by the SPC according to law, shall be reported to the SPC for examination and approval. The local people's court, i.e., the higher people's court at provincial level, shall no longer enjoy the power to approve the judgment of cases involving the death penalty.

316. The creation of the system of the death penalty with a two-year suspension of execution:

> For those who shall be sentenced to death, if the immediate execution of a criminal punishable by death is not deemed necessary, a two-year suspension of execution may be pronounced simultaneously with the imposition of the death sentence (Art. 48 of the Criminal Code of 1997).

It has been proven that most of the criminals sentenced to death with a two-year suspension of execution will, during execution of the sentence, admit their guilt and show true repentance and so the execution of these criminals is extremely rare. The system of the death penalty with a two-year suspension has been proven to be an effective way to control and eventually de facto abolish the death penalty in China.

317. It should be noted that the death sentence with a two-year suspension of execution is a system to execute the death penalty and not an independent punishment. The criminal who should not be sentenced to death cannot be announced as sentenced to death with suspension of execution.

318. If a person sentenced to death with a suspension of execution shows true repentance during the period of suspension, his punishment shall be commuted as follows in accordance with the law (Article 50):

- if he commits no intentional crime during the period of suspension, his punishment shall be commuted to life imprisonment upon the expiration of the two-year period;
- if he has truly performed major meritorious service, his punishment shall be, upon the expiration of the two-year period, commuted to fixed-term imprisonment of twenty-five years, which had been regulated as fifteen-twenty years but was amended in 8th Amendment of 2011.

For a recidivist or a criminal who has committed murder, rape, robbery, abduction, arson, explosion, dissemination of hazardous substances or organised violence and who is sentenced to death with a suspension, the people's court may decide to put restrictions on commutation of his sentence in light of the circumstances of the crime committed.

The term of suspension of execution of a death penalty shall be counted from the date the judgment becomes final. The term of a fix-term imprisonment that is commuted from a death penalty with suspension of execution shall be counted from the date the suspension of execution expires (Article 51 of the Criminal Code of 1997).

319. If it is verified that he has committed an intentional crime, the death penalty shall be executed upon verification and approval of the SPC (Article 50). The condition of 'an intentional crime' was added to the Criminal Code of 1997 to clarify the condition of execution in the Criminal Code of 1979 that the person sentenced to death with a suspension shall resist reform in a flagrant manner. Accordingly, if the criminal commits only a negligent crime or only violates the regulation of prison, he shall not therefore be executed (for execution of death penalty, also cf. *infra*, paragraph 584).

In order to further restrict the execution of death penalty, the 9th Amendment of 2015 provides an additional condition of 'with execrable circumstance' for immediate execution. Whether a circumstance is execrable or not shall be subject to the approval of the SPC. When the crime is committed intentionally but the immediate execution is not approved, the period of death penalty with two-years suspension shall be recalculated and reported to the SPC for recording.

In the 9th Amendment of 2015, there is a specific arrangement for the death penalty in the crime of embezzlement. In the case where a convicted person of the crime of embezzlement shall be sentenced to death with two-years suspension, he may be given a condition that no commutation or parole is possible after his sentence was reduced to life imprisonment upon expiration of the two-year period. It is generally believed that the death penalty in the crime of embezzlement is de facto abolished (Article 383, paragraph 4 and *supra* 289).

II. The Accessory Penalties

A. Fines

320. A fine is the lightest pecuniary penalty in Chinese criminal law. It is principally provided for in the crimes of gaining profits, such as tax evasion, gambling, or violation of trademark. However, it can also be seen in some other crimes, e.g., intentionally destroying property or obstruction of justice.

Generally, a fine is imposed in addition to another form of punishment. When independently imposed, it can only be applied to the lighter crimes such as obtaining registration by deceiving the competent company registration authority.

321. With respect to the amount of fine, the Chinese Criminal Code of 1997 provides three types of fine imposition:

- A fine to be imposed by percentage. For example, Article 140 provides that any producer or seller who mixes impurities into or adulterates the products, passes a fake product off as a genuine one, passes a defective product as a high-quality one, or a substandard product as a standard one, who has made the amount of earnings from sales of more than CNY 50,000 but less than CNY 200,000, shall be additionally or independently fined not less than half, but not more than two times the amount of earnings from sales. Paragraph 1 of Article 153 provides that for the crime of smuggling in which the payable duties evaded or dodged reaches the amount of more than CNY 500,000, the fine to be imposed shall be not less than one time but not more than five times the amount of payable duties evaded or dodged.

- A fine imposed by a concrete amount. For example, Article 172 provides that whoever knowingly holds or uses counterfeit currencies shall additionally or independently be fined not less than CNY 10,000 but not more than CNY 100,000; in the case where a large amount is involved, the fine shall be not less than CNY 20,000 and not more than CNY 200,000; and in the case of an amount which is especially large, the fine shall be not less than CNY 50,000 and not more than CNY 500,000 in addition to the confiscation of property.
- A fine to be imposed is not specified. For example, Article 322 provides that whoever, in violation of the laws or regulations on administration of the national border (frontier), illegally crosses the national border (frontier), shall be fined additionally. The SPC says that, in this case, the minimum fine shall be no less than CNY 1,000 for adults and CNY 500 for minor delinquents.

Article 52 of the Criminal Code of 1997 provides a general guideline for fine imposition: 'the amount of any fine imposed shall be determined according to the circumstances of the crime.'

322. A fine may be paid in a lump sum or in instalments within the time limit specified in the judgment. If a fine is not paid upon the expiration of that time limit, the payment shall be compelled. If a person is not able to pay the fine in full, the people's court shall demand the payment whenever it finds the person has property for execution of the fine.

If a person has true difficulties in paying due to an unavoidable disaster or other reason, his payment of the fine may be postponed, reduced or even exempted in light of the actual circumstances. The 9th Amendment of 2015 adds that any change of the payment required in a judgment needs the people's court to render a ruling.

B. Deprivation of Political Rights

323. Deprivation of political rights refers to deprivation of the following rights:

- the right to vote and to stand for election;
- the right of freedom of speech, of the press, of assembly, of association, of procession and of demonstration;
- the right to hold a position in a state organ; and
- the right to hold a leading position in any state-owned company, enterprise, institution or people's organisation.

Those who are convicted without also being deprived of their political rights can have the right to vote in the prison.

324. The deprivation can be either independently or imposed additionally. When independently imposed, it is a kind of relatively light punishment without deprivation of personal freedom. When imposed in addition, however, it is a kind of relatively serious punishment to be imposed upon the serious crimes.

There are three circumstances in which this punishment would be imposed (Articles 56 and 57):

- anyone who commits the crime of endangering national security shall be sentenced to deprivation of political rights as a supplementary punishment;
- anyone who commits the crime of seriously undermining public order by intentional homicide, rape, arson, explosion, poisoning or robbery may be sentenced to deprivation of political rights as a supplementary punishment;
- independent imposition of deprivation of political rights shall be applied according to the Specific Part of the Criminal Code;
- any criminal who is sentenced to death or to life imprisonment shall be deprived of his political rights for life.

325. The term of deprivation of political rights shall be determined as follows (Articles 55 and 57):

- the term of deprivation of political rights shall be not less than one year but not more than five years, unless otherwise stipulated in the Criminal Code;
- anyone who is sentenced to public surveillance is deprived of political rights as a supplementary punishment, the term of deprivation of political rights shall be the same as the term of public surveillance, and the penalties shall be executed simultaneously;
- the term for criminals who have been sentenced to death or to life imprisonment shall be life-long;
- for criminals whose sentence of death with a suspension of execution is commuted to a fixed-term imprisonment, or where life imprisonment is commuted to a fixed-term imprisonment, the term of deprivation of political rights shall be changed from the term of lifelong to not less than three years and not more than ten years.

326. A term of deprivation of political rights as a supplementary punishment shall be counted from the date on which imprisonment or criminal detention ends or from the date on which parole begins. Deprivation of political rights shall, as a matter of course, be in effect during the period in which the principal punishment is being executed.

Any criminal who is deprived of his political rights shall, during the period of execution, observe laws, administrative rules and regulations and other regulations governing supervision and control stipulated by the department of public security under the state council and submit to supervision. He shall not exercise any of the rights listed in Article 54 (*supra*, paragraph 324).

C. *Confiscation of Property*

327. Confiscation of property refers to the confiscation of part or all of the property owned by a criminal.

Although confiscation can theoretically be imposed independently, this rarely occurs. It is the order of the day to impose it additionally upon the crimes with serious characteristics.

328. The property to be confiscated should be owned by the criminal himself. When a sentence of confiscation of property is imposed, the amount necessary for the daily expenses of the criminal himself and the family members supported by him shall be taken out. When a sentence of confiscation of property is imposed, property that the criminal's family members own or should own shall not be subject to confiscation (Article 59). This provision is a reflection of the principle of being responsible for one's own crime (*supra*, paragraph 77).

329. Article 64 provides that all money and property illegally obtained by a criminal shall be recovered, or compensation shall be ordered. The lawful property of the victim shall be returned without delay and the contrabands and possessions of the criminal that are used in the commission of the crime shall be confiscated.

However, confiscation of property is not the same as the confiscation of the ill-gotten gains and contrabands. The latter is not a punishment, rather, an administrative compulsory measure.

330. Confiscation of property shall also protect the rights of the lawful creditor. Where it is necessary to use part of the confiscated property to repay the legitimate debts that the criminal incurred before his property is confiscated, the debts shall be repaid at the request of the creditors (Article 60).

§3. General Principles Concerning Sentencing

I. The General Principle

331. As a concrete reflection of Article 5, the principle of proportionality (*supra*, paragraph 74), Article 61 of the Criminal Code of 1997 provides the general principle for sentencing is as follows: 'when sentencing a criminal, a punishment shall be meted out on the basis of the facts, nature and circumstances of the crime, the degree of harm done to society and the relevant provisions of this Code.'

The Chinese Criminal Code and its supplementary regulations have provided each criminal offence with an applicable penalty. The prescribed punishment usually has a scope between the maximum and the minimum. The judge is supposed to choose an appropriate sentence based upon the factors prescribed by law for each crime.

In the criminal law theory, the purpose of criminal punishment is an important topic. There are various arguments. However, a unified theory has become influential which is based upon prevention, with the consideration of different types of punishment and different stages in the development of punishment. This theory is based upon prevention but absorbs the theoretical elements of justified retribution and all positive elements of preventions. On one hand, it combines the theory of justified retribution, which is generally reflected in the punishment of death penalty, with the theories of prevention, which are generally reflected in other types of penalties. On the other hand, it reflects the theory of general prevention in the legislative stage, the theories of special prevention and retribution in the judicial stage, and the theory of special prevention in the stage of implementation. This new theory will be conducive to the new exploration for the Chinese criminal law theory in modern times. Unfortunately, this theory will not advocate the total abolition of death penalty. However, it will restrict the imposition of death penalty to an extremely limited area, which reflects the reality in China today and the near future, but also provides a good basis for further total abolition. Regardless, prevention is the basic characteristics for this type of theory.

332. In cases where the circumstances of a crime call for a heavier or lighter punishment under the provisions of the Criminal Code, the criminal shall be sentenced to a punishment within the limits of the prescribed punishment (Article 62).

333. In cases where the circumstances of a crime call for a mitigated punishment under the provisions of the Criminal Code, the criminal shall be sentenced to a punishment less than the prescribed punishment. In cases where the circumstances of a crime do not warrant a mitigated punishment under the provisions of the Criminal Code, however, in the light of the special circumstances of the case, and upon verification and approval of the SPC, the criminal may still be sentenced to a punishment less than the prescribed punishment (Article 63). The new criminal legislation adds that if there are two or more ranges of sentencing under the Criminal Code, the penalty shall be given within the range immediately below the statutory range.

II. Circumstances Affecting Sentencing

334. Circumstance is of significance in sentencing. It refers to the various situations which can be used to determine the severity of punishment. Circumstances can be divided into prescribed circumstances and discretional circumstances.

A. Prescribed Circumstances

335. Prescribed circumstances refer to the circumstances explicitly prescribed in criminal law. There are four types of circumstances with respect to two aspects: increasing punishment and decreasing punishment, in the Criminal Code of 1997.

336. With respect to increasing punishment, there is a kind of circumstance:

- Heavier circumstances, which shall lead to a heavier punishment.
  The heavier circumstances in the General Part of the Criminal Code are two: the criminal who instigates a person under the age of 18 to commit a crime (Article 29, *supra*, paragraph 275) and recidivists (Articles 65 and 66, *infra*, paragraph 341). Although the principal criminal (Article 26, *supra*, paragraphs 247 et seq.) is not an explicit heavier circumstance, he will certainly receive a heavier punishment than his accomplice in a case, since he shall be responsible for all the crimes that the criminal organisation has committed, when he is a ringleader,

or all the crimes that he participates in or that he organises or directs (Article 26, *supra*, paragraph 269).
There are numerous heavier circumstances provided in the Specific Part of the Criminal Code of 1997. Many of them are designed to punish the crimes committed by a state functionary. For example, a heavier punishment shall be given in the case of a state functionary who takes advantage of his office to commit unlawful detaining (Article 238), any state functionary who commits the crime of false accusation (Article 243), or who extorts a confession by torture and causes injury or disability to a person through corporal punishment (Article 247), and so on.
The aggravating circumstance, which shall lead to a sentence beyond the maximum prescribed punishment, is no longer included in the Chinese criminal law. It was provided in the Decision Regarding the Criminals Who Escape or Commit New Crimes (*supra*, paragraph 32) for the criminals who commit new crimes after escaping from the prison, use violence or retaliate against their accusers, victims, relevant judicial personnel and cadres or other people who try to stop their unlawful criminal acts. However, this type of circumstance was totally deleted in the 1997 CCC.

337. With respect to decreasing punishment, there are three relevant circumstances:

- lighter circumstances, which shall or may call for a lighter punishment within the limits of the prescribed punishment;
- mitigated circumstances, which shall or may call for a mitigated punishment less than the prescribed punishment;
- exempting circumstances, which shall or may exempt a criminal from criminal punishment.

These circumstances for decreasing punishment are almost all prescribed in the General Part of the Criminal Code, which we have mentioned above (*supra*, paragraphs 96, 130–133, 155 et seq., 210 et seq., 222 et seq., 225 et seq., 231 et seq., 249–250, 251 et seq.).

There are not many provisions of the circumstances for decreasing punishment in the Specific Part of the Criminal Code. The only examples are as follows:

- any person who bribes another (or any person who introduces a bribe) who, before he is investigated for criminal responsibility, voluntarily confesses his act of offering bribes may be given a mitigated punishment or exempted from punishment (Articles 390, 392 and 164);
- if an individual who embezzles not less than CNY 5,000 but less than CNY 10,000, shows true repentance after committing the crime, and gives up the embezzled money of his own accord, he may be given a mitigated punishment, or he may be exempted from criminal punishment but shall be subjected to administrative sanctions by his work unit or by the competent authorities at a higher level (Article 383);

- persons who illegally cultivate opium poppy or any mother plants of other narcotic drugs but voluntarily uproot them before harvest may be exempted from punishment (Article 351).

B. Discretional Circumstances

338. Discretional circumstance refers to the circumstances which may be used at the discretion of judge. It is a summation from the legal practice experiences according to the legislative spirit.

Discretional circumstances are usually very general. For example, when the law requires giving a heavier or lighter punishment, the discretional circumstances should be relied upon to determine how heavy or how light the sentence should be adjusted to because the law cannot stipulate so in detail.

Actually, every case has its own discretional circumstances, though it should necessarily have a prescribed circumstance as well. Therefore, the discretional circumstances are of importance in the sentencing.

339. It is hard to say how many discretional circumstances there are in Chinese legal practice. However, the most common or the most frequently mentioned discretional circumstances are the following:

- The criminal motive (*supra*, paragraphs 150 et seq.). Since criminal motive may explain why the criminal committed the crime, e.g., he stole in order to buy some necessities of life for the family or to buy a luxury for himself, it can display the degree of the subject malice of the criminal. The more malicious criminal motive shall be given heavier punishment.
- The criminal method (*supra*, paragraph 150). In the case that a criminal method is not a constitutive element, it can still affect the severity of punishment though not the conviction. For example, in the case of rape, the extremely cruel rape shall be more heavily punished than the rape with usual compulsory measures.
- The time and place of committing the crime (*supra*, paragraph 150). For example, the crime committed in a disaster area should be more dangerous than in other areas.
- The criminal target (*supra*, paragraph 131). The criminal who has attacked a patient, a disabled person, a minor, an aged person, or a pregnant woman shall definitely be given a heavier punishment.
- The consistent manifestation of the criminal. This is the circumstance for seeing if the criminal commits the crime casually. The criminal who often violates regulations and makes trouble everywhere will usually be given a heavier punishment.
- The criminal's manner after committing the crime. Those who voluntarily admit their guilt, actively give up ill-gotten gains, effectively lighten or eliminate the harmful consequences shall be given a lighter punishment.

III. Recidivist

340. Recidivists can generally be described as the criminals who commit a certain criminal offence after having been convicted previously of another criminal offence. A criminal's recidivist nature is the typical prescribed circumstance leading to a heavier punishment. Recidivists shall be given a heavier punishment according to Article 65 of the Criminal Code of 1997.

341. In accordance with the provision of the Criminal Code, the recidivists can be divided into two types: the ordinary recidivist and the special recidivist.

342. The ordinary recidivist refers to the criminal who commits another crime punishable by fixed-term imprisonment or heavier penalty within five years after serving his sentence of not less than fixed-term imprisonment or receiving a pardon.

In accordance with Article 65, the ordinary recidivist shall have the following conditions:

- There must have been two intentional crimes. Recidivist shall not apply to cases involving negligent crime.
- The sentences for either the former or the latter crime must be the fixed-term imprisonment or a heavier penalty.
- The latter crime shall occur within five years after serving his sentence of the former crime or receiving a pardon.

Here, for the criminals who are paroled, the period shall be counted from the date the parole expires.

343. Before 2011, the special recidivist only refers to the recidivist of endangering national security. In the 8th Amendment of the 1997 CCC, the special recidivist was expanded to cover the recidivists who commit crimes against national security, the crime of terrorist activities or the crimes related to underground societies. Now, the special recidivist refers to those criminals who commit again, any of the crimes against national security, the crime of terrorist activities or the crimes with the nature of an underground society at any time after serving his sentence or receiving a pardon.

In accordance with Article 66, the special recidivist shall have the following conditions:

- Both the former and latter crimes are crimes against national security, the crime of terrorist activities or the crimes related to underground societies. If, however, either of them is not one of these crimes, the criminal shall only become the ordinary recidivist, as long as he conforms to the conditions.
- There is no restriction upon the severity of the punishment.
- There is no restriction upon the requirement of five-year period between the former and latter crimes.

IV. Voluntary Surrender

344. In accordance with Article 67 of the Criminal Code, voluntary surrender refers to the act of voluntarily delivering oneself up to justice and truthfully confessing one's crime after one has committed the crime. Voluntary surrender is the typical prescribed circumstance leading to a lighter punishment or even exemption of punishment.

A voluntary surrender shall have the following conditions according to the Criminal Code and the relevant judicial explanation.

345. The first condition requires that a criminal shall voluntarily give himself up to the authorities, while the crime committed may not be discovered or, though discovered, he has not yet been interrogated or a compulsory measure has not yet been adopted against him.

Usually, the criminal is supposed to surrender himself to the police or to the judicial organs. However, the person who reports his own crime to other authorities such as his working units, the street residents committee or the committee leaders, who entrusts other people to report because he himself is sick, injured, or is trying to prevent the harmful consequence from occurring or from getting more serious, who reports by mail and will show up soon afterwards, and who is arrested on the way to surrender himself will be deemed to have given up voluntarily in Chinese legal practice. Those who are brought or accompanied to the police or judicial organs by their parents or relatives will usually be deemed to have given up voluntarily, as long as they conform to other conditions.

346. The second condition requires that a criminal shall honestly confess his crime. At least, he is supposed to confess the principal criminal conduct. In the joint crime, the criminal is supposed to give information on his accomplice and the principal criminal shall expose another criminal's guilt.

In the development of the Chinese criminal law, it is policy to encourage criminals to surrender themselves. In the 1979 CCC, Article 63 provides that anyone who voluntarily surrenders after committing a crime may be given a lighter punishment. Those whose crimes are relatively minor may be given a mitigated punishment or be exempted from punishment; those whose crimes are relatively serious but who have performed meritorious service may also be given a mitigated punishment or be exempted from punishment. But in the 1997 CCC, Article 67 provides a clear legal definition: The act of voluntarily giving oneself up to the police, and giving a true account of one's crime after committing it, is an act of voluntary surrender. In addition, Article 67 also provides that if a criminal suspect or a defendant under compulsory measures or a criminal serving a sentence truthfully confesses his other crimes that the judicial organ does not know, his act shall be regarded as voluntary surrender.

In the 1997 CCC, there is a regulation on meritorious service (*infra* paragraph 348), which is different but somewhat better than voluntary surrender.

It has been a criminal policy in China to encourage confession. 'Lenient treatment for confession' has been well known in China for a long time. In 2011, the 8th Amendment enacted this policy fully in the criminal law. Now, Article 67 of the 1997 CCC provides that a criminal suspect who truthfully confesses to his crime may be given a lighter penalty although there is no voluntary surrender as mentioned in the preceding two paragraphs of this Article; and he may be given a mitigated penalty if any especially serious consequence is avoided for his truthful confession.

347. The third condition requires that a criminal shall show that he willingly subjects himself to the investigation and judgment. He cannot try to escape or to avoid the investigation and trial. But the new research argues that this condition is not absolutely necessary, since the meaning of this condition is already included in the second condition (*supra* paragraph 346).

348. The punishment of voluntary surrender shall follow the rule below (Articles 67, 68):

- Criminals who voluntarily surrender may be given a lesser punishment or a mitigated punishment.
- Those among them whose crimes are relatively minor may be exempted from punishment.
- Criminals who perform meritorious service by exposing an offence committed by another, which is verified through investigation, or producing important clues for solving other cases may be given a lighter or mitigated punishment; The meritorious service usually refers to the act of exposing serious crimes committed by others which have been verified, to provide the important hints which are helpful in uncovering other big cases, or to help the police or judicial organs to have other criminals arrested. If a criminal provides several hints about crimes, although ordinary ones, as long as they have been verified, he shall be deemed to have provided the meritorious service.
- Criminals who perform major meritorious services may be given a mitigated punishment or be exempted from punishment.
- Criminals who not only voluntarily surrender after committing the crime but also perform major meritorious services shall be given mitigated punishment or be exempted from punishment.
- Criminals who truthfully confess to their crimes may be given a lighter penalty although there is no voluntary surrender as mentioned in the preceding two paragraphs.
- He may be given a mitigated penalty if any especially serious consequence is avoided for his truthful confession.

V. Combined Punishment for More than One Crime

A. The Principle to Combine Penalties

349. When a criminal commits more than one crime, Chinese criminal law does not simply add the sentences for each crime up together, rather, it adopts the approach that the principle of limited aggravation and the principles of absorption and addition help, as follows.

350. When there is a crime for which the sentence shall be life imprisonment or the death penalty among the several crimes, the principle of absorption shall be applied. Only life imprisonment or the death penalty will be executed and other penalties will no longer be executed (Article 69 of the Criminal Code of 1997).

351. When there is a fixed-term imprisonment, criminal detention or public surveillance respectively for each crime in a case, the principle of limited aggravation shall be applied, which means that his term of punishment shall be decided in such a way that it may not exceed the total of the terms for all the crimes and must be longer than the maximum term for any one of the crimes, depending on the circumstances of each case. However, the decided term of public surveillance may not exceed three years, the decided term of criminal detention may not exceed one year, and fixed-term imprisonment may not exceed twenty years (Article 69). In the 8th Amendment, the maximum term for fixed-term imprisonment was changed. Now, the decided fixed-term imprisonment shall not exceed twenty years if the sum of terms of fixed-term imprisonment for all of the crimes is less than thirty-five years or shall not exceed twenty-five years if the sum of terms is thirty-five years or more (*supra*, paragraph 308).

When the sentences entail different penalties, e.g., a fixed-term imprisonment for one crime and a criminal detention for another crime, the sentence shall be considered as the same punishment, i.e., the criminal detention shall be considered as fixed-term imprisonment.

Fixed-term imprisonment and public surveillance, according to a judicial Expl. of SPC of 7 April 1958, cannot be considered as one punishment, since they have different characteristics. According to the opinion of the SPC, public surveillance shall be carried out after the execution of the fixed-term imprisonment. However, this opinion is of little practical significance.

352. When there is one or more supplementary punishments in a case, the principle of addition shall be applied. Every supplementary punishment shall be executed according to the requirement of the Criminal Code (Article 69).

B. The Concrete Methods to Combine Penalties for Several Crimes

353. Crime may be committed before, during or after the judgment. The Chinese Criminal Code provides different accounting methods for combining the penalties.

354. For a criminal who commits several crimes before a judgment is pronounced, the accounting method shall follow the principles described above (*supra*, paragraphs 328–331).

355. If after a judgment has been announced but before the punishment has been completely executed, it is discovered that before the judgment was announced, the criminal committed another crime for which he was not sentenced, a judgment shall also be rendered for the newly discovered crime; the punishment to be executed shall be determined on the basis of the punishments imposed in the former and latter judgments and according to the principles described above (Article 69, *supra*, paragraphs 328–331). Any portion of the term that has already been served shall count towards the fulfilment of the term imposed by the latest judgment (Article 70).

356. If after a judgment has been announced but before the punishment has been completely executed the criminal again commits a crime, another judgment shall be rendered for the newly committed crime; the punishment to be executed shall be decided on the basis of the punishment that remains to be executed for the former crime and the punishment imposed for the latter crime and according to the principle described above (*supra*, paragraphs 328–331, Article 71).

357. The differences between Article 70 (*supra*, paragraph 356) and Article 71 (*supra*, paragraph 357) rest on two aspects:

- On the accounting method, Article 70 is to add the punishment imposed in the former and latter judgments together before subtracting the portion of the term that has already been served; Article 71 is to subtract the portion of the term that has been served before adding the newly imposed punishment and the remainder of the former punishment together.
- On the significance of the punishment, the minimum term of actual execution according to Article 71 will be higher than that according to Article 70; and the total of the actual execution according to Article 71 may respectively exceed the prescribed maximum term of fixed-term imprisonment, criminal detention and public surveillance provided in Article 69 (*supra*, paragraph 352). Obviously, the accounting method in Article 71 is harsher than that in Article 70 for the criminals.

C. Concurrence of Criminal Offences

358. Obviously, combined punishment presupposes more than one crime and therefore more than one punishment. Chinese criminal law theory commonly agrees that the standard to determine whether one or more crimes exist is in the theory of criminal constitution (*supra*, paragraphs 101–151). When a criminal offence conforms to the constitution of one crime, it shall constitute one crime.

However, there are the following situations in which more than one criminal conduct or consequence, or even more than one crime is dealt with as one crime, in order to avoid that an unreasonable amount or unworkable term of punishment is imposed.

359. A continuous crime refers to the situation in which the criminal conduct retains its continuity within a certain period of time. For example, the crime of unlawful detention of other persons and the crime of abandonment are the typical examples of this type of crime.

Since this offence has been provided as a crime in a specific criminal provision with a specific prescribed punishment, and given that Article 89 of the Criminal Code also mentions continuous crime (*infra*, paragraph 384), it shall be dealt with as one crime, no matter how long the criminal conduct lasts.

360. The habitual criminal refers to those who take a certain crime as their profession or make their living based upon what they get from committing a crime. Naturally, a habitual criminal shall be one who has cultivated the bad habit of committing a certain crime and usually has a relatively long criminal history. Chinese criminal law provides more serious penalties for habitual criminals, e.g., Article 303 provides that whoever, for the purpose of profit, gathers people to engage in gambling, runs a gambling house or makes gambling his profession shall be guilty of gambling. However, the Chinese criminal law and criminal law theory have gradually abandoned this term. In 1997 CCC, the legislation stopped using the terms of habitual theft and habitual fraud in the offences of theft and fraud (Article 152 of the 1979 CCC). In the 1997 CCC, for instance, Article 264 stipulated that committing several thefts shall be deemed as an offence, though the new criminal legislation adds burglary and carrying lethal weapons to steal or to pick pockets as the new forms of theft in this article.

361. Combined crime refers to the situation in which criminal law combines two independent offences into a new crime with a more serious punishment. The crime of robbery is the typical combined crime in Chinese criminal law, when it causes grievous bodily injury or death and takes the property of someone else. However, scholars began to discuss whether the combinations should be of offences or acts. A transitorily opinion for acts seems to gain influence. In the case of robbery, for instance, either an attempt of bodily injury or killing or an attempt of taking other's property away shall be qualified to fulfil the requirement of the criminal conduct of robbery.

362. Continual crime refers to the situation in which a criminal, with general criminal intent, continually commits a criminal act on several occasions and violates the same criminal provision. For example, to rob the same storehouse several times will be deemed as an offence, though the amount of the stolen goods and the acts in each commitment shall be cumulatively considered.

What the continual crime violates is the same criminal provision, so it shall be dealt with as one crime, even though the criminal conduct is committed several times. However, this is only true when all criminal conducts have been discovered before a judgment is pronounced. If the case shall be tried by applying Articles 70 and 71 (*supra*, paragraphs 334 and 335), it shall be a case of more than one crime.

363. Implicated crime refers to the situation in which a criminal, while intending to commit one crime, is responsible for another crime by his criminal method or because of the criminal result. The typical implicated crime in Chinese legal practice is the case in which a criminal stole a gun and concealed it at home. His conduct constitutes the crime of stealing weapons (Article 127) and the result constitutes the crime of secretly keeping firearms (Article 128).

Although the Criminal Code does not provide specific rules for implicated crime, theoretical circles and the legal practice commonly agree that the principle of combined punishment for more than one crime shall not be applied to an implicated crime, rather, it shall be treated as the crime with the most serious punishment. In the case mentioned above, for example, what the thief committed is the crime of stealing a weapon, since the former crime has more serious prescribed punishment than the latter one.

364. Absorbed crime refers to the situation in which one criminal offence was absorbed by another criminal offence. Therefore, it shall only constitute one crime. The absorbable relation between two or more criminal offences exists because these conducts usually belong to the same proceedings of a certain crime. The former conduct may be the necessary step for the latter conduct and the latter conduct may be the natural result of the former conduct. For example, the executing conduct will usually absorb the preparing conduct.

365. In Chinese criminal law theory, the problems similar to *Idealkonkurenz* and *Gesetzeskonkurrenz* in German criminal law theory have been discussed. Many arguments have arisen from the discussion. However, scholars and judges commonly agree that these problems shall not be dealt with as more than one crime, rather, only as one crime, i.e., the more serious one.

§4. Concrete Application of Punishment

366. There are three specific areas related to the concrete application of punishments, which are specifically provided for by the criminal law: probation, commutation of punishment and parole.

I. Probation

367. In Chinese criminal law, probation refers to the system where a criminal, upon whom certain types of punishment have been imposed, shall not undergo, under certain conditions, the sentence imposed upon him.

368. In accordance with the Criminal Code of 1997, the grant of probation requires the following conditions, which also reflect the latest development of criminal legislation:

- The punishment imposed upon the criminal can only be criminal detention or fixed-term imprisonment of not more than three years (Article 72).
- The criminal to be granted probation shall not be the recidivist or the ringleader of criminal organisations (Article 74). However, a probation shall be announced for those who are under the age of 18, pregnant or who reached the age of 75, if they meet the condition listed in the next paragraph.
- It is considered that the probation will not result in further harm to society, according to the circumstances of his crime and his demonstration of repentance (Article 72). In order to make this condition more applicable, the new criminal legislation provides the detailed circumstances for the requirement as follows:

  (1) the circumstances of the crime are minor;
  (2) he shows repentance;
  (3) he is not likely to commit any offence again; and
  (4) announcing the probation will not have any major adverse impact on the community where he lives.

When probation is announced, in light of the crime committed, the convict may also be prohibited from engaging in certain activities, entering certain areas or places or contacting certain persons during probation (Article 72). Only when these three conditions are simultaneously fulfilled can probation be granted.

369. The probation period for suspension of criminal detention shall be not less than the term originally decided but not more than one year. However, it may not be less than two months.

The probation period for suspension of fixed-term imprisonment shall be not less than the term originally decided but not more than five years. However, it may not be less than one year.

The probation period for suspension of sentence shall be counted from the date the judgment is made final (Article 73).

370. A criminal whose sentence is suspended shall observe the following regulations:

- to observe laws and administrative rules and regulations, and to accept supervision, including obeying the order of prohibition given by the people's court in its judgment;
- to report on his own activities as required by the observing organ;
- to observe the regulations for receiving visitors stipulated by the observing organ;
- to obtain approval from the observing organ for any departure from the city or county he lives in or for any change in residence (Article 75).

371. Any criminal whose sentence is suspended shall, during the probation period, be subjected to social correction (*supra* paragraph 303), and in the absence of the circumstances prescribed in Article 77 of this Code (below), the punishment originally decided shall cease to be executed upon the expiration of the probation period for suspension of sentence, which shall be made known publicly (Article 76).

If, during the probation period for suspension of sentence, a criminal whose sentence is suspended commits a crime again or it is discovered that before the judgment is pronounced, he has committed another crime for which he is not sentenced, the suspension shall be revoked and another judgment rendered for the newly committed or discovered crime; the punishments to be executed shall be decided on the basis of the punishments for the old crime and the new crime and according to the provisions of Article 69 of this Code (*supra*, paragraph 351).

If, during the probation period for suspension of sentence, a criminal whose sentence is suspended violates laws, administrative rules and regulations or regulations relating to supervision and control over suspension of sentence stipulated by the relevant departments under the State Council or the order of prohibition in the judgment of the people's court for the probation and if the circumstances of this violation are serious, the suspension shall be revoked and the original punishment shall be executed (Article 77).

It is noticeable that the Chinese criminal law provides nothing about the type and severity of the crime which can revoke the probation.

372. Article 449 of the Criminal Code of 1997 provides that:

> if during wartime a serviceman is sentenced to fixed-term imprisonment of not more than three years for a crime he commits and is granted suspension of sentence because he presents no real danger, he may be allowed to atone for his crime by performing meritorious deeds. If he truly performs meritorious deeds, the original sentence may be rescinded and he shall not be regarded as a criminal.

This is a specific probation only for servicemen.

II. Commutation of Punishment

373. Commutation of punishment refers to the system to commute the term of the originally imposed punishment being served by the criminal for his demonstration of repentance. Actually, this system is a kind of reward to criminals for their good reform.

374. According to Article 78 of the Criminal Code of 1997, commutation of punishment shall be applied under the following conditions:

- any criminal sentenced to public surveillance, criminal detention, fixed-term imprisonment or life imprisonment, including those who have been granted probation;
- the criminal shall conscientiously observe prison regulations, accept education and reform and show true repentance or perform meritorious services while serving his sentence;
- within certain limits, i.e., after one or more commutations, the term of punishment actually to be served by those sentenced to public surveillance, criminal detention or fixed-term imprisonment may not be less than half of the term originally decided upon; for those sentenced to life imprisonment, it may not be less than thirteen years; for those who used to be sentenced to the death penalty with two-years suspension and has been legally commuted to life imprisonment upon expiration of the suspension, it may not be less than twenty-five years and for those who has been legally commuted to twenty-five years imprisonment, it may not be less than twenty years where the people's court has put restrictions on commutation of the death penalty with a suspension according to paragraph 2, Article 50 of the 1997 CCC (*supra*, paragraph 318).

The criminal shall be commuted if he performs any of the following major meritorious services:

- preventing another person from conducting major criminal activities;
- providing information about major criminal activities conducted inside or outside prison which is then verified through investigation;
- having inventions or important technical innovations to his credit;
- coming to the rescue of another in everyday life and production at the risk of losing his own life;
- performing remarkable services in fighting against natural disasters or curbing major accidents; or
- making other major contributions to the country and society.

375. The term of the commuted punishment, whose original sentence is public surveillance, criminal detention, or fixed-term imprisonment shall be counted from the date of the execution of the original sentence. The portion of the term having been served shall be included into the term of the commuted punishment. The term of fixed-term imprisonment that is commuted from a life imprisonment shall be counted from the date on which the order of commutation is issued (Article 80).

376. If punishment to a criminal is to be commuted, the executing organ shall submit to a people's court at or above the intermediate level, a written proposal for the commutation of punishment. The people's court shall form a collegiate panel for examination and, if the criminal is found to have shown true repentance or performed meritorious services, issue an order of commutation. However, no punishment shall be commuted without going through the correct legal procedure (Article 79).

III. Parole

377. Parole, or conditional relief, may be applied under the following conditions (Article 81 of the Criminal Code of 1997):

- only the criminals who are sentenced to fixed-term imprisonment or life imprisonment may be granted parole;
- only after a certain period of punishment has been served can a parole be granted, i.e., criminals sentenced to fixed-term imprisonment have served more than half of the term of their original sentence, criminals sentenced to life imprisonment have served no less than thirteen years of their term; however, if special circumstances exist, the restrictions relating to the term served may be disregarded with the verification of the SPC;
- the criminal to be granted parole shall conscientiously observe prison regulations, accept education and reform and show true repentance while serving his sentence.

No parole shall be granted to recidivists or criminals who are sentenced to more than ten years of imprisonment or life imprisonment for crimes of murder, rape, robbery, abduction, arson, explosion, dissemination of hazardous substances or organised violent crime.

During the making of a parole decision for a criminal, the judges shall consider the impact of the parole for the criminal on the community where he lives.

378. The probation period for parole in the case of fixed-term imprisonment shall be equal to the portion of the term that has not been completed; the probation period for parole in the case of life imprisonment shall be ten years.

The probation period for parole shall be counted from the date when the criminal is released on parole (Article 83).

379. Parole shall be granted to a criminal through the procedure prescribed in Article 79 of the 1997 CCC (*supra*, paragraph 376). No parole shall be granted without going through the legal procedure (Article 82).

Any criminal who is granted parole shall observe the laws and regulations, which are also applicable to a criminal who is probated (*supra*, paragraph 370). However, there is not yet a regulation for parolees to accept the order of prohibition.

380. Any criminal who is granted parole shall be subjected to social correction (*supra* paragraph 303) during the probation period for parole. If he is not found in any of the circumstances prescribed in Article 86 of the 1997 CCC (below), the punishment originally decided shall be considered to have been fully executed upon the expiration of the probation period for parole, which shall be made known publicly (Article 85).

According to Article 86, a criminal who is granted parole and who commits another crime during the probation period for parole, shall have their parole revoked, and he shall be given a combined punishment for several crimes as provided in Article 71 of the Criminal Code (*supra*, paragraph 357).

If a criminal who is granted parole is discovered to have committed, before the judgment is pronounced, other crimes for which no punishment has been imposed, the parole shall be revoked and a combined punishment for several crimes shall be given according to the provisions of Article 70 of this Code (*supra*, paragraph 356).

If a criminal who is granted parole, during the probation period for parole, violates laws, administrative rules and regulations or regulations relating to supervision and control over the parole stipulated by the relevant department under the State Council, but the violation does not constitute a new crime, the parole shall be revoked in accordance with legal procedure and he shall be put back into prison to serve the remaining part of the criminal punishment (Article 86).

§5. Limitation

381. Article 87 of the Criminal Code of 1997 provides that crimes shall not be prosecuted if the following periods have elapsed:

- five years, when the maximum punishment prescribed is fixed-term imprisonment of less than five years;
- ten years, when the maximum punishment prescribed is fixed-term imprisonment of not less than five years but less than ten years;
- fifteen years, when the maximum punishment prescribed is fixed-term imprisonment of not less than ten years; and
- twenty years, when the maximum punishment prescribed is life imprisonment or death penalty. If after twenty years it is considered necessary to prosecute a crime, the matter shall be submitted to the Supreme People's Procuratorate for examination and approval.

382. No limitation on the period for prosecution shall be imposed with respect to a criminal who escapes from investigation or trial after a people's procuratorate, public security organ or national security organ files the case or a people's court accepts the case.

No limitation on the period for prosecution shall be imposed with respect to a case which should have been, but is not filed by a people's court, people's procuratorate or public security organ after the victim brings a charge within the period for prosecution (Article 88).

The regulation on the statute of limitation in the Chinese criminal law will not provide an unreasonable restriction against prosecution of the serious offences.

383. The limitation period for prosecution shall be counted from the date when the crime is committed; if the criminal act is of a continual or continuous nature, it shall be counted from the date the criminal act is terminated.

If further crime is committed during a limitation period for prosecution, the limitation period for prosecution of the old crime shall be counted from the date when the new crime is committed (Article 89 of the Criminal Code of 1997).

Part II. Criminal Procedure

Chapter 1. General Characteristics

§1. Organisation of Criminal Jurisdiction

384. The term 'judicial personnel' in the Chinese law has been used to refer to personnel engaged in the functions of investigating, prosecuting, adjudicating, supervising and controlling offenders (Article 94 of the 1997 CCC).

In accordance with the Chinese Code of Criminal Procedure of 2012 (CCP), the public security organs shall be responsible for investigation, detention, execution of arrests and preliminary inquiry in criminal cases. The people's procuratorates shall be responsible for procuratorial work, authorising approval of arrests, conducting investigation and initiating public prosecution of cases directly accepted by the procuratorial organs. The people's courts shall be responsible for adjudication. Except as otherwise provided by law, no other organs, organisations or individuals shall have the authority to exercise such powers (Article 3).[1]

In the Chinese Criminal Procedure, Article 290 provides that the security departments of the armed forces shall have the authority to investigate criminal cases that occur within the armed forces, while crimes committed by inmates within a prison shall be investigated by the prison.

385. The Constitution provides that the people's courts shall exercise judicial power independently and the people's procuratorates shall exercise procuratorial power independently, in accordance with the provisions of the law, and are not subject to interference by any administrative organ, public organisation or individual (Articles 126 and 131 Const. (Constitution of the PRC)).

I. Trial Jurisdiction

386. In accordance with Article 123 of the Constitution and Article 1 of OLPC, the people's courts of the PRC are the judicial organs of the state. Article 3 of the Criminal Procedure of 2012 provides that the people's courts shall be responsible for adjudication. Article 12 also stresses that no person shall be found guilty without being

1. In this Part, all articles which do not mention the name of the law shall refer to the Chinese Criminal Procedure of 2012.

judged as such by a people's court according to law. Article 4 states that national security authorities shall, in accordance with law, handle criminal cases regarding endangering national security and perform the same functions as those of public security authorities.

A. Organisational System of the People's Court

387. The people's court of the PRC is a complete organisational system of adjudication composed of the SPC, local people's courts and the special people's courts (including, e.g., the military court) (*supra*, paragraphs 38 et seq.).

In accordance with the Constitution, the SPC is the highest judicial organ, and it shall have the power to supervise the administration of justice by the people's courts at various local levels and by the special people's courts. The people's courts at higher levels supervise the administration of justice by those at lower levels (Article 127).

There may be certain instances of co-operation and assistance between the local people's courts, such as delivering summons, notices and other court documents for other people's court or running investigations, entrusted by other people's court.

B. Trial Organisations

388. In accordance with the provisions of the Chinese Criminal Procedure of 2012, there are three types of trial organisations in the Chinese criminal adjudication system: trial by a single judge, the collegial panel, and the judicial committee.

389. Article 178 of the CCP, states that the cases in which summary procedures are applied, in the basic people's courts, may be tried by a single judge alone.

390. Trial by the collegial panel is the basic organisational form in the PRC. The collegial panel shall be structured and applied in the following ways:

- trials of cases of first instance in the basic and intermediate people's court shall be conducted by a collegial panel composed of either; three judges or of judges and people's assessors totalling three;
- trial of cases of first instance in the higher people's courts or the SPC shall be conducted by a collegial panel composed of either; three to seven judges or of judges and people's assessors totalling seven;
- trial of appealed and protested cases in the people's courts shall be conducted by a collegial panel composed of between three to five judges (Article 178);
- reviews by the SPC of cases involving death sentences and reviews by a higher people's court of cases involving death sentences with a suspension of execution, shall be conducted by collegial panels, each composed of three judges (Article 238).

The people's assessors shall enjoy equal rights with the judges when performing their functions in the people's courts. In the Decision of the Standing Committee of the NPC Regarding Perfecting the System of People's Assessors, Article 4 provides that any citizens who uphold the Constitution of PRC, have reached the age of 23, are of good ethics, upright and decent; and are in good health, may serve as a people's assessor. As a general rule, one shall have an educational background of junior college or higher education. In addition, Article 6 states that those who have been subjected to criminal punishment for committing a crime or have been dismissed from public posts may not serve as people's assessors.

The members of a collegial panel shall be odd in number.

The president of the people's court or the chief judge of a division shall designate one judge to be the presiding judge of the collegial panel. If the president of the court or the chief judge of a division participates in a trial, he himself shall serve as the presiding judge.

If there is any dissenting opinion in a collegial panel during its deliberations, a decision shall be made in accordance with the opinions of the majority, but the opinion of the minority shall be entered in the records. The records of the deliberations shall be signed by the members of the collegial panel.

For a case remanded for retrial, a new collegial panel shall be formed and the judicial personnel in the original proceedings shall not be allowed to participate in the new collegial panel.

391. In accordance with Article 10 of the OLPC, people's courts at all levels shall set up judicial committees which practice democratic centralism. The task of the judicial committees is to sum up judicial experience and to discuss important or difficult cases and other issues relating to the judicial work.

The judicial committee is not, by nature, a pure trial organisation. It is only so when it discusses the important or difficult cases. Article 180 of the Criminal Procedure sets that after the hearings and deliberations, the collegial panel shall render a judgment. With respect to a difficult, complex or major case, on which the collegial panel considers it difficult to make a decision, the collegial panel shall refer the case to the president of the court for him to decide whether to submit the case to the judicial committee for discussion and decision. The collegial panel shall execute the decision of the judicial committee.

The system of the judicial committee is under reform in China. The tendency of the reform is clearly towards judges taking full responsibility to try cases and to undertake the responsibility for their judgments.

II. Investigating Jurisdiction

392. It is true that the main investigating jurisdiction rests in the hands of the public security organs, however, the people's procuratorates shall also have their own scope of investigating jurisdiction (*supra*, paragraph 385) and the people's courts shall in a certain sense have the power of investigation.

A. Public Security Organs

393. The public security organ is the state organ responsible for protection of the public security of this country. It is also the enforcement organ for executive administration. In the criminal proceedings, the public security organ is the main organ for criminal investigation.

The Ministry of Public Security is the leading organ for public security in the state. The local public security organs are either established according to the administrative areas, i.e., the organs at the level of province, prefecture and country, or according to industrial system, i.e., military forces, railway and civil aviation. The public security station is an agency of the basic public security organs.

The relationship between the upper and lower level of the public security organs is one of leadership and subordination and the relationship between the organs at the same level is co-operative. Article 81 of the CCP provides that when a public security organ is to detain or arrest a person in another place, it shall inform the public security organ in the place where the person to be detained or arrested stays, and the public security organ there shall co-operate in the action.

394. The Criminal Procedure provides full authority to the public security organ. The following are the principal authorities they hold:

- to decide to file cases for investigation within the scope of their jurisdiction (Article 18);
- to carry out inquest and examination, search and seizure, to organise expert evaluation, to inquire into or freeze criminal suspects' deposits or remittances, to question witnesses and victims and to interrogate the criminal suspect (Article 113ff.);
- to issue a warrant to compel the appearance of the criminal suspect or defendant or to detain him, to order him to obtain a guarantor pending trial or subject him to residential surveillance (Articles 64 et seq.);
- to submit a request of arrest to the people's procuratorate for examination and approval and to make an arrest, and to issue a wanted order (Articles 64ff.–153ff.).

395. The CCP also states that state security organs shall perform the same functions and powers as the public security organs according to law in handling cases of crimes that endanger state security (Article 4). The security departments of the Army shall exercise the power of investigation with respect to criminal offences that have occurred in the Army. Crimes committed by inmates in prison shall be investigated by the prison (Article 225).

B. The People's Procuratorate

396. In accordance with the Constitution, the people's procuratorates of the PRC are state organs for legal supervision (Article 129). As mentioned above (*supra*, paragraphs 35 and 36), the people's procuratorates are headed by the Supreme People's Procuratorate and composed of the local and special people's procuratorates with three levels; province, prefecture and county.

People's procuratorates at the provincial or county level may, according to work requirements and upon the approval of the standing committee of the people's congress at the corresponding level, establish people's procuratorates as their agencies in industrial and mining areas, agricultural reclamation areas, forest zones, etc. (Article 2 of the OLPP).

In accordance with Article 3 of the OLPP, people's procuratorates at all levels shall each set up a procuratorial committee. The procuratorial committee shall apply the system of democratic centralism and, under the direction of the chief procurator, hold discussion and make decisions on important cases and other major issues. In the case of the chief procurator disagreeing with the majority's opinion over a decision on an important issue, the matter may be reported to the standing committee of the people's congress at the corresponding level for final decision.

397. The CCP provides the people's procuratorates with their functions and judicial position in criminal proceedings:

- The people's procuratorates are one of the state organs which can exercise investigatory powers. Article 18 of the Criminal Procedure provides that crimes of embezzlement and bribery, crimes of dereliction of duty committed by state functionaries, and crimes involving violations of a citizen's civil or personal rights such as illegal detention, extortion of confessions by torture, retaliation, frame-up and illegal search and crimes involving infringement of a citizen's democratic rights, committed by state functionaries by taking advantage of their functions and powers, shall be placed on file for investigation by the people's procuratorates. If cases involving other grave crimes committed by state functionaries by taking advantage of their functions and powers need be handled directly by the people's procuratorates, they may be placed on file for investigation by the people's procuratorates upon decision by the people's procuratorates at or above the provincial level.
  It is obvious that the jurisdiction of the people's procuratorate and of the public security organ might overlap in some situations. According to the Provisions of the SPC, the Supreme People's Procuratorate, the Ministry of Public Security, the Ministry of State Security, the Ministry of Justice, and the Legislative Affairs Commission of the Standing Committee of the NPC on Several Issues concerning the Implementation of the Criminal Procedure Law, as of effective on 1 January 2013 (Provision of 2013), where a criminal case investigated by a public security authority involves bribery or corruption and is within the jurisdiction of a people's procuratorate, the bribery or corruption case shall be transferred to the people's procuratorate; and where a bribery or corruption case investigated by a people's procuratorate involves a criminal case that is within the jurisdiction of a public security authority, the criminal case shall be transferred to them. Where there is conflict regarding jurisdiction, the public security authority shall be the primary investigating authority; if the primary suspect of the offence is within the jurisdiction of the public security authority, the people's procuratorate shall provide only co-operation; or if the primary suspect of the offence is within the jurisdiction of the people's procuratorate, the people's procuratorate shall be the primary investigating authority and the public security authority shall provide their co-operation (Article 1 of the Provision of 2013).
- The people's procuratorates are the only state organs which can exercise the power of prosecution (*infra*, paragraphs 402 and 514).
- Article 8 of the Criminal Procedure states that the people's procuratorate shall, in accordance with law, exercise legal supervision over criminal proceedings.

When finding any mistake or misconduct in the criminal proceedings, the people's procuratorate may, in the areas where the criminal procedure grants power for legal supervision, exercise its power of legal supervision. The Chinese Criminal Procedure provides the people's procuratorate with the power in relation to, particularly, the following areas: the filing of a case (Article 110), investigation and interrogation (Articles 85, 98, 171), the trial (Article 203), protest for the second instance (Article 217), protest for the retrial (Article 243), the execution of a death sentence (Article 252), those temporarily serving sentence outside an incarceration facility (Article 255), commutation or parole (Article 263) and over the authorities of implementation (Article 265).

- The people's procuratorate is the principal organ to examine arrest. In accordance with Article 78 of the CCP, arrests of criminal suspects or defendants shall be subject to approval by a people's procuratorate, except for those decided by a people's court.

C. *The People's Courts*

398. The people's courts can exercise certain powers of investigation in accordance with the Criminal Procedure. Article 191 states that:

> during a court hearing, if the collegial panel has doubts about the evidence, it may announce an adjournment, in order to carry out investigation to verify the evidence. When carrying out investigation to verify evidence, the people's court may conduct inquest, examination, seizure, expert evaluation, as well as inquiry and freeze.

In order to avoid the conflict of jurisdiction, the Provision of 2013 provides a resolution: a people's court, a people's procuratorate, or a public security authority may handle cases concurrently within its functions when: (1) one person committed more than two offences; (2) there is a joint crime; (3) a criminal suspect or defendant in a joint crime additionally committed other crimes; (4) the offences committed by more than one suspects or defendants are linked with each other and handling these cases concurrently will facilitate the finding of case facts (Article 2 of the Provision of 2013).

§2. Participants in the Proceedings

399. The judicial organisations are not a party in the criminal proceedings according to the theory of the Chinese criminal procedure. The participants in the proceedings refer to the parties, legal representatives, agents *ad litem*, defenders, witnesses, expert witnesses and interpreters (item 4, Article 82). In theory, they are classified into two categories: the parties and other participants in the proceedings.

I. The Parties

400. The parties refer to victims, private prosecutors, criminal suspects, defendants and the plaintiffs and defendants in incidental civil actions (item 2, Article 82).

A. Victims

401. The 'victim' refers to the person who directly suffered from the criminal activities. The victim can be a natural person, a legal person or another organisation without the status of legal person. If a victim brings an incidental civil action in a public prosecution, he is then the plaintiff of the incidental civil action as well as the victim. In the case of private prosecution, the victim is the private prosecutor and, if he brings an incidental civil action, he is then also the plaintiff.

The victim's position in the proceedings is a party exercising the function of prosecution. His rights in the proceedings are as follows:

- to ask for the filing of the case for investigation;
- to apply for withdraw;
- to entrust an agents *ad litem*;
- to request compensation for damages or to bring an incidental civil action during criminal procedures;
- to submit complaint to the people's procuratorate at a level higher when a people's procuratorate made a decision of not filing a case, or to bring a private prosecution directly to a people's court;
- to appear in court and to state circumstances of the case, to question the defendant, to participate in the investigation and examination of evidence, and to request new witnesses to be summoned, new material evidence to be obtained, new evaluations to be made and another inquest to be held;
- to participate in the debates in court;
- to ask for protection due to his position as a witness in the proceedings and for the suffering of threats to his own or his relative's personal safety (*infra* paragraph 412);
- to request the people's procuratorate to present a protest within the time limit prescribed by law, to present a petition regarding a legally effective judgment or ruling and to request a retrial;
- to receive any property illegally obtained by the defendant.

The minor victim will have the right to present their opinion with the presentation of their legal representatives.

B. Private Prosecutor

402. The private prosecutor refers to the person who brings a criminal lawsuit directly to a people's court in his own name to prosecute a defendant's criminal liability. The private prosecutor is the plaintiff in the case of private prosecution and usually is also the victim. In accordance with Article 88 of the CCP, if the victim is dead, or has lost his ability of conduct, his legal representatives and near relatives shall have the right to bring a suit to a people's court and the people's court shall accept it according to law.

The private prosecutor's rights in the proceedings are as follows:

- to bring a private prosecution directly to a people's court and to entrust an agents *ad litem*;
- to bear the burden of proof to demonstrate the guilt of the defendant;
- to apply for the withdrawal of a private prosecution;
- to bring an incidental civil action in the criminal proceedings;
- to arrange a settlement with the defendant;
- to appear in court as the plaintiff and to participate in the trial of a case and to debate with the defendant;
- to apply for withdraw;
- to appeal;
- to present a petition regarding a legally effective judgment or ruling and to request a retrial.

A private prosecutor shall bear the burden of proof. If he invents a story and forges evidence, he shall bear the criminal responsibility. A private prosecutor shall participate in the proceedings personally. If a private prosecutors, having been served twice with a summons according to law, refuses to appear in court without justifiable reasons, or if he withdraws from a court session without permission of the court, the case may be considered withdrawn by him (Article 205).

C. Criminal Suspects and Defendants

403. A criminal suspect refers to the criminal party who is being investigated and examined for potential prosecution in a case of public prosecution.

A defendant refers to the criminal party who is being prosecuted by a public or a private prosecutor for criminal charge.

The terms of criminal suspect and defendant are terms for a person who is at the different stages in the criminal proceedings.

404. As a criminal suspect, he shall have the principal rights in the criminal proceedings as follows:

- to apply for withdraw;
- to appoint a lawyer to provide legal assistance for him during investigation;
- to meet with his lawyer without being monitored and to correspond with his lawyer;
- to have the right to refuse to answer any questions that are irrelevant to the case;
- to apply for obtaining a guarantor pending trial;
- to request a new expert evaluation or another inquest;
- to entrust a defender during prosecution and in trial (*infra*, paragraph 552);
- to present a petition according to law for the decision not to initiate a prosecution.

A criminal suspect's basic obligations are to accept investigation and examination for prosecution, and to observe the lawful compulsory measures.

405. As a defendant, he shall have the principal rights in the criminal proceedings as follows:

- to apply for withdraw;
- to defend himself or to entrust a person to defend him;
- to refuse his defender and to entrust a new defender;
- to present statements regarding the crime accused;
- to participate in court for investigation and examination for facts and evidences and present his opinions;
- to request new witnesses to be summoned, a new expert evaluation to be made or another inquest to be held;
- to debate with the prosecutor;
- to make the final statement;
- to appeal for the judgment which is not yet final;
- to present a petition for the legally effective judgment.

The private defendant shall have the right to bring a counter-claim against the private prosecutor.

D. Plaintiff and Defendant in an Incidental Civil Action

406. The plaintiff in an incidental civil action refers to the person who suffers economic damages because of the defendant's criminal activities and requests compensation according to law in the criminal proceedings. He is usually the victim or the private prosecutor, but may be the agent *ad litem* or the successor of the dead victim. It may also be a 'unit' or corporate body (*supra*, paragraph 156).

407. The defendant in an incidental civil action refers to the person who shall bear the responsibility of compensation for the economic damages caused by the criminal activities of the defendant. He usually is the criminal defendant but may also be the agent *ad litem* of him or other person or organisation that shall bear the responsibility of compensation for the losses caused by the criminal defendant.

408. In criminal proceedings, the plaintiff and defendant in an incidental civil action may commonly have the following rights:

- to apply for withdraw;
- to participate in court for investigation and examination for facts and evidences relating to the part of the incidental civil action and to debate;
- to entrust an agent *ad litem*;
- to appeal the judgment of the civil action;

In addition, the plaintiff shall have the right to request mediation and to arrange a settlement with the defendant, to bring a request for compensation or to withdraw this request. But he shall also have a duty to provide evidence to support his request.

II. Other Participants

409. As mentioned above, other participants in the criminal proceedings refer to legal representatives, agents *ad litem*, defenders, witnesses, expert witnesses and interpreters (*supra*, paragraph 400).

A. Legal Representatives

410. Legal representatives refer to the parents, foster parents or guardians of a person being represented and representatives of the state organ or public organisation responsible for that person's protection (item 3, Article 106 of the CCP).

When the legal representative is more than one person, only one may be allowed to participate in the proceedings.

A legal representative shall enjoy the same rights in criminal proceedings as the person he represents, except for those of personal characteristics such as statement.

B. Agent ad litem

411. Agent *ad litem* refers to persons entrusted by victims and their legal representatives or near relatives in cases of public prosecution and by private prosecutors and their legal representatives in cases of private prosecution, to participate in legal proceedings on their behalf, and persons entrusted by parties in incidental civil actions and their legal representatives to participate in legal proceedings on their behalf (item 5, Article 106).

C. Witnesses

412. Witnesses refer to the participants in the criminal proceeding, other than the parties, who are aware of the circumstances of the case and who provide testimony to the public security organ or the judicial organ.

A witness must be a natural person. Any person who has information regarding a case shall have the obligation to testify. However, physically or mentally handicapped persons or minors who cannot distinguish right from wrong or cannot properly express themselves shall not be qualified as witnesses (Article 60).

The people's courts, the people's procuratorates and the public security organs shall ensure the safety of witnesses and their near relatives. Anyone who intimidates, humiliates, beats or retaliates against a witness or his near relatives, if his act constitutes a crime, shall be investigated for criminal responsibility according to law; if the case is not serious enough for criminal punishment, he shall be punished for violation of public security in accordance with law (Article 61). For witnesses who testify in cases involving the crime of endangering national security, terrorist activities, organised crime with the nature of underground society or a drug crime, Specific protection shall be given through methods such as not disclosing his true name, residence address, his look, true voice and so on, when he takes the stand (Article 62). The witness performing his obligation to testify shall be financially supported by the Chinese government. The costs of travel, board and lodging and other expenses for the testimony shall be ensured by the treasury of the government at the same level. When a working witness testifies, his or her employer may not directly or indirectly deduct his or her salary, bonus, welfare and other remunerations (Article 63).

The testimony of a witness may be used as a basis for deciding the outcome of a case only after the witness has been questioned and cross-examined in the courtroom by both sides, that is, the public prosecutor and victim as well as the defendant and defenders, and after the testimonies of the witnesses on all sides have been heard and verified. If a court discovers through investigation that a witness has intentionally given false testimony or concealed criminal evidence, it shall handle the matter in accordance with the law (Article 59).

D. Expert Witnesses

413. An expert witness refers to the participant in the criminal proceedings who is assigned or invited by a public security organ or judicial organ to evaluate certain special problems relating to a case with his professional knowledge or skills. The opinion of an expert witness is called the conclusion of expert evaluation and is a kind of independent evidence.

An expert witness shall be subject to the conditions of withdrawal. If he has any relation to a party in the said case that could affect the impartiality of his work, he is expected to withdraw voluntarily. The parties and their legal representatives shall also have right to request him to withdraw.

An expert witness shall have right to know the materials of the case relating to the expert evaluation and to reject to provide his opinion when he thinks that the conditions are not sufficient enough for him to do so. He shall also have right to receive fees and compensation for his work.

The expert witness shall bear legal responsibility for intentional false evaluation with the purpose to frame another person or conceal criminal evidence and shall have a duty to keep confidential about what he knows in the case and those facts relating to another's privacy.

After 2012, technical investigation measures were stipulated in the Chinese Criminal Procedure. These measures may be used by the public security organ after following strict approval formalities for those cases regarding the crime of endangering national security, crimes of terrorist activities, organised crime with the nature of underground society, serious drug crimes, or any other crime seriously endangering the society. They may also be used by the request of the people's procuratorate after undergoing strict approval formalities for the cases regarding the serious crimes of embezzlement or bribery or a serious crime committed by taking advantage of one's powers to gravely infringe upon the personal rights of citizens. When in the process of capturing a wanted or a fugitive criminal suspect or defendant whose arrest has been approved or decided, technical investigation measures necessary for capture may be taken with approval (Articles 148 et seq.).

The expert witness shall enjoy the same protection as the witness mentioned above (*supra*, paragraph 412).

E. Interpreters

414. Interpreters in criminal proceedings refer not only to the translation of language but also to that of sign language for deaf and dumb. The rights and duties an interpreter shall have are similar to an expert witness (*supra*, paragraph 414).

F. Defenders

415. In accordance with Article 32 of the CCP, the following persons may be entrusted as defenders:

- lawyers;
- persons recommended by a public organisation or the 'unit' (i.e., corporate body) to which the criminal suspect or the defendant belongs; and
- guardians, relatives and friends of the criminal suspect or defendant.

Persons who are under criminal punishment or whose personal freedom is deprived of or restricted according to law shall not serve as defenders.

416. In Chinese legal practice, lawyers are the most common defenders in criminal cases. We have discussed the qualification of lawyers above (*supra*, paragraph 48). The Chinese Lawyers Law was primarily stipulated in 1996, which replaced the Interim Regulations on Lawyers of 1980. However, the Chinese Lawyers Law was again revised in 2001, 2007 and 2012. As a general tendency, the legal position of lawyers has been strengthened in the Chinese legal system. Lawyers enjoy more rights than before.

In the Lawyers Law, it also is stated that active working personnel of a state organ shall not concurrently practice as a lawyer. A lawyer shall not practice law while serving as a member of a standing committee of a people's congress at any level (Article 11 of the Lawyers Law of 2012). A lawyer who once served as a judge or prosecutor shall not act as agent *ad litem* or defend clients for two years after leaving his post in the people's court or the people's procuratorate (Article 41 of the Lawyers Law of 2012).

Although both lawyers and people without a lawyer's licence can act as defenders for a defendant, those who have not obtained a lawyer's practice certificate shall not practice law under the title of 'lawyer', act as agent *ad litem* or defend a client for the purpose of seeking economic benefit (Article 13 of the Lawyers Law of 2012).

417. In accordance with the Criminal Procedure, a criminal suspect in a case of public prosecution shall have the right to entrust persons as his defenders from the date when the criminal suspect is interrogated by a criminal investigation authority for the first time or from the day when a compulsory measure is taken against the criminal suspect. A defendant in a case of private prosecution shall have the right to entrust persons as his defenders at any time (Article 33). A criminal suspect or a defendant may entrust one or two persons as his defenders, in addition to exercising the right to defend himself (Article 32). These two people may both be lawyers or just one lawyer and one citizen. During the period of criminal investigation, a criminal suspect may only retain a lawyer as a defender. After the prosecution is initiated, a defendant shall have the right to retain a defender at any time (Article 33).

In a case of joint crime, one defender shall not defend two or more defendants in the same case.

418. The responsibility of a defender shall be to present, according to the facts and law, materials and opinions proving the innocence of the criminal suspect or defendant, the pettiness of his crime and the need for a mitigated punishment or exemption from criminal responsibility, thus safeguarding the lawful rights and interests of the criminal suspect or defendant (Article 35 of the Criminal Procedure and Article 31 of the Lawyers Law).

419. The defenders may enjoy the following rights in criminal proceedings according to laws:

- A lawyer appointed by a criminal suspect, who is interrogated by an investigative organ for the first time or from the day when compulsory measures (*infra*, paragraphs 433 et seq.) are taken against him, shall have the right to find out from the investigative organ about the crime his client is suspected of, and may meet with the criminal suspect in custody to enquire about the case (Articles 33, 36).
- A defence lawyer may meet and correspond with a criminal suspect or defendant in custody. As permitted by the people's court or people's procuratorate, a defender other than a defence lawyer may also meet and correspond with a criminal suspect or defendant in custody. When a defence lawyer files a request for a meeting with a criminal suspect or defendant in custody on the basis of the lawyer's practising licence, a certificate issued by the law firm and a power of attorney or an official legal aid document, a jail shall arrange a meeting in a timely manner, no later than 48 hours after the request is filed. Where a defence lawyer files a request during the period of criminal investigation for a meeting with a criminal suspect in custody who is suspected of endangering national security, terrorist activities, or extraordinarily serious bribery, the meeting shall be subject to the permission of the criminal investigation authority. In such a case, the criminal investigation authority shall issue a prior notice to the jail. When meeting with a criminal suspect or defendant in custody, a defence lawyer may learn relevant case information and provide legal advice and other services, and from the day when the case is transferred for examination and prosecution, may verify relevant evidence with the criminal suspect or defendant. A meeting between a defence lawyer and a criminal suspect or defendant shall not be monitored. Where a defence lawyer meets or correspond with a criminal suspect or defendant under residential surveillance, he shall enjoy the rights hereof (Article 37).
- Defence lawyers may, from the date when the people's procuratorate begins to examine a case for prosecution, consult, extract and duplicate the judicial documents pertaining to the current case and the technical verification material. Other defenders, with permission of the people's procuratorate or people's court, may also consult, extract and duplicate the above-mentioned material (Article 38).
- Defence lawyers may, with the consent of the witnesses or other units and individuals concerned, collect information pertaining to the current case from them and they may also apply to the people's procuratorate or the people's court

for the collection and obtainment of evidence, or request the people's court to inform the witnesses to appear in court and give testimony (Article 41).

- When examining a case, the people's procuratorate shall interrogate the criminal suspect and hear the opinions of the victim and of the persons entrusted by the criminal suspect and the victim. The written opinions of the defender, victim, and litigation representative, if any, shall be attached to the case file (Article 170).
- Defenders shall have the right to participate in court investigation and court debate, including the right to question the defendant (Article 186), to question witnesses or expert witnesses (Article 189), to raise objection to a witness statement or an expert opinion (Article 187), to request new witnesses to be summoned, new material evidence to be obtained, new expert evaluation to be made and another inquest to be held (Article 192), and to debate with the prosecutor (Articles 193, 210 and 212).
- With the consent of the defendant, defenders may file appeals (Article 216).
- If the compulsory measures adopted by a people's court, a people's procuratorate or a public security organ exceed the time limit prescribed by law, the criminal suspect or defendant, his legal representatives, near relatives, or the lawyers or other defenders entrusted by the criminal suspect or defendant shall have the right to demand cancellation of the compulsory measures. The people's court, the people's procuratorate, or the public security organ shall release the criminal suspect or defendant when the compulsory measures adopted against him have exceeded the time limit prescribed by law, terminate the period for awaiting trial after obtaining a guarantor or organising residential surveillance, or take different compulsory measures according to law (Article 97).
- If the matter authorised by a client violates law, the client uses the services provided by the lawyer to engage in illegal activities or the client deliberately conceals facts related to the case, the lawyer shall have the right to refuse to defend or to represent the client (Article 32 of the Lawyers Law of 2012).

420. The defenders should undertake the following obligations in criminal proceedings according to laws:

- To observe the regulations of the custody place when meeting the criminal suspect or the defendant in custody.
- To observe the regulation of court when participating the trial in court.
- Not to collect material pertaining to the case from the victim or the witnesses provided by the victim without the permission of the people's procuratorate or the people's court.
- Not to help the criminal suspect or the defendant to do anything that would undermine the judicial activities, such as to destroy or forge evidence.
- Not to commit conduct prohibited in laws and regulations, such as bribing or meeting a judge, prosecutor or arbitrator in violation of regulations.
- Not to accept authorisation or charging fees privately, or accept property or any other benefit from a client and not to seek the disputed rights and interests of a party by taking advantage of the provision of legal services.

- Not to disclose to the public any state secrets or confidential trade information or any privacy of clients which the defender knows from his practice. However, a defence lawyer shall inform a judicial authority in a timely manner of the facts and information of a crime endangering national security or public security or seriously endangering the safety of the body of a person, which a client or other person prepares to commit or is committing (Article 46 of the Criminal Procedure of 2012 and Article 38 of Lawyers Law of 2012).
- Not to refuse defence without justifiable reasons.

421. A defender, including a lawyer, is not allowed to help his client unlawfully. Article 306 of the 1997 CCC provides that, during the course of the criminal procedure, any defender or law agent alone destroys or falsifies evidence or assists parties concerned in destroying or falsifying evidence, threatening or luring witnesses to contravene facts, change their testimony or make false testimony shall be criminally punished. In order to prevent the misuse of this article, however, Article 42 of the CCP provides that the case where a defender or other person helps a criminal suspect or defendant illegally shall be handled by a criminal investigation authority other than the one handling the case in which the defender provides representation. If the defender is a lawyer, the law firm employing the lawyer or the bar association to which the lawyer belongs shall be informed in a timely manner.

§3. Principles Concerning Criminal Procedure

422. The principles in the criminal procedure refer to the basic norms governing the criminal proceedings carried by the public security organ, the people's procuratorate and the people's court and followed by the participants in criminal proceedings.

The first important revision of the 2012 Criminal Procedure is to add a legal requirement for the respect for and protection of human rights into the Chinese Criminal Procedure (Article 2 of the CCP, *supra*, paragraph 69). This is not a simple repetition of the Chinese Constitution. Article 33 of the Chinese Constitution provides that the State respects and protects human rights but the Chinese Criminal Procedure shall set out this constitutional requirement in detailed regulations.

In accordance with the CCP, the principles in the criminal procedure are generally recognised as follows.

I. The Principle of Division of Investigatory, Prosecutorial and Adjudicative Powers

423. Article 3 of the Chinese Code of Criminal Procedure of 2012 provides contains the principle that the power of investigation, prosecution and adjudication shall be exercised by separate, specialised organs (*supra*, paragraph 385).

According to this principle, only the public security organs, the people's procuratorates and the people's court shall have the authority to exercise the powers of investigation, prosecution and adjudication. And these three organs shall have a definite division of work and shall not obscure their powers and works with others.

II. The Principle of the Independence of the People's Court and the People's Procuratorate

424. This principle also comes from the Constitution (*supra*, paragraph 386) and is laid down in Article 5 of the CCP. Accordingly, no other administrative organs, social organisations or individuals shall have the right to interfere in pending cases.

Indeed, China is a communist country, and the Chinese Communist Party is the ruling party. However, even the CCP cannot legally directly intervene into the trials of criminal cases.

III. The Principle of 'Relying upon the Masses'

425. In conducting criminal proceedings, the people's courts, the people's procuratorates and the public security organs must rely on the masses. Only this way a crime can be correctly discovered and proven. It is true that criminal investigation, prosecution and trial are highly professional procedures. However, this principle stresses how the professionals should also be relying on social reality. This principle also reflects the good tradition of people's revolution in China.

IV. The Principle of 'Taking Facts as the Basis and Law as the Criterion'

426. This principle directly reflects the requirement of the constitutional principle of legality (*supra*, paragraphs 67–68). It is probably the most popular slogan in China and has become an easy way for people to understand how their acts will be judged in accordance with the law.

With respect to the requirement of taking facts as the basis, stress is placed on having the evidence and the facts ascertained. The subjective imagination, inference and the accusation without evidence shall not become the basis of conviction.

With respect to the requirement of taking law as the criterion, it shall only follow the criminal law and the criminal procedure in conducting criminal proceedings and shall not violate the laws.

V. The Principle of Equal Treatment

427. Article 6 of the Criminal Procedure provides that the law applies equally to all citizens and no privilege whatsoever is permissible before law. Broadly speaking, this principle is only applicable in criminal proceedings. However, it reflects the constitutional principle as a whole.

Accordingly, the people's court, the people's procuratorate and the public security organ must, in conducting criminal proceedings, protect the legitimate interests of all citizens according to law without exception, no matter what their nationalities, races, sex, professions, social and family background, religious belief, levels of education, state of property and residential time limit. And anyone's unlawful criminal conduct shall be investigated according to law.

VI. The Principle of Dividing Responsibilities, Co-ordinating Efforts and Checking Each Other

428. Article 7 of the CCP provides that in conducting criminal proceedings, the people's courts, the people's procuratorates and the public security organs shall divide responsibilities, co-ordinate their efforts and check each other to ensure the correct and effective enforcement of law.

In recent years, the function of checking has been stressed. Legal supervision (*infra*, paragraph 429) and the supervision of social consensus have been also included.

VII. The Principle of Exercising Legal Supervision over Criminal Proceedings

429. Article 8 of the Criminal Procedure provides that the people's procuratorates shall exercise legal supervision over criminal proceedings in accordance with law. This legal supervision shall include the supervision over whether the criminal proceedings conducted by the public security organs, the people's courts and prisons, as well as the participants in the criminal proceedings, are according to law or not (e.g., *supra*, paragraph 397).

VIII. The Principle of Native Spoken and Written Languages in Court Proceedings

430. In accordance with this principle, citizens of all nationalities shall have the right to use their native spoken and written languages in court proceedings. The people's court, the people's procuratorates and the public security organs shall provide translations for any party to the court proceedings who is not familiar with the spoken or written language commonly used in the locality. Where people of a minority nationality live in a concentrated community or where a number of nationalities live together in one area, court hearings shall be conducted in the spoken language commonly used in the locality, and judgments, notices and other documents shall be issued in the written language commonly used in the locality (Article 9 of the CCP).

IX. The Principle of Public Trial

431. This is the requirement of the CCP as well as the Constitution. Cases in the people's courts shall be heard in public, unless otherwise provided by the law.

The cases which cannot be heard in public are, in accordance with Article 183, as follows:

- Cases involving state secrets.
- Cases involving the private affairs of individuals. In China, the offences involving sexual matters are included in this category.
- Cases involving any trade secrets. They may be heard in public if a party files such a request (Article 183).
- Cases involving crimes committed by minors who have not reached the age of 18 at the time of trial. However, with the consent of the juvenile defendant or his legal representative, the juvenile defendant's school and a juvenile protection organisation may send representatives to be present (Article 274). If a juvenile has been sentenced to a fixed-term imprisonment of five years or a lighter punishment, the related criminal records shall be sealed with an exception only for judicial authority, subject to keeping confidential obligations (Article 275).

X. The Principle of the Right to Defence

432. It is also the requirement of the Criminal Procedure as well as the Constitution that a defendant shall have the right to defence (Article 125 of the Constitution and Article 11 of the Criminal Procedure). The people's court shall have the duty to guarantee the defence (cf. *supra*, paragraph 393ff.).

XI. The Principle of Presumption of Innocence

433. This principle is very noticeably added into the CCP.

'No person shall be found guilty without being judged as such by a people's court according to law.'

Although the legal wording is not the same as the presumption of innocence, the Chinese academic circle commonly recognise this principle. However, the Chinese principle does not automatically recognise the right of silence. According to the CCP, the criminal suspect shall truthfully answer the questions of the investigators, though he has the right to refuse to answer questions irrelevant to the case (Article 118). Interestingly, there is no provision in the Chinese criminal law or criminal procedure that provides criminal liability for a criminal suspect who keeps silence during an interrogation.

XII. The Principle of Guaranty of the Procedural Rights

434. It is the requirement of the Criminal Procedure that the people's courts, the people's procuratorates and the public security organs shall safeguard the procedural rights to which participants in proceedings are entitled according to law. In cases where a minor under the age of 18 commits a crime, the criminal suspect and the legal representative of the defendant may be notified to be present at the time of interrogation and trial. Participants in proceedings shall have the right to file charges against judges, procurators and investigators whose acts infringe on their citizen's procedural rights or subject their persons to indignities (Article 14).

XIII. The Principle of Non-prosecution According to Law

435. Article 15 of the CCP identifies the following circumstances where criminal responsibility shall not be investigated.

If investigation has already been undertaken, the case shall be dismissed, or prosecution shall not be initiated, or the handling shall be terminated, or innocence shall be declared:

- if an act is obviously minor, causing no serious harm, and is therefore not deemed a crime;
- if the limitation period for criminal prosecution has expired;
- if an exemption of criminal punishment has been granted in a special amnesty decree;
- if the crime is to be handled only upon complaint according to the criminal law, but there has been no complaint or the complaint has been withdrawn;
- if the criminal suspect or defendant is deceased; and
- if other laws provide an exemption from investigation of criminal responsibility.

XIV. The Principle of Applying the Chinese Law for Foreigners' Criminal Responsibility

436. When China has jurisdiction over foreigners who have committed crimes, the Chinese criminal procedure shall, obviously, apply. However, if foreigners with diplomatic privileges and immunities commit crimes, those cases shall be resolved through diplomatic channels (Article 16 of the CCP).

437. Besides the basic principles mentioned above, Article 17 of the CCP provides that in accordance with the international treaties which the PRC has concluded or acceded to or on the principle of reciprocity, the judicial organs of China and those of other countries may request judicial assistance from each other in criminal affairs.

§4. The Rules of Evidence

I. Concept of Evidence

438. Article 48 of the Criminal Procedure of 2012 provides that all materials that may be used to prove the facts of a case are evidence.

The theory of the Chinese criminal procedure generally holds that evidence can play the following roles in criminal proceedings:

- evidence is the only method to find out the circumstances of a case;
- evidence is the basis for handling a case correctly;
- evidence is the foundation for criminal proceedings;
- evidence is the powerful weapon to force a criminal to confess his guilt;
- evidence is the safeguard to protect the innocent from being prosecuted;
- evidence is the tool for the socialist legal education.

439. The objects of proof, and where evidence shall be used as proof in criminal proceedings, have been issues in the theoretical circle. In the CCP, there are no clear regulations on this issue. However, the following articles are relevant to this issue: Article 193 provides that in a court session, any fact or evidence relating to conviction or sentencing shall be investigated and debated. Article 50 requires that judges, prosecutors, and criminal investigators must, under legal procedures, gather various kinds of evidence that can prove the guilt or innocence of a criminal suspect or defendant and the gravity of crime. Generally speaking, the objects of proof refer to those facts which can or cannot constitute a crime.

For individual offences, which facts are there in the scope of object to be proven? The Supreme People's Procuratorate has been trying to create guidance. For instance, the Supreme People's Procuratorate issued a Trial Criterion for reference on Examination of the Evidence for Arrest in 2003, in which only the criterion for ten offences was listed such as intentional killing, injury, theft, traffic violation, etc.

Accordingly, these requirements are around the facts required by a criminal constitution (*supra*, paragraphs 101 et seq.), i.e., the facts indicating criminal object, criminal objective aspect, criminal subject, criminal subjective aspect (*supra*, paragraphs 106 et seq.), in addition to any problems in the criminal proceedings. These facts can be summarised as 'who', 'when', 'where', 'why', 'how', 'which', 'what'. The facts which can make criminal punishment heavier, lighter, mitigated or exempted are mentioned above (*supra*, paragraphs 313 et seq.). The individual circumstances of a criminal suspect or defendant, such as pregnancy, any former convictions or consistent showings, as well as the after-case performance, are important in certain cases.

II. Burden of Proof

440. In accordance with the theory of Chinese criminal procedure and the statutory Criminal Procedure, the burden of proof shall rest upon the side of the prosecutor. Article 50 of the Criminal Procedure sets that:

> judges, procurators and investigators must, in accordance with the legally prescribed process, collect various kinds of evidence that can prove the criminal suspect's of defendant's guilt of innocence and the gravity of his crime.

In addition, Article 49 of the CCP clearly states that the burden of proof of demonstrating the guilt of the defendant in a public prosecution case shall fall on the people's procuratorate, while that in a private prosecution, case shall fall on the private prosecutor.

Articles 204 and 205 of the CCP also provide that the private prosecutor shall support his accusation with evidence when he brings it to a people's court. If criminal evidence is lacking and the private prosecutor cannot present supplementary evidence, the court shall persuade him to withdraw his prosecution or order its rejection. If the defendant in the private prosecution brings a counter-claim against the private prosecutor, he shall also provide evidence to support the counter-claim.

441. According to the theory of Chinese criminal procedure and the statutory Criminal Procedure, a criminal suspect or defendant shall not have the right of silence. Article 118 of the Criminal Procedure provides that a criminal suspect shall answer the investigator's questions truthfully (*supra*, paragraph 433). However, this provision does not mean to shift the burden of proof to the criminal suspect or defendant.

442. Indeed, there is an exception to the rule that the burden of proof rests upon the defendant. In accordance with Article 395 of the Criminal Code of 1997:

> any state functionary whose property or expenditure obviously exceeds his lawful income, if the difference is enormous, may be ordered to explain the sources of his property. If he cannot prove that the sources are legitimate, the part that exceeds his lawful income shall be regarded as illegal gains, and he shall be sentenced to.

In this kind of case, obviously, it is the judicial organ that shall undertake the burden of proof. Only when the judicial organ collects sufficient evidence which can prove that a state functionary's property or expenditure has obviously exceeded his lawful income and the difference is enormous, the burden of proof shall be shifted to the criminal suspect or the defendant, who must then show that the source of his property is legitimate. This inverted burden of proof is designed to fight against corruption of governmental officials.

However, Article 14 of the 7th Amendment to the Chinese Criminal Code in 2009 revised Article 395 as follows: where the property or expenditure of any state functionary obviously exceeds his legitimate income, and the difference is huge, he shall be ordered to explain the sources. If he fails to do so, the difference shall be determined as illegal income, and he shall be criminally punished. This revision sparks the discussion of whether this article is an exception to the rules on the burden of proof.

III. Classification of Evidence

443. In accordance with Article 48 of the CCP, there shall be the following eight categories of evidence:

- material evidence;
- documentary evidence;
- testimony of witnesses;
- statements of victims;
- statements and exculpations of criminal suspects or defendants;
- expert opinion;
- transcripts of crime scene investigation, examination, identification, and investigative re-enactment; and
- audio-visual recordings and electronic data.

However, any of the above-mentioned evidence must be verified before it can be used as the basis for deciding cases.

444. In the theory of the Chinese criminal procedure, there are the following categories of evidence:

- According to the source, evidence can be classified as original evidence, e.g., the testimony of eyewitnesses, original documents or the statement of the victim, and secondary evidence, e.g., hearsay and copies of materials. The rules generally accepted are that (1) material with an unknown source cannot be used as evidence, (2) people cannot be convicted only by secondary evidence, (3) secondary evidence shall be used only when the original is difficult to obtain, and (4) secondary evidence can have the same evidentiary power as the original only when it has been verified with the original or evaluated as authentic.
- According to the function, evidence can be divided into evidence for guilt or innocence. Only when evidence for guilt is reliable and sufficient and the evidence for innocence is completely removed, can the criminal suspect and the defendant be convicted. If evidence for innocence cannot be disproved, the case shall be dealt with according to the principle used in 'the suspect case', i.e., the defendant shall be innocent.
- According to its form, evidence can be divided into oral and material evidences. Material evidence will include witnesses and material evidences. Oral evidence is easy to change, so collection of it shall be timely and verified and fixed by signature according to law. Material evidence shall be inspected or evaluated. It is extremely difficult to convict a person with only oral evidence or only material evidence, if not impossible.
- According to the relationship with the main facts of a case, evidence can be divided into direct and indirect evidence. The evidence which can directly prove

the main facts of a case independently is the direct evidence. For example, the confession of a defendant, the testimony of a witness indicating that the defendant is the criminal who committed the crime as charged. If an evidence cannot prove the main fact of a case independently, it shall be indirect evidence. For example, a corpse cannot be a direct evidence because it proves only a crime occurred but cannot prove who the criminal is. Usually, indirect evidence is used as a means to strengthen direct evidence. When only indirect evidence has to be used, the entirety of the indirect evidence must be formed as a complete system of proof and shall not be conflicting in nature and, particularly, the proof system must exclude other possibilities and the conclusion of this proof shall be the sole and conclusive one.

IV. Collection of Evidence

445. Collection of evidence shall be carried out by the judicial organs and the parties and their defenders.

Article 52 of the Criminal Procedure of 2012 provides that the people's courts, the people's procuratorates and the public security organs shall have the authority to collect or obtain evidence from the 'units' (i.e., corporate bodies) and individuals concerned. The units and individuals concerned shall provide truthful evidence. Physical evidence, documentary evidence, audio-visual recordings, electronic data, and other evidences gathered by an administrative authority in the process of law enforcement and case investigation may be used as evidence in criminal procedures.

Article 37 of the Criminal Procedure states that defence lawyers may, with the consent of the witnesses or other units and individuals concerned, collect information pertaining to the current case from the people's courts, the people's procuratorates and the public security organs. With permission of the people's procuratorate or the people's court and with the consent of the victim, his near relatives or the witnesses provided by the victim, defence lawyers may collect information pertaining to the current case from them also.

In the case of private prosecution, the private prosecutor shall provide sufficient evidence to support his claim. He may also collect evidence for that purpose.

446. Collection of evidence shall observe legal procedures. Article 50 of the Criminal Procedure of 2012 provides that it shall be strictly forbidden to extort confessions by torture and to collect evidence by threat, enticement, deceit or other unlawful means. It is forbidden to force anyone to commit self-incrimination. Article 247 of the Criminal Code of 1997 sets that any judicial officer who extorts confession from a criminal suspect or defendant by torture or extorts testimony from a witness by violence shall be sentenced to fixed-term imprisonment of not more than three years or criminal detention. If he causes injury, disability or death to the victim, he shall be convicted and given a heavier punishment in accordance with the provision of Article 234 (intentional injury) or 232 (intentional homicide) of this Code.

447. When evidence is collected, evidence involving state secrets, trade secrets and personal privacy shall be kept confidential (Article 52 of the Criminal Procedure of 2012).

448. Collection of evidence shall be thorough and complete.

During the collecting of evidence, judges, procurators and investigators must protect all citizens who are involved in a case or who have information about the circumstances of a case can be able to objectively and fully furnish evidence. When the circumstances of the case allow, these citizens may be invited to help the investigation (Article 50 of the CCP).

Article 61 of the Criminal Procedure provides that the people's courts, the people's procuratorates and the public security organs shall ensure the safety of witnesses and their near relatives. Anyone who intimidates, humiliates, beats or retaliates against a witness or his near relatives, if his act constitutes a crime, shall be investigated for criminal responsibility according to law; if the case is not serious enough for criminal punishment, he shall be punished for violation of public security in accordance with law.

Article 62, which is a new addition into the CCP, provides that the people's court, people's procuratorate, and public security authority shall take one or more of the following protective measures to protect the witness, identification or evaluation expert or victim who testified in a crime of endangering national security, a crime of terrorist activities, an organised crime with the nature of underground society, or a drug crime from the threat to their own personal safety or that of their close relatives:

(1) not disclosing his or her true personal information, such as name, residence address, and employer;
(2) not exposing his or her look, true voice, and so on, when he or she takes the stand;
(3) prohibiting particular persons from contacting the witness, identification or evaluation expert, or victim and his or her close relatives;
(4) providing special protection for his or her person and residence; and
(5) other necessary protective measures.

Where a witness, identification or evaluation expert, or victim believes that his or her personal safety or that of his or her close relatives is endangered by his or her testimony in criminal procedures, he or she may request protection from the people's court, people's procuratorate, and public security authority. The relevant entities and individuals shall co-operate with a people's court, people's procuratorate, or public security authority in taking protective measures in accordance with law.

V. Admissibility of Evidence

449. The public security organ's requests for approval of arrest, the people's procuratorate's bill of prosecution and the people's court's written judgments must be faithful to the facts. The responsibility of anyone who intentionally conceals the facts shall be investigated (Article 51 of the Criminal Procedure of 2012).

450. As mentioned above (*supra*, paragraph 446), any evidence must be verified before it can be used as the basis for deciding cases.

In addition, Article 59 stresses that the testimony of a witness may be used as a basis for deciding a case only after the witness has been questioned and cross-examined in the courtroom by both sides, that is, the public prosecutor and victim as well as the defendant and defenders, and after the testimonies of the witnesses on all sides have been heard and verified.

451. In the decisions of all cases, stress shall be placed on evidence, investigation and study; credence shall not be readily given to oral statements. A defendant cannot be found guilty and sentenced to a criminal punishment if there is only his statement but no evidence; the defendant may be found guilty and sentenced to a criminal punishment if evidence is sufficient and reliable, even without his statement (Article 53 of the Criminal Procedure of 2012).

In the CCP, one important paragraph, Article 53, was added as follows: Evidence shall be deemed as reliable and sufficient when the following conditions are fulfilled:

(1) all facts for conviction and sentencing are supported by evidence;
(2) all evidences used to decide a case has been verified under legal procedures; and
(3) all facts found are beyond reasonable doubt based on all evidence of the case.

It is an important step for the development of the Chinese criminal procedure to accept the criterion of 'beyond reasonable doubt'.

452. Any illegally obtained evidence shall be excluded from trial proceedings in the Chinese criminal procedure. In the theoretical circle of the Chinese criminal procedure, however, there are disputes on whether all types of illegally obtained evidence shall be excluded. There are opinions that the illegally obtained evidence in kind, such as material evidence and documentary evidence shall not be excluded because there are usually no substitutes for them, but the illegally obtained evidence in words such as statements of defendants or victims or testimony of witnesses shall be excluded. This opinion is supported by the Chinese Criminal Procedure of 2012. Article 54 provides that a confession of a criminal suspect or defendant extorted by torture or obtained by other illegal means and a witness or victim statement obtained by violence, threat, or other illegal means shall be excluded. Any physical or documentary evidence which was not gathered under the statutory procedure and may seriously affect justice shall be corrected or justified; otherwise, such evidence shall be excluded. If it is discovered during the criminal investigation, examination and prosecution, or trial of a case that any evidence shall be excluded, such evidence shall be excluded and not be used as a basis for a prosecution proposal, a prosecution decision, or a sentence. In Article 58, it provides that where, at trial, any illegal obtainment of evidence as described in Article 54 of the Criminal Procedure is confirmed or cannot be ruled out, the relevant evidence shall be excluded.

The exclusive rules in the Chinese criminal procedure have become much more strict, especially for the capital cases, in order to prevent any mistakes and wrong judgments.

§5. Coercive Measures

453. Coercive or compulsory measures refer to the legal coercive methods taken by the public security organs, the people's procuratorates and the people's courts to temporarily restrict or strip personal freedom of a criminal suspect or a defendant, in order to safeguard the smooth progress of criminal proceedings.

The Criminal Procedure provides five coercive measures as follows:

- a warrant to compel the appearance;
- an order to obtain a guarantor pending trial;
- an order to subject to residential surveillance;
- detainment;
- arrest.

I. Warrant to Compel the Appearance

454. In accordance with Article 64 of the CCP, the people's courts, the people's procuratorates and the public security organs may issue a warrant to compel the appearance of the criminal suspect or defendant. This is the lightest coercive measure.

455. A warrant to compel appearance is usually issued after serving a summons. However, the judicial organs shall, according to the circumstances, have right to issue the warrant without serving a summons.

456. The time for interrogation through summons or forced appearance shall not exceed 12 hours. If a criminal suspect in an extraordinarily significant or complicated case is necessary to be detained or arrested, the duration of interrogation by summons or forced appearance may not exceed 24 hours. A criminal suspect shall not be detained under the disguise of successive summons or forced appearance. During the period of interrogation by summons or forced appearance, the meals and necessary rest time of the criminal suspect shall be ensured (Article 117 of the Criminal Procedure of 2012).

II. Order to Obtain a Guarantor Pending Trial

457. In accordance with Article 65 of the Criminal Procedure, the people's courts, the people's procuratorates and the public security organs may allow criminal suspects or defendants under any of the following conditions to obtain a guarantor pending trial or subject them to residential surveillance:

- they may be sentenced to public surveillance, criminal detention or simply imposed with supplementary punishment;
- they may have been given a punishment of at least fixed-term imprisonment but they would not endanger society if they were allowed to obtain a guarantor pending trial or were placed under residential surveillance; or
- the criminal suspect or defendant suffers a serious illness and cannot live by himself or herself or is a pregnant woman or a woman who is breastfeeding her own baby and will not cause danger to the society if granted bail; or
- The term of custody of the criminal suspect or defendant has expired but the case has not been closed, and it is necessary for them to obtain a guarantor pending trial.

458. The public security organs shall execute the decision on allowing a criminal suspect or defendant to obtain a guarantor pending trial (Article 65).

A criminal suspect or defendant in custody and his legal representatives or near relatives shall have the right to apply for the obtainment of a guarantor pending trial.

459. If the people's courts, the people's procuratorates or the public security organs decide to allow a criminal suspect or defendant to obtain a guarantor pending trial, they shall order the criminal suspect or defendant to provide a guarantor or pay guaranty money.

The authority deciding on a guaranty shall decide the amount of guaranty money after fully considering the need to ensure normal legal proceedings, the danger of the person to the society, the nature and circumstances of the case, the gravity of the possible punishment, the financial condition of the person, and other factors. The person providing guaranty money shall deposit the guaranty money into a special account at a bank designated by the execution authority (Article 70 of the CCP).

It is the legal requirement that a guarantor must be a person who meets the following conditions:

- to be not involved in the current case;
- to be able to perform a guarantor's duties;
- to be entitled to political rights and not subjected to restriction of personal freedom; and
- to have a fixed domicile and steady income (Article 67 of the Criminal Procedure of 2012).

460. A guarantor shall perform the following duties:

- to see to it that the person under his guarantee observes the provision of Article 69 (*infra*, paragraph 463); and
- to promptly report to the executing organ when finding that the person under his guarantee may commit or has already committed acts in violation of the provision of Article 69.

If the guarantor fails to perform his duty of a guarantor, when the person under his guarantee has committed an act in violation of the provision of Article 69, he shall be fined. If the case constitutes a crime, criminal responsibility shall be investigated according to law (Article 68 of the Criminal Procedure of 2012).

461. If a criminal suspect or defendant has obtained a guarantor pending trial, he shall according to law observe the following provisions:

- not to leave the city or county where he resides without the permission of the executing organ;
- to report any change of his address, working unit or contact information to the execution authority within 24 hours;
- to be present in time at a court when summoned;
- not to interfere in any form with the witness when the latter gives testimony; and
- not to destroy or falsify evidence or tally confessions.

In addition, a people's court, a people's procuratorate, and a public security authority may according to the circumstances of a case, order the criminal suspect or defendant under guaranty to comply with one or more of the following provisions:

- not entering particular places;
- not meeting or communicating with particular persons;
- not engaging in particular activities; and
- delivering his or her passport and other international travel credentials and driver's licence to the execution authority for preservation.

If the criminal suspect or defendant violates any of these provisions, the guaranty money paid shall be partly or fully confiscated. In addition, in light of specific circumstances, the criminal suspect or defendant shall be ordered to write a statement of repentance, pay guaranty money or provide a guarantor again, or shall be subjected to residential surveillance or arrested. Where the criminal suspect or defendant violates the guaranty regulation and needs to be arrested, he may be detained first (Article 69 of the Criminal Procedure of 2012).

Where a criminal suspect or defendant has not violated the provisions of Article 69 during the period of waiting for trial under guaranty, he may receive a refund of the guaranty money to his bank on the basis of relevant legal instrument at the end of that period.

462. The period granted by a people's court, people' procuratorate or public security organ to a criminal suspect or defendant for awaiting trial after obtaining a guarantor shall not exceed twelve months, in accordance with Article 77 of the Criminal Procedure of 2012 (cf. *infra*, paragraph 469).

III. Residential Surveillance

463. In accordance with Article 65 of the Criminal Procedure, the people's courts, the people's procuratorates and the public security organs may allow criminal suspects or defendants to be under residential surveillance, too (*supra*, paragraph 459).

In practice, residential surveillance may be applied to a person who cannot provide a guarantor or guaranty money.

According to the new legislation, Article 72 provides that a people's court, a people's procuratorate, and a public security authority may put a criminal suspect or defendant who meets the conditions for arrest into residential surveillance. This will be so if any of the following circumstances are met:

- the criminal suspect or defendant suffers a serious illness and cannot live by himself or herself;
- the criminal suspect or defendant is a pregnant woman or a woman who is breastfeeding her own baby;
- the criminal suspect or defendant is the sole supporter of a person who cannot live by himself or herself;

- considering the special circumstances of the case or as needed for handling the case, residential confinement is more appropriate; or
- the term of custody has expired but the case has not been closed, and residential confinement is necessary.

Residential confinement shall be executed by a public security authority.

464. A criminal suspect or defendant under residential surveillance shall observe the following legal provisions:

- not to leave his domicile without permission of the executing organ or, if he has no fixed domicile, not to leave the designated residence without permission;
- not to meet with others without the permission of the executing organ;
- to be present in time at a court when summoned;
- not to interfere in any form with the witness when the latter gives testimony;
- not to destroy or falsify evidence or tally confessions; and
- to deliver his or her passport and other international travel credentials and driver's licence to the execution authority for preservation.

If a criminal suspect or defendant under residential surveillance violates any of these provisions and if the case is serious, he shall be arrested (Article 75 of the Criminal Procedure of 2012).

Execution authorities may oversee criminal suspects or defendants under residential surveillance regarding their compliance with the regulations by electronic monitoring, random inspection, and other surveillance means. In addition, during the period of criminal investigation, Execution authorities may monitor their communications (Article 76 of the Criminal Procedure of 2012).

465. Residential surveillance shall be executed at the residence of a criminal suspect or defendant; or may be executed at a designated residence if the criminal suspect or defendant has no fixed residence. Where execution of residential surveillance at the residence of a criminal suspect or defendant in a case regarding endangering national security, terrorist activities, or extraordinarily serious bribery may obstruct criminal investigation, it may be executed at a designated residence with the approval of the people's procuratorate or public security authority at the next higher level. However, residential surveillance may not be executed at a place of custody or a place specially used for handling cases (Article 73).

The period for residential surveillance shall not exceed six months. However, the term of residential surveillance at a designated residence shall be calculated into the term of punishment. For a sentence of public surveillance (*supra*, paragraph 280ff.), one day of residential surveillance shall be counted as one day of the term of punishment. For a sentence of criminal detention (*supra*, paragraph 284ff.) or fixed-term imprisonment (*supra* paragraph 308), two days of residential confinement shall be counted as one day of the term of punishment (Article 74).

During the period for awaiting trial after obtaining a guarantor or of residential surveillance, investigation, prosecution and handling of the case shall not be suspended. If it is discovered that the criminal suspect or the defendant shall not be investigated for criminal responsibility or when the period for awaiting trial after obtaining a guarantor or the period of residential surveillance has expired, such period shall be terminated without delay. The person who has obtained a guarantor pending trial or who is under residential surveillance and the units concerned shall be notified of the termination immediately.

IV. Detention

466. The detention as a compulsory measure is not the same as criminal detention (*supra*, paragraph 284ff.) or a criminal punishment. The detention in criminal proceedings is only a kind of compulsory measure which temporarily deprives an active criminal or a major suspect of his personal freedom.

467. In accordance with Article 80, public security organs may initially detain an active criminal or a major suspect under any of the following conditions:

(1) if he is preparing to commit a crime, is in the process of committing a crime or is discovered immediately after committing a crime;
(2) if he is identified as having committed a crime by a victim or an eyewitness;
(3) if criminal evidence is found on his body or at his residence;
(4) if he attempts to commit suicide or escape after committing a crime, or he is fugitive;
(5) if there is likelihood of his destroying or falsifying evidence or tallying confessions;
(6) if he does not tell his true name and address and his identity is unknown; and
(7) if he is strongly suspected of committing crimes from one place to another, repeatedly, or in a gang.

468. The people's procuratorate shall have the right to make a decision to detain a criminal suspect as well as arrest, which shall then be executed by a public security organ, in the cases of the conditions (4) and (5) in paragraph 467 when necessary, in the case directly accepted by it (Article 163 of the Criminal Procedure of 2012, cf. *supra*, paragraph 397).

469. In accordance with the CCP, the public security organ shall observe the following procedure and legal requirements in detaining a person:

- When detaining a person, the public security organ shall produce a detention warrant (Article 83).
- Within 24 hours after a person has been detained, his family or the unit to which he belongs shall be notified of the reasons for detention and the place of custody, unless such notification is impossible or such notification may obstruct criminal investigation in a case regarding endangering national security or terrorist activities. However, once such a situation that obstructs criminal investigation disappears, the family of the detainee shall be immediately notified (Article 83).
- A public security organ shall interrogate a detainee within 24 hours after detention. If it is found that the person shall not have been detained, he must be immediately released and issued a release certificate (Article 84).

- If the public security organ deems it necessary to arrest a detainee, it shall, within three days after the detention, submit a request to the people's procuratorate for examination and approval. Under special circumstances (this refers to the very complicated cases and the remote areas where it is difficult to submit the request within three days), the time limit for submitting a request for examination and approval may be extended by one to four days. As to the arrest of a major suspect involved in crimes committed from one place to another, repeatedly, or in a gang, the time limit for submitting a request for examination and approval may be extended to thirty days (Article 89).
- The people's procuratorate shall decide either to approve or disapprove the arrest within seven days from the date of receiving the written request for approval of arrest submitted by a public security organ. If the people's procuratorate disapprove the arrest, the public security organ shall, upon receiving notification, immediately release the detainee and inform the people's procuratorate of the result without delay. If further investigation is necessary, and if the released person meets the conditions for obtaining a guarantor pending trial or for residential surveillance, he shall be allowed to obtain a guarantor pending trial or subjected to residential surveillance according to law (Article 89).

470. If the public security organ considers the people's procuratorate's decision to disapprove an arrest to be incorrect, it may request a reconsideration but must immediately release the detainee. If the public security organ's opinion is not accepted, it may request a review by the people's procuratorate at the next higher level. The people's procuratorate at the higher level shall immediately review the matter, decide whether or not to make a change and notify the people's procuratorate at the lower level and the public security organ to implement its decision (Article 90).

V. Arrest

471. Arrest is the most serious compulsory measure in the Chinese criminal proceedings.

The Chinese Criminal Procedure provides that arrests of criminal suspects or defendants shall be subject to approval by a people's procuratorate or decision by a people's court and shall be executed by a public security organ (Article 78). This is also the provision of the Chinese Constitution (Article 37 of the Chinese Constitution).

472. In accordance with Article 79 of the Criminal Procedure, an arrest shall be immediately applied to a criminal suspect or defendant who fulfils the following conditions:

- there is evidence to support the facts of crime committed by the criminal suspect or defendant;
- this criminal suspect or defendant could be sentenced to a punishment of not less than imprisonment;

- the measures such as allowing him to obtain a guarantor pending trial or placing him under residential surveillance would be insufficient to prevent the occurrence of following danger to society, his arrest is thus then necessary:

  (1) the criminal suspect or defendant may commit a new crime;
  (2) there is an actual danger to national security, public security, or social order;
  (3) the criminal suspect or defendant may destroy or forge evidence, interfere with the testimony of a witness, or make a false confession in collusion;
  (4) the criminal suspect or defendant may retaliate against a victim, informant, or accuser; or
  (5) the criminal suspect or defendant attempts to commit suicide or escape.

Where there is evidence to prove the facts of a crime which shall make the criminal suspect or defendant sentenced to a punishment of more than ten years fixed-term imprisonment or where there is evidence to prove the facts of a crime which shall lead to the criminal suspect or defendant being sentenced to imprisonment, or a heavier punishment and the fact that he used to commit an intentional crime have not been identified, the criminal suspect or defendant shall be arrested.

If a criminal suspect or defendant who should be arrested is seriously ill or is a pregnant woman or a woman breastfeeding her own baby, however, he or she may be allowed to obtain a guarantor pending trial or could be placed under residential surveillance (Article 72, cf. *supra*, paragraph 463). Where a criminal suspect or defendant waiting for trial on a guaranty or under residential surveillance seriously violates the regulations, he may be arrested (Article 79). In April of 2014, a new legislative explanation was given to this situation. Accordingly, a criminal suspect or defendant awaiting trial on guaranty or under residential surveillance who may be sentenced to a penalty lighter than imprisonment may be arrested, if he violates the regulations on guaranty or under residential surveillance and seriously affects the normal process of litigation.

473. An arrest shall observe the following procedure which is prescribed in the Chinese Criminal Procedure:

- When a public security organ wishes to arrest a criminal suspect, it shall submit a written request for approval of arrest together with the case file and evidence to the people's procuratorate at the same level for examination and approval. When necessary, the people's procuratorate may send procurators to participate in the public security organ's discussion of a major case (Article 85).
- When the people's procuratorate examines and approves the arrest of a criminal suspect, the decision shall be made by the chief procurator. Major cases shall be submitted to the procuratorial committee for discussion and decision (Article 87). After a people's procuratorate has examined a case with respect to which a public security organ has submitted a request for approval of arrest, it shall decide according to the circumstances of the case either to approve the arrest or disapprove the arrest. If it decides to approve the arrest, the public security organ shall execute it immediately and inform the people's procuratorate of the result without delay. If the people's procuratorate disapproves the arrest, it shall give its reasons therefor;

and if it deems a supplementary investigation necessary, it shall at the same time notify the public security organ of this need (Article 90).

- When making an arrest, a public security organ must produce an arrest warrant (Article 91).
- Like the requirement for detention, his family or the unit to which he belongs shall, within 24 hours after a person has been detained, be notified of the reasons for detention and the place of custody, unless such notification is impossible (Article 91 and cf. *supra*, paragraph 469).
- Interrogation must be conducted within 24 hours after the arrest, by a people's court or people's procuratorate with respect to a person it has decided to arrest, and by a public security organ with respect to a person it has arrested with the approval of the people's procuratorate. If it is found that the person should not have been arrested, he must be immediately released and issued a release certificate (Article 92).

If the public security organ considers the people's procuratorate's decision to disapprove an arrest to be incorrect, it may request reconsideration but must immediately release the detainee. If the public security organ's opinion is not accepted, it may request a review by the people's procuratorate at the next higher level. The people's procuratorate at the higher level shall immediately review the matter, decide whether or not to make a change and notify the people's procuratorate at the lower level and the public security organ to implement its decision (Article 90).

In the cases which are directly accepted by the people's procuratorate (*supra*, paragraph 397), the people's procuratorate shall make a decision within fourteen days after detention if believing it necessary to arrest a detainee. Under special circumstances, the time limit for deciding an arrest may be extended for one to three days. If arrest is not necessary, the detainee shall be released immediately; or if further investigation is necessary and the detainee meets the conditions for guaranty pending trial or residential surveillance, the compulsory measure shall be changed in accordance with law (Article 165).

In order to strengthen the legal supervision, the CCP added Article 86 as follows: During the examination and approval of an arrest request, a people's procuratorate may interrogate the criminal suspect; and, under any of the following circumstances, must interrogate the criminal suspect:

(1) it has any doubt on whether the arrest conditions have been met;
(2) the criminal suspect requests a statement before prosecutors; or
(3) any gross violation of law might have occurred during the criminal investigation.

During the examination and approval of an arrest request, a people's procuratorate may interview a witness and other litigation participants and hear the opinion of a defence lawyer. If a defence lawyer files a request to present an opinion, the people's procuratorate shall hear his opinion.

474. When a public security organ is to detain or arrest a person in another place, it shall inform the public security organ in the place where the person to be detained or arrested stays, and the public security organ there shall co-operate in the action (Article 81).

VI. Change and Termination of Coercive Measures

475. If a people's court, a people's procuratorate or a public security organ finds that the coercive measures taken against a criminal suspect or defendant are inappropriate, such measures shall be cancelled or modified without delay. If a public security organ releases a person arrested or substitutes the measure of arrest with a different measure, it shall notify the people's procuratorate that approved the arrest.

After arresting a criminal suspect or defendant, a people's procuratorate shall continue to examine the necessity of custody. If custody is no longer necessary, the people's procuratorate shall suggest a release of the arrestee or change the compulsory measure for the arrestee. The relevant authority shall notify the people's procuratorate of the result within ten days (Article 93).

A criminal suspect or defendant or his or her legal representative, close relative, or defender shall have the right to apply for changing a compulsory measure. A people's court, people's procuratorate, or public security authority shall make a decision within three days after receiving such an application. If a disapproval decision is made, the applicant shall be informed of the decision and reasons for disapproval (Article 95).

476. If a case involving a criminal suspect or defendant in custody cannot be closed within the time limit stipulated by the Criminal Procedure for keeping the criminal suspect or defendant in custody for the sake of investigation, for conducting examination before prosecution, or for the procedure of first or second instance and thus further investigation, verification and handling are needed, the criminal suspect or defendant may be allowed to obtain a guarantor pending trial or be subjected to residential surveillance.

477. When the statutory term of a compulsory measure taken against a criminal suspect or defendant expires, the people's court, the people's procuratorate, or the public security organ shall release the criminal suspect or defendant, terminate the period for awaiting trial after obtaining a guarantor or being placed under residential surveillance, or take different compulsory measures according to law. A criminal suspect or defendant or his or her legal representative, close relative, or defender shall have the right to require termination of a compulsory measure taken by a people's court, a people's procuratorate, or a public security authority when the term of the compulsory measure expires (Article 97).

478. If in the process of examining and approving arrests, a people's procuratorate discovers illegalities in the investigatory activities of a public security organ, it shall notify the public security organ to make corrections, and the public security organ shall notify the people's procuratorate of the correction it has made.

VII. Seizure by Citizen

479. The Chinese Criminal Procedure explicitly provides that the persons listed below may be seized outright by any citizen and delivered to a public security organ, a people's procuratorate or a people's court for handling:

- any person who is committing a crime or is discovered immediately after committing a crime;
- any person who is wanted for arrest;
- any person who has escaped from prison; and
- any person who is being pursued for arrest (Article 63).

Seizure by citizen is not a type of compulsory measures. But it does legalise the seizure of criminals by any ordinary citizen and is good for the struggle against crime.

§6. Stages of Criminal Process

I. General Criminal Process

480. Generally, these are the next stages in the Chinese criminal process:

- the pretrial proceedings;
- the prosecution; and
- the inquiry in court.

However, the following processes may also occur in certain cases in the Chinese criminal proceedings:

- incidental civil actions;
- cases of private prosecution;
- summary procedure;
- procedure of second instance;
- procedure for review of death sentences;
- procedure for trial supervision and special procedures (*infra* paragraph 490 and more).

II. Incidental Civil Actions

481. If a victim has suffered material losses as a result of the defendant's criminal act, he shall have the right to file an incidental civil action during the course of the criminal proceeding.

If the victim is dead or has lost capacity of conduct, his or her legal representative or close relative shall have the right to institute an incidental civil action.

If losses have been caused to state property or collective property, the people's procuratorate may file an incidental civil action while initiating a public prosecution.

482. An incidental civil action shall be heard together with the criminal case. Only for the purpose of preventing excessive delay in a trial of the criminal case may the same judicial organisation, after completing the trial of the criminal case, continue to hear the incidental civil action.

483. When necessary, the people's court may take a preservative measure to seize, impound, or freeze the property of a defendant. In an incidental civil action, the plaintiff or the people's procuratorate may apply to the people's court to have them enforce a preservative measure. Where a people's court takes a preservative measure, the relevant provisions of the Civil Procedure Law shall apply.

When trying an incidental civil case, a people's court may conduct mediation or render a judgment or ruling based on the material loss (Article 101).

The parties in an incidental civil action shall be responsible for the provision of evidence to respectively support their arguments.

III. Case of Private Prosecution

484. In accordance with Article 204 of the Criminal Procedure, cases of private prosecution include the following:

- cases to be handled only upon complaint, i.e., insult and defamation (Article 246 of the Criminal Code of 1997, except where serious harm is done to public order or to the interests of the state), interference with another person's freedom of marriage by violence (Article 257 of the Criminal Code of 1997), maltreating a member of his family (Article 260 of the Criminal Code of 1997), misappropriation (Article 270 of the Criminal Code of 1997);
- cases for which the victims have evidence to prove that their claims amount to minor criminal cases, i.e., intentional injury (Article 234 of the Criminal Code of 1997), unlawful intrusion into another person's residence (Article 245 of the Criminal Code of 1997), violation of citizen's right to freedom of correspondence (Article 252 of the Criminal Code of 1997), bigamy (Article 258 of the Criminal Code of 1997), refusing to fulfil one's duty to support an aged person, minor, sick person or any other person who cannot live independently (Article 261 of the Criminal Code of 1997), crimes of producing and marketing fake or substandard commodities (Section I of the Specific Part of the Criminal Code of 1997, except where serious harm is done to public order or to the interests of the state), crimes against intellectual property rights (Section VII of the Specific Part of the Criminal Code of 1997, except where serious harm is done to public order or to the interests of the state), the crimes in Chapter IV (crimes infringing upon citizens' civil and democratic rights) and V (property crimes) which might be sentenced to fixed-term imprisonment of not more than three years;
- cases for which the victims have evidence to prove that the defendants should be investigated for criminal responsibility according to law because their acts have infringed upon the victims' personal or property rights, whereas, the public security

organs or the people's procuratorates has made the decision not to investigate the criminal responsibility of the accused.

485. After examining a case of private prosecution, the people's court shall handle it in different manner according to the different circumstances as follows:

- if the facts of the crime are clear and the evidence is sufficient, the case shall be tried at a court session;
- if criminal evidence is lacking and the private prosecutor cannot provide supplementary evidence, the court shall persuade him to withdraw his prosecution or order its rejection;
- if a private prosecution, having been served twice with a summons according to law, refuses to appear in court without justifiable reasons, or if he withdraws from a court session without permission of the court, the case may be considered withdrawn by him.

486. A people's court may conduct mediation in a case of private prosecution. The private prosecutor may arrange a settlement with the defendant or withdraw his prosecution before a judgment is pronounced. However, the third type of the cases mentioned in paragraph 488 shall not be mediated according to law. The period for a people's court to try a case of private prosecution is usually two months or three months at latest, if the defendant is in custody. If the defendant is not in custody, a sentence shall be announced within six months after the case is accepted (Articles 206 and 202 of the CCP).

IV. Summary Procedure

487. The typical nature of a summary procedure is to try a case with a simplified procedure and usually will be heard by an individual judge. The general tendency of summary procedures in the Chinese criminal procedure is that they are expensive. In the Criminal Procedure of 1996, summary procedures shall be used in the following cases and tried by a lone judge:

- cases of public prosecution where the defendants may be lawfully sentenced to fixed-term imprisonment of not more than three years, criminal detention, public surveillance or punished with fines, where the facts are clear and the evidence is sufficient, and for which the people's procuratorate suggests or agrees to the application of summary procedure;
- cases to be handled only upon complaint (cf. the first type of the cases in *supra*, paragraph 484); and
- cases prosecuted by the victims, for which there is evidence to prove that they are also minor criminal cases (cf. the second type of the cases in *supra*, paragraph 484).

In the Criminal Procedure of 2012, however, it is required that a case under the jurisdiction of a basic people's court may be heard under summary procedures if the following conditions are met:

- the facts of a case are clear and evidence is sufficient;
- the defendant confesses to his or her crime and raises no objection to the charges; and
- the defendant raises no objection to the application of summary procedures.

It is even required that a people's procuratorate suggest that the people's court apply summary procedures when initiating a public prosecution (Article 208).

However, the following cases shall not be eligible for the application of summary procedures (Article 209):

- where the defendant is blind, deaf, or dumb or is a mental patient who has not yet completely lost the ability to recognise or control his behaviour;
- if the case has a significant social impact;
- in a joint crime, some defendant pleads not guilty or raises an objection to the application of summary procedures; or
- the application of summary procedures is otherwise inappropriate, e.g., those cases where a defender raises an innocent defence.

488. In accordance with the CCP, a case under summary procedures may be tried by a collegial panel or a sole judge, if the defendant is to be sentenced to fixed-term imprisonment of less than three years. If the defendant may be sentenced to fixed-term imprisonment of more than three years, a collegial panel must be formed to try the case.

For a case of public prosecution under summary procedures, the people's procuratorate shall send procurators to appear before court.

489. In the summary procedure, the defendant's rights shall be guaranteed. The judge shall ask for the defendant's opinion on the charges, inform the defendant of the legal provisions on the application of summary procedures, and confirm whether the defendant agrees to the application of summary procedures (Article 211). In the summary procedure, the defendant and his defender may, with the permission of a judge, debate with the public prosecutor or private prosecutor and his litigation representative (Article 212). Although the regulations on time limits for service of process and the procedures for questioning the defendant, witnesses, and identification or evaluation experts, adducing evidence and debating in court might be not so strictly applied, the closing statement of the defendant shall be heard before a sentence is announced (Article 213).

For a case to be tried using summary procedures, the people's court shall conclude it within twenty days after accepting it. If the defendant may be sentenced to fixed-term imprisonment of more than three years, the above period may be extended to one and a half months (Article 214).

If, however, the people's court discovers that the summary procedure is not appropriate for the case in the course of trying the case, it shall try it anew according to the law (Article 215).

V. Procedures for Legal Remedies and Special Procedures

490. The procedure of second instance, the procedure for review of death sentences and the procedure for trial supervision are the procedures for legal remedies. For details of each procedure, *see* relevant paragraphs (*infra*, paragraphs 550 et seq.). Special procedures are now stipulated in the CCP. They are procedures for juvenile criminal cases, procedures for public prosecution cases where parties have reached settlement, confiscation procedures for illegal income in cases where a criminal suspect or defendant escapes or dies and procedures for involuntary medical treatment of mental patients legally exempted from criminal liability.

Chapter 2. The Pretrial Proceedings

491. Strictly speaking, neither the Chinese Criminal Procedure itself nor the theory of the Chinese criminal procedure formally adopts the term of 'the pretrial proceedings' in their texts. However, before Part Three of the CCP, there is a specific part labelled 'trial' CCP. This Part Two includes Filing a Case, Investigation, and initiation of Public Prosecution. The proceedings thereof can be considered as 'the pretrial proceedings' in the Chinese criminal procedure.

§1. Filing a Case

492. Filing a case is the primary stage of criminal proceedings.

As a procedure, filing a case refers to the system where the public security organ, the people's procuratorate or the people's court examines the materials it receives in order to ascertain whether there are criminal facts and whether the case shall be investigated and tried as a criminal case to determine criminal responsibility.

493. The premise of filing a case is the existence of the materials to be examined by the people's security organ, the people's procuratorate and the people's court. In accordance with the Criminal Procedure, these materials may come from the following sources:

- The criminal facts or the criminal suspect discovered by the public security organ or the people's procuratorate during their daily works or in investigating other criminal cases.
- The reports or information from the relevant units or citizens. Article 108 of the CCP provides that any 'unit' (i.e., corporate body) or individual, upon discovering facts of a crime or a criminal suspect, shall have the right and duty to report the case or provide information to a public security organ, a people's procuratorate or a people's court.
- The complaint or report of victims. Article 108 of the CCP also provides that the victim shall have the right to report to a public security organ, a people's procuratorate or a people's court the facts of the crime or bring a complaint to it against the criminal suspect, when his personal or property rights are infringed upon. Besides that, Article 112 provides that as to a case of private prosecution, the victim shall have the right to bring a suit directly to a people's court. If the victim is dead or has lost his ability of conduct, his legal representatives and near relatives shall have the right to bring a suit to a people's court. The people's court shall accept it according to law.
- The confession of an offender who has voluntarily surrendered.

The public security organ, the people's procuratorate or the people's court shall accept all reports, complaints and information. If a case does not fall under its jurisdiction, it shall refer the case to the competent organ and notify the person who made the report, lodged the complaint or provided the information. If the case does not fall under its jurisdiction but calls for emergency measures, the original organ shall take emergency measures before referring the case to the competent organ.

494. Reports, complaints and information may be filed in writing or orally.

The officer receiving an oral report, complaint or information shall make a written record of it, which, after being read to the reporter, complainant or informant and found free of error, shall be signed or sealed by him or her.

The officer receiving the complaint or information shall clearly explain to the complainant or the informant the legal responsibility that shall be incurred for making a false accusation. However, a complaint or information that does not accord with the facts, or even a mistaken complaint shall be strictly distinguished from a false accusation, as long as no fabrication of facts or falsification of evidence is involved.

It is the duty of the public security organs, the people's procuratorates and the people's courts to ensure the safety of reporters, complainants and informants as well as their near relatives. If the reporters, complainants or informants wish not to make their names and acts of reporting, complaining or informing known to the public, these shall be kept confidential (Article 109 of the Criminal Procedure of 2012).

495. A people's court, people's procuratorate or public security organ shall, within the scope of its jurisdiction, promptly examine the materials provided by a reporter, complainant or informant and the confession of an offender who has voluntarily surrendered.

If it believes that there are facts of a crime and criminal responsibility shall be investigated, it shall file a case.

496. If after examination, a people's court, people's procuratorate or public security organ believes that there are no facts of a crime or that the facts are obviously incidental and do not require investigation of criminal responsibility, it shall not file a case and shall notify the complainant of the reason. If the complainant does not agree with the decision, he may ask for reconsideration.

497. Where a people's procuratorate considers that a case shall be filed for investigation by a public security organ but the latter has not done so, or where a victim considers that a case shall be filed for investigation by a public security organ but the latter has not done so and the victim has brought the matter to a people's procuratorate, the people's procuratorate shall request the public security organ to state the reasons for not filing the case. The public security organ shall submit a report to the people's procuratorate within seven dates. If the people's procuratorate considers that the reasons for not filing the case given by the public security organ are untenable, it shall notify the public security organ to file the case, and upon receiving the notification, the public security organ shall make a decision to file the case within fifteen days and submit that decision to the people's procuratorate (Article 111 of the Criminal Procedure of 2012).

§2. Investigation

I. General Description

498. In accordance with Article 106 of the CCP, 'investigation' means the specialised investigatory work and related compulsory measures carried out according to law by the public security organs and people's procuratorates in the process of handling cases.

Investigation is an independent stage in criminal proceedings. The tasks in this aspect are to collect evidence, find out criminal facts and catch the criminal suspect, so that the crime can be prevented or stopped and the legal interests can be protected.

499. Investigation can be carried out only by the following investigatory organs or departments specified by the Criminal Procedure:

- the public security organs;
- the people's procuratorates (Articles 18, 163 and cf. *supra*, paragraphs 375, 445 and 449);
- the state security organs (Article 4 and cf. *supra*, paragraph 395);
- the security department of the Army (Article 225 and cf. *supra*, paragraph 395);
- the prison (Article 225 and cf. *supra*, paragraph 395).

500. In accordance with Articles 113 and 114, investigation is composed of two phases: the phase of investigation and the phase of preliminary inquiry.

In the phase of investigation, the public security organ shall carry out investigation, collect and obtain evidence which can prove the criminal suspect guilty or innocent or prove the crime to be minor or grave. Active criminals or major suspects may be detained first according to law, and criminal suspects who meet the conditions for arrest shall be arrested according to law (Article 113).

In the phase of preliminary inquiry, the public security organ shall start a preliminary inquiry in the case for which there is evidence to support the facts of a crime, so that the evidence which has been collected and obtained can be verified (Article 114).

501. During the investigation, the investigators may carry out the following investigatory activities:

- interrogation the criminal suspect;
- questioning the witnesses;
- inquest and examination;
- search;
- seizure and impoundment of material evidence and documentary evidence;
- expert evaluation;
- technical investigation measures; and
- wanted orders.

In order to prevent the misconducts of the judicial personnel during the investigation, the Chinese Code of Criminal Procedure of 2012 contains a new Article 115. Accordingly, a party, a defender, agent *ad litem* or an interested party shall have the right to file a petition or accusation with a judicial authority regarding any of the following conduct of the judicial authority or any of its personnel:

- refusing to release a criminal suspect or defendant or terminate or modify a compulsory measure taken, when the statutory term of the compulsory measure expires;
- refusing to refund a guaranty money that should be refunded;
- seizing, impounding, or freezing any property irrelevant to a case;
- refusing to terminate a measure of seizing, impounding, or freezing property that shall be terminated; or
- embezzling, misappropriating, distributing in private, replacing, or illegally using any seized, impounded, or frozen property.

The authority accepting the petition or accusation shall handle it in a timely manner. Against the handling result, the party, the defender, any agents *ad litem* or the interested party may file a petition with the people's procuratorate at the same level. If the case is directly accepted by the people's procuratorate, the interested party may file a petition with the people's procuratorate at the next higher level. The people's procuratorate shall examine the petition in a timely manner and, if it is true, notify the relevant authority to make corrections.

II. Interrogation of the Criminal Suspect

502. During an interrogation, the investigators shall have the following principal powers and duties, in accordance with the Criminal Procedure:

- Interrogation of a criminal suspect must be conducted by the investigators of a people's procuratorate or public security organ.
- There must be no fewer than two investigators participating in an interrogation.
- After a criminal suspect is transferred to a jail for custody, the investigators shall conduct interrogation of the criminal suspect inside the jail. For the criminal suspect who need not be arrested or detained, they may be summoned to a designated place in city or county where the criminal suspect stays for interrogation, or he may be interrogated at his residence. However, the interrogators shall produce their papers issued by a people's procuratorate or a public security organ. The interrogators may verbally give summons to a criminal suspect discovered on the scene after producing their work passes. However, this shall be noted in the interrogation transcript.
- The time for interrogation through summons or forced appearance shall not exceed 12 hours. A criminal suspect shall not be detained under the disguise of successive summons or forced appearance. If it is necessary to detain or arrest a criminal suspect in an extraordinarily grave or complicated case, the duration of interrogation

by summons or forced appearance may not exceed 24 hours. During the period of interrogation by summons or forced appearance, the meals and necessary rest time of the criminal suspect shall be ensured (Article 117).

- When interrogating a criminal suspect, the investigators shall first ask the criminal suspect whether or not he has committed any criminal act, and let him state the circumstances of his guilt or explain his innocence, then they ask him questions. When interrogating a criminal suspect, the investigators shall inform the criminal suspect of the legal provisions on leniency for a truthful confession (Article 118).
- During the interrogation of a minor criminal suspect under the age of 18, his legal representative may be notified to be present at the time of interrogation. If such notification is impossible, the legal representative is unable to be present, or the legal representative is an accomplice, any other adult relative of the juvenile criminal suspect or defendant or a representative of his or her school or employer, a basic organisation at the place of his or her residence, or a juvenile protection organisation may be notified to be present, and relevant circumstances shall be recorded. The legal representative who is present may exercise the procedural rights of the juvenile criminal suspect or defendant on his or her behalf. Believing that the case-handling personnel have infringed upon the juvenile's lawful rights and interests in the course of interrogation or trial, the present legal representative or other person may present an opinion. The interrogation or court transcripts shall be handed over to the legal representative or other person for reading or shall be read out to the legal representative or other person who is present. When a female juvenile criminal suspect is interrogated, there shall be a female staff member present (Article 270).
- For the deaf or mute criminal suspect, a person who has a good command of sign language shall participate. For the criminal suspect who is not familiar with the spoken or written language commonly used in the locality, the foreign or stateless criminal suspect, an interpreter shall be provided for him. And such circumstances shall be noted in the record.
- When interrogating a criminal suspect, the investigators may keep an audio or visual record of the interrogation process; and, in a case regarding a crime punishable by life imprisonment or death penalty or any other significant crime, the investigators shall keep an audio or visual record of the interrogation process. An audio or visual record shall cover the entire process of interrogation to ensure integrity (Article 121).
- After interrogation, the record shall be shown to the criminal suspect for checking. If the criminal suspect cannot read, the record shall be read to him. When necessary, the investigators may also ask the criminal suspect to write a personal statement (Article 120).

503. During an interrogation, the criminal suspects shall have the following rights and duties, in accordance with the Criminal Procedure:

- The criminal suspect shall answer the investigators' questions truthfully, but he shall have the right to refuse to answer any questions that are irrelevant to the case, such as those regarding issues of personal privacy or state secrets he may know (*supra*, paragraph 433).

- When checking the record at the end of the interrogation, the criminal suspect may make additions or corrections, if there are omissions or errors in the record. When he acknowledges that the record is free from error, he shall sign or affix his seal to it (Article 120).
- From the day when the criminal suspect is interrogated by an investigation organ or from the day when compulsory measures are adopted against him, he may appoint a lawyer to provide him with legal advice and to file petitions and complaints on his behalf. If the criminal suspect is arrested, the appointed lawyer may apply on his behalf to obtain a guarantor pending trial. If a case involves state secrets, the criminal suspect shall have to obtain the approval of the investigative organ in the appointment of a lawyer (*supra*, paragraphs 395, 397).
- The conversation between a criminal suspect and his defence lawyer shall not be monitored (*supra*, paragraph 419).

III. Questioning of the Witnesses

504. Witnesses are the persons who are aware of the circumstances of the case and provide testimony to the public security organ or the judicial organ (*supra*, paragraphs 391 et seq.).

In accordance with the Criminal Procedure, investigators may question a witness on the crime scene, at the place of the witness' employer or his residence, but they must produce a work pass or certificate issued by a people's procuratorate or public security organ. If necessary, the investigators may also notify the witness to give testimony at the people's procuratorate of public security organ.

In a criminal case, witness may be more than one. However, regardless of how many witnesses there are, they shall be questioned individually.

505. When a witness is questioned, he shall be instructed to provide evidence and give testimony truthfully and shall be informed of the legal responsibility that shall be incurred for intentionally giving false testimony or concealing criminal evidence.

506. When a witness under the age of 18 is questioned, his legal representative may be notified to be present (Article 270, cf. *supra*, paragraph 502). For a witness who needs an interpreter (cf. *supra*, paragraph 502, item 7), said interpreter shall be provided for him. For a witness who wishes to remain nameless to the public, the investigators are bound to confidentiality in accordance with Article 109 of the Criminal Procedure (*supra*, paragraph 498). In the cases of endangering national security, terrorist activities, organised crime with the nature of underground society, or a drug crime, the judicial organs shall take special protective measures for them (Article 62, cf. *supra*, paragraph 412). Their assumed name may be used in the legal document. However, the true situation shall be recorded in a separate file to which the defence lawyer may consult only after signing the letter of commitment to confidentiality.

507. Strictly speaking, victims are not the same as witnesses (*supra*, paragraphs 380 et seq.). However, the provision applicable for questioning witnesses shall also apply to questioning victims (Article 125 of the Criminal Procedure).

508. After the questioning of a witness, the record shall be shown to him for checking and signing (Article 120, cf. *supra*, paragraphs 479).

IV. Inquest and Examination

509. Investigators shall conduct an inquest or examination of the sites, objects, people and corpses relevant to a crime. When necessary, experts may be assigned or invited to conduct an inquest or examination under the direction of the investigators.

Any 'unit' (i.e., corporate body) or individual shall have the duty to preserve the scene of a crime and to immediately notify a public security organ to send officers to hold an inquest.

510. The Code of Criminal Procedure provides for the following types of inquest and examination:

- Inquest of the sites.
- Examination of objects.
- Examination of corpses. Article 129 provides that if the cause of a death is unclear, a public security organ shall have the power to order an autopsy and shall notify the family members of the deceased to be present.
- Examination of a person's body. Article 130 provides that a full body examination of the victim or criminal suspect may be conducted in order to determine certain characteristics, condition of injuries, or physiological conditions of a victim or criminal suspect. Fingerprint information, blood, urine, and other biological samples may be collected. If a criminal suspect refuses to be examined, the investigators, when they deem it necessary, may conduct a compulsory examination. However, examination of a woman's body shall be conducted by female officers or doctors.
- Investigative experiments. Article 133 provides that when necessary and with the approval of the responsible person of a public security bureau, investigative experiments may be conducted in order to clarify the circumstances of a case. Transcripts shall be prepared for an investigative re-enactment, to which the signatures or seals of participants in the investigative re-enactment shall be affixed. In conducting investigative experiments, it shall be forbidden to take any action which is hazardous, humiliating to anyone, or offensive to public morals.

511. If, in reviewing a case, a people's procuratorate deems it necessary to repeat an inquest or examination that has been done by a public security organ, it may ask the latter to conduct another inquest or examination and may send procurators to participate in it (Article 107).

V. Search

512. In accordance with Article 134 of the CCP, investigators may search the person, belongings and residence of the criminal suspect and anyone who might be hiding a criminal or criminal evidence, as well as other relevant places, in order to collect criminal evidence and track down an offender.

513. When a search is to be conducted, a search warrant must be shown to the person that is to be searched. However, if an emergency occurs when an arrest or detention is being made, a search may be conducted without a search warrant. The emergency refers to instances such as where the criminal suspect is holding a lethal weapon or explosives or the criminal evidence is possibly destroyed or hidden (Article 136 of the CCP).

Any unit or individual shall have the duty, as required by the people's procuratorate or the public security organ, to hand over evidence such as material evidence, documentary evidence or audio-visual material which may prove the criminal suspect guilty or innocent.

514. It is a legal requirement that the person that is to be searched or his family members, neighbours or other eyewitnesses shall be present at the scene during a search. But searches of a woman's body shall be conducted by female officers (Article 137 of the CCP).

515. After a search, a record of the circumstances of said search shall be made, signed and sealed by the investigators and the person who was searched or his family members, neighbours or other eyewitnesses. If the person who was searched or his family members have become fugitives or refuse to sign or affix their seals to the record, this shall be noted in the record.

VI. Seizure and Impoundment

516. In accordance with Article 139 of the Criminal Procedure of 2012, any articles and documents discovered during an inquest or search that may be used to prove a criminal suspect's guilt or innocence shall be seized or impounded.

However, articles and documents which are irrelevant to the case may not be seized.

517. All seized articles and documents shall be carefully checked by the investigators jointly with the eyewitnesses and the holder of the articles. A detailed list shall be made in duplicate on the spot and shall be signed or sealed by the investigators, the eyewitnesses and the holder. One copy of the list shall be given to the holder, and the other copy shall be kept on file for reference.

The seized articles and documents shall be properly kept or sealed for safekeeping and may not be utilised, changed or damaged.

518. If the investigators deem it necessary to seize the mail or telegrams of a criminal suspect, they may upon approval of a public security organ or a people's procuratorate, notify the post and telecommunications offices to check and hand over the relevant mails and telegrams for seizure.

519. The people's procuratorates and the public security organs may, as required by investigation of crimes, inquire into or freeze criminal suspects' deposits or remittances, as well as bonds, stocks, fund shares, and other property according to regulations. The relevant entities and individuals shall provide co-operation. Where the deposits, remittances, bonds, stocks, fund shares, and other property of a criminal suspect have been frozen, repeat freezing shall be prohibited (Article 117).

520. If any seized articles, documents, mails, telegrams, frozen deposits and remittances, bonds, stocks, fund shares, and other property of criminal suspect are proved, through investigation, to be truly irrelevant to a case, the seizure and freeze shall be cancelled within three days, and the things shall be returned to their original owners or the original post and telecommunications offices (Article 143).

VII. Expert Evaluation

521. In accordance with Article 144 of the CCP, the investigation organ shall assign or invite experts to give their evaluation, when certain special problems relating to a case need to be solved in order to clarify the circumstances of the case.

522. The administration of judicial authentication was strengthened in 2005. The Standing Committee of the NPC issued the Decision on the Administration of Judicial Authentication (Decision on Judicial Authentication).

Accordingly, The term 'judicial authentication' refers to those activities where the authenticators identify, make judgments and offer expertise on the special issues involved in litigation by using scientific technologies or special knowledge.

In China, the authenticators and authentication institutions shall be subject to special management.

The qualifications which should be held by an authenticator are as follows:

- holding a senior professional technical title relating to the judicial authentication in which he applies for engaging; or
- having professional practising qualifications relating to the judicial authentication in which he applies for, engaging or having a university diploma of relevant speciality or above, and having pertinent working experience for five or more years; or
- possessing ten or more years of working experience relating to the judicial authentication in which he applies for engaging and having relatively strong professional skills.

Anyone who has record of a criminal punishment for an intentional crime or duty-related crime, has ever been sanctioned or being dismissed from a government organ, or is a de-registered authenticator shall not engage in judicial authentication.

The qualification of a judicial authentication institution is as follows:

- having definite business scope;
- having instruments and equipment that can meet the needs of judicial authentication within its business scope;

- having a test lab which has passed measurement certification or laboratory accreditation and can meet the needs of judicial authentication within its business scope; and
- having three or more authenticators for each judicial authentication business.

An authentication institution established by an investigating organ for the purpose of investigation may not accept the entrustment of the general public to make judicial authentications. No authentication institution may be established by the people's court or judicial administrative organ.

523. In accordance with the Decision on Judicial Authentication, judicial authentication shall include the following types of activities:

- the forensic or medico-legal authentication;
- the authentication of physical evidences;
- the authentication of audio and visual materials; and
- other authentication matters determined by the judicial administrative department of the State Council in consultation with the SPC or Supreme Peoples' Procuratorate.

In legal practice, 'expert evaluations' usually encompass the following:

- forensic (legal medicine) expert evaluation;
- psychiatric expert evaluation;
- toxicity expert evaluation;
- criminal technical expert evaluation;
- accounting expert evaluation;
- general technical expert evaluation.

524. After evaluating a matter, the experts shall write a conclusion of expert evaluation and affix their signature to it.

Re-verification necessitated by disputes over medical evaluation of personal injuries and medical evaluation of mental illness shall be conducted by a hospital designated by a people's government at the provincial level. After verification and evaluation, the expert shall make a conclusion in writing, to which his signature and the hospital's seal shall be affixed.

The investigative organ shall notify the criminal suspect and the victim of the conclusion of the expert evaluation which will be used as evidence in his case. A supplementary expert verification or another expert verification may be conducted upon application submitted by the criminal suspect or the victim.

The period of mental illness evaluation of a criminal suspect shall not be counted in the case-handling period.

VIII. Technical Investigative Measures

525. This is a new matter, added by the CCP. Accordingly, technical investigative measures may be adopted by the public security authority after undergoing strict approval formalities for the cases regarding the endangerment of national security, terrorist activities, organised crime with the nature of underground society, serious drug crime, or any other crimes seriously endangering the society. The people's procuratorate may also adopt these measures after undergoing strict approval formalities for the offences regarding serious cases of embezzlement or bribery or serious crimes committed by taking advantage of one's powers to gravely infringe upon the personal rights of citizens. However, the technical investigative measures decided by the people's procuratorate shall be executed by relevant authorities according to relevant legal provisions. In order to capture a wanted criminal suspect or defendant or a fugitive criminal suspect or defendant whose arrest has been approved or decided, technical investigative measures necessary for capture may be taken with approval (Article 148).

The approval decision for the application of the technical investigative measures is only valid for three months from the date issued. Extension shall be subject to approval again, and each may not exceed three months (Article 149).

When necessary, criminal investigation may be conducted by relevant personnel anonymously as decided by the chief of a public security authority. However, such personnel shall not induce others to commit a crime and shall not use a method which may compromise public security or cause any serious danger to personal safety. For criminal activities involving the delivery of drugs and other contraband or properties, a public security authority may, as needed for criminal investigation, conduct controlled delivery according to relevant legal provisions (Article 151).

IX. The Wanted Orders

526. In accordance with the CCP, a public security organ may issue a wanted order and take effective measures to pursue a person for arrest and bring him to justice, if the criminal suspect who shall be arrested is a fugitive (Article 123).

527. Public security organs at any level may directly issue wanted orders within the areas under their jurisdiction. They shall request a higher level organ with the proper authority to issue such orders for areas beyond their jurisdiction.

X. Conclusion of Investigation

528. The Chinese Criminal Procedure of 2012 imposes the following time limits for conclusion of investigation:

(1) the time limit for holding a criminal suspect in custody during investigation after arrest shall not exceed two months (Article 154);
(2) if the case is complex and cannot be concluded within two months, an extension of one month may be allowed with the approval of the people's procuratorate at the next higher level (Article 154);
(3) if due to special reason, it is not appropriate to hand over a particularly grave and complex case for trial even within a relatively long period of time, the Supreme

People's Procuratorate shall submit a report to the Standing Committee of the NPC for approval to postpone the hearing of the case (Article 155);

(4) if the investigation of the following cases cannot be concluded within the time limit specified in (1) and (2) of this paragraph (Article 154), an extension of two months may be allowed upon approval or decision by the people's procuratorate at the provincial level:

- grave and complex cases in outlying areas where traffic is most inconvenient;
- grave cases that involve criminal gangs;
- grave and complex cases that involve people who commit crimes from one place to another; and
- grave and complex cases that involve various quarters and for which it is difficult to obtain evidence (Article 156);

(5) if in the case of a criminal suspect who may be sentenced to fixed-term imprisonment of ten years at least, investigation of the case can still not be concluded upon expiration of the extended time limit as provided in Article 156 (item 4 of this paragraph), another extension of two months may be allowed upon approval or decision by the people's procuratorate at the provincial level (Article 157).

However, if during the period of investigation a criminal suspect is found to have committed other major crimes, the time limit for holding the criminal suspect in custody during investigation shall be recalculated from the date on which such crimes are found. If a criminal suspect does not tell his true name and address and his identity is unknown, the identity investigation shall be conducted but the time limit for holding him in custody during investigation shall be calculated from the date on which his identity is found out. However, before then, the investigation into his crime and the obtaining of evidence shall not cease. Where the facts of a crime are clear and evidence is hard and sufficient, even if the identity of the criminal suspect cannot be established, the criminal suspect may be prosecuted and tried by the name claimed by the criminal suspect (Article 158).

529. In accordance with the CCP, the conclusion of investigation shall be made in the following situations:

- If the criminal facts are clear and the criminal evidence is reliable and sufficient, the public security organ shall conclude its investigation and make a written recommendation for prosecution, which shall be transferred, together with the case file and evidence, to the people's procuratorate at the same level for examination and decision. At the same time, the criminal suspect and the defence lawyer thereof shall be informed of the transfer (Article 160). Before the investigation of a case is closed, the criminal investigation authority shall hear the opinion of the defence lawyer and record it, if the defence lawyer files a request to present an opinion. A written opinion of the defence lawyer, if any, shall be attached to the case file (Article 159).
- If it is discovered during investigation that a criminal suspect's criminal responsibility shall not have been investigated, the case shall be dismissed (Article 15 and *supra*,

paragraph 435). If the criminal suspect is under arrest, he shall be released immediately and issued a release certificate, and the people's procuratorate that originally approved the arrest shall be notified (Article 161).

XI. Supplementary Investigation

530. In accordance with the CCP, supplementary investigation may be conducted in the following circumstances:

- During examination and approval of an arrest. After a people's procuratorate has examined a case with respect to which a public security organ has submitted a request for approval of arrest and if it disapproves the request, it shall give its reasons thereof. If it deems a supplementary investigation necessary, it shall at the same time notify the public security organ of the need (Article 88).
- During examination and approval of prosecution. In examining a case that requires supplementary investigation, the people's procuratorate may remand the case to a public security organ for supplementary investigation or conduct the investigation itself. The people's procuratorate may require a public security authority to explain the legality of the obtainment of evidence, if they believe that any evidence may have been illegally obtained. However, in cases where supplementary investigation is to be conducted, it shall be completed within one month. Supplementary investigation may be conducted twice at most. When supplementary investigation is completed and the case is transferred to the people's procuratorate, the time limit for examination and prosecution shall be recalculated by the people's procuratorate (Article 171).
- During trial in court. Among the situations listed in Article 198 that may affect the conduct of the trial and therefore allow a hearing to be postponed, one is that the procurators find that a case for which public prosecution has been initiated requires supplementary investigation and makes a proposal to that effect. The people's procuratorate shall complete the supplementary investigation within one month (Articles 198 and 199).

531. There are two types of supplementary investigation:

- To remand the case to a public security organ for supplementary investigation. Among the three types of supplementary investigation (*supra*, paragraph 530), the first type, which occurs during examination and approval of an arrest, can only be conducted in this way. The other two types of supplementary investigation can be conducted by either this way or the way mentioned below.
- To conduct the investigation by the people's procuratorate itself.

§3. Initiation of the Public Prosecution

I. General Description

532. According to the subject who initiates the prosecution, prosecution can be divided into two categories: the public prosecution and the private prosecution (for the private prosecution, cf. *supra*, paragraphs 461–463). The system of Chinese prosecution is that public prosecution is the principal and private prosecution is supplementary.

Initiation of public prosecution has two meanings: the narrow meaning is that it is a judicial act in criminal proceedings (*supra*, paragraph 480) and the broad meaning is that it is a stage, including the act of prosecution, in criminal proceedings.

533. The power to initiate a public prosecution is only held by the people's procuratorate (*supra*, paragraphs 400, 401). Article 167 of the CCP provides that all cases requiring initiation of a public prosecution shall be examined for decision by the people's procuratorate.

II. Examination of the Initiation of Prosecution

534. A people's procuratorate shall make a decision within one month on a case that a public security organ has transferred to it with a recommendation to initiate a prosecution. An extension of a half month may be allowed for major or complex cases.

When examining a case, the people's procuratorate shall interrogate the criminal suspect and heed the opinion of the victim and of the persons entrusted by the criminal suspect and the victim. The people's procuratorate shall also request a public security organ to provide the evidence that is essential to a trial in court. When necessary, it may remand the case for supplementary investigation or conduct the investigation itself (*supra*, paragraphs 397, 505–507).

535. In examining a case, a people's procuratorate shall ascertain the following items:

- whether the facts and circumstances of the crime are clear, whether the evidence is reliable and sufficient and whether the charge and the nature of the crime has been correctly determined;
- whether there are any crimes that have been omitted or other persons whose criminal responsibility shall be investigated;
- whether it is a case in which criminal responsibility shall not be investigated;
- whether the case has an incidental civil action; and
- whether the investigation of the case is being lawfully conducted (Article 168 of the CCP).

III. Decision to Initiate the Prosecution

536. In accordance with the CCP, the people's procuratorate shall make two types of decisions concerning initiation of prosecution: a decision to initiate a prosecution and a decision not to initiate a prosecution.

The decision to exempt a person from prosecution, which was provided in the Criminal Procedure of 1979, has now been abolished. It used to be applied to cases in which a defendant was deemed as guilty by the people's procuratorate but it was not necessary to impose a criminal punishment upon him or he could be exempted from adjudication according to law. The abolition of the decision to exempt from prosecution is to comply with the requirement of legality, especially the principle of presumption of innocence (*supra*, paragraph 433).

537. When a people's procuratorate considers that the facts of a criminal suspect's crime have been ascertained, that the evidence is reliable and sufficient and that criminal responsibility shall be investigated according to law, it shall make a decision to initiate a prosecution and shall, in accordance with the provision for trial jurisdiction, initiate a public prosecution in a people's court. The case file and evidence shall be transferred to the people's court (Article 172).

For cases of public prosecution where the defendants may be lawfully sentenced to fixed-term imprisonment of not more than three years, criminal detention, public surveillance or punished with fines exclusively, provided that the facts are clear and the evidence is sufficient, the people's procuratorate may suggest or agree to the application for summary procedure, in which the case shall be tried by a single judge alone (*supra*, paragraphs 464 et seq.).

538. The Criminal Procedure of 1996 sets out three types of decision not to initiate a prosecution:

- statutory decision not to initiate a prosecution;
- discretional decision not to initiate a prosecution;
- decision not to initiate a prosecution due to having a doubtful case.

539. Statutory decision not to initiate a prosecution is provided in paragraph 1, Article 173 of the Criminal Procedure. It provides that if a criminal suspect was found that no criminal fact had been committed, most often due to short of evidence, or falls under one of the circumstances provided in Article 15 of the Criminal Procedure (*supra*, paragraph 435), the people's procuratorate shall make a decision not to initiate a prosecution.

540. Discretional decision not to initiate a prosecution is provided in paragraph 2, Article 173 of the Criminal Procedure. It provides that, with respect to a case that is minor and so it is not necessary to give the offender criminal punishment or there is need to exempt the offender from it according to the Criminal Code, the people's procuratorate may decide not to initiate a prosecution. This decision involves the following provisions of the Criminal Code of 1997:

- Article 37 of the 1997 CCC, if the circumstances of a person's crime are minor and do not require criminal punishment (*supra*, paragraph 238).

- Article 10 of the 1997 CCC, if a criminal has already received criminal punishment in a foreign country, he may be exempted from punishment in China (*supra*, paragraph 115).
- Article 19 of the 1997 CCC, provides that any deaf-mute or blind person who commits a crime may be exempted from punishment (*supra*, paragraph 154).
- Article 20 of the 1997 CCC, if the defence obviously exceeds the limits of necessity and causes undue harm, consideration may be given to an exemption from punishment (*supra*, paragraph 193).
- Article 21 of the 1997 CCC, if necessity exceeds the limits of necessity and causes undue harm, consideration shall be given to an exemption from punishment (*supra*, paragraph 205).
- Article 22 of the 1997 CCC, preparation of a crime (*supra*, paragraph 237).
- Article 24 of the 1997 CCC, discontinuation of a crime (*supra*, paragraph 253).
- Article 27 of the 1997 CCC, accomplice (*supra*, paragraph 272).
- Article 28 of the 1997 CCC, anyone who is coerced to participate in a crime (*supra*, paragraph 273).

541. Making a decision not to initiate a prosecution due to having a doubtful case is provided in paragraph 4, Article 140. It provides that with respect to a case for which supplementary investigation has been conducted, if the people's procuratorate still believes that the evidence is insufficient and the case does not meet the conditions for initiation of a prosecution, the people's procuratorate may decide not to initiate a prosecution. This provision reflects the requirement of presumption of innocence (*supra*, paragraph 433).

After the decision not to initiate a prosecution is made, however, the decision to initiate a prosecution can still be made, if new evidence is found and the condition for initiating a prosecution is fulfilled, according to Article 405 of the Rules for Criminal Procedure of the People's Procuratorate enacted by the Supreme People's Procuratorate in 2012.

542. Decision not to initiate a prosecution shall be announced publicly, and the decision shall be delivered, in written form, to the person who is not to be prosecuted and his 'unit' (i.e., corporate body). If the person is under custody, he shall be released immediately. At the same time, the people's procuratorate shall cancel the seizure or freeze of the property or things of value seized or frozen during the period of investigation.

If the person against whom prosecution is not to be initiated needs to be given administrative penalty or administrative sanction or his illegal gains need be confiscated, the people's procuratorate shall make suggestions to such an effect and transfer the case to the competent organ for handling. The competent organ shall, without delay, inform the people's procuratorate of how it has handled the case.

IV. Review of the Decision Not to Prosecute

543. If the people's procuratorate decides not to initiate the prosecution of a case transferred by a public security organ for prosecution, it shall deliver the decision in writing to the public security organ. If the public security organ considers that the decision not to initiate a prosecution is wrong, it may demand reconsideration, and if the demand is rejected, it may submit the matter to the people's procuratorate at the next higher level for review (Article 175 of the CCP).

544. If the people's procuratorate decides not to initiate a prosecution to a case that involves a victim, it shall send the decision in writing to the victim. If the victim refuses to accept the decision, he may, within seven days after receiving the written decision, present a petition to the people's procuratorate at the next higher level and request the latter initiates a public prosecution. The people's procuratorate shall notify the victim of its decision made after re-examination. If the people's procuratorate upholds the decision not to initiate a prosecution, the victim may bring a lawsuit to a people's court. The victim may also bring a lawsuit directly to a people's court without presenting a petition first. After the people's court has accepted the case, the people's procuratorate shall transfer the relevant case file to the people's court (Article 176 of the CCP).

545. If the person against whom a people's procuratorate makes the discretional decision not to initiate a prosecution (*supra*, paragraph 544) still refuses to accept the decision, he may present a petition to the people's procuratorate within seven days of receiving the written decision. The people's procuratorate shall make a decision to conduct a re-examination, notify the person against whom no prosecution is to be initiated and at the same time send a copy of the decision to the public security organ (Article 177 of the CCP).

Chapter 3. The Procedure of First Instance

546. As we discussed before, according to the subject that initiates a prosecution, the criminal process can be divided into, the cases of public prosecution and the cases of private prosecution (*supra*, paragraphs 461 et seq.); according to the completeness of the procedure in first instance, the criminal process can be divided into the cases using the ordinary procedure and the cases using the summary procedure (*supra*, paragraphs 464 et seq.).

In this Chapter, what we will discuss are only the cases of public prosecution in the ordinary procedure.

§1. Decision to Open a Court Session

547. In accordance with the CCP, a people's court shall decide to open the court session and try the case, after it has examined a case in which public prosecution has been initiated and if the bill of prosecution contained clear facts of the crime accused (Article 181).

548. In comparison to the Criminal Procedure of 2012, the regulations on the decision to open a court session have changed in the following ways:

- The people's court does not require anymore materials to support the decision to open the court session. For those cases where the people's procuratorate contained clear facts of the crime accused with the case file and evidence in its bill of prosecution, the people's court shall make the decision to open the court session and shall not take it as an excuse that the evidence is not sufficient. For those cases where there is not such file and evidence, the people's court may ask the people's procuratorate to supplement and the people's procuratorate shall do it within three days.

The people's court shall make the decision within seven days.

549. In accordance with Article 181 of the CCP (*supra*, paragraph 548), the detailed items a people's court shall check in deciding to open a court are the followings:

- Whether the case is under the jurisdiction of that court. For instances where the case shall be upon complaint, the case shall be returned to the people's procuratorate and the victim shall be informed of the right of private prosecution. For those where the court has no jurisdiction to deal with the case or the accused person is not present, the case shall also be returned back to the people's procuratorate.
- Whether the bill of prosecution contains new facts or evidence. For instances where the people's procuratorate has withdrawn the case with the agreement of the people's court, the people's court will not accept them, except where there are new facts or evidence. However, the people's court shall accept the case if the people's procuratorate initiates the prosecution with new facts or evidence

even though the accused person was announced not guilty on the grounds that there was not strong enough evidence according to paragraph 3, Article 195.

- Whether there are any circumstances listed in paragraph 2–6, Article 15 (*supra*, paragraph 435, item 2–6) for terminating a criminal case which apply. When yes, the case shall be given back to the people's procuratorate.
- Whether the facts of the case are clear with sufficient evidence for those where the identification of the accused is not clear (*supra*, paragraph 528). When yes, the people's court shall accept it.

550. In a case where the people's court finds that anything is wrong, it can, of course, return the bill of prosecution back to the people's procuratorate for supplement. However, this is only of procedural, not of substantial, control in nature anymore.

§2. Preparation to Open a Court Session

551. In accordance with Article 182 of the CCP, a people's court shall proceed with the following actions after a people's court has decided to open a court session:

(1) to determine the members of the collegial panel;
(2) to deliver to the defendant and the defender thereof a copy of the people's procuratorate's bill of prosecution, no later than ten days before the opening of the court session;
(3) to call together the public prosecutor, parties, defenders, and litigation representatives to gather information and hear opinions on trial-related issues, such as withdraw, a list of witnesses to testify in court, and exclusion of illegally obtained evidence before a court session is opened;
(4) to notify the people's procuratorate of the time and place of the court session three days before the opening of the session;
(5) to summon the parties and notify the defenders, agents *ad litem*, witnesses, expert witnesses and interpreters, and deliver the summons and notices no later than three days before the opening of the court session; and
(6) to announce, three days before the opening of the session, the subject matter of the case to be heard in public, the name of the defendant and the time and place of the court session.

552. The CCP also provides that the people's court, the people's procuratorate and public security organ shall notify a legal aid agency to designate a lawyer to defend the accused person.

According to Article 34 and Article 267 of the CCP and some judicial explanations of the SPC, the people's court shall do the following for a defendant for the sake of defence:

- Where a defendant is the blind, deaf or mute or is a mental patient who has not completely lost the ability to recognise or control his or her behaviour, if he has not retained a defender, the people's court, as well as the people's procuratorate, and public security authority shall notify a legal aid agency to designate a lawyer to defend him.

- Where a case involves a juvenile defendant who has not retained a defender, the people's court, as well as the people's procuratorate, or the public security authority shall notify a legal aid agency to assign a lawyer to defend him.
- Where a defendant who may be sentenced to life imprisonment or death penalty has not retained a defender, the people's court, as well as the people's procuratorate and public security authority shall notify a legal aid agency to designate a lawyer to defend him.
- Where a defendant has not retained a defender for financial hardship or other reasons, the defendant or his close relative may file an application with a legal aid agency. If the legal aid conditions are met, the legal aid agency shall designate a lawyer to defend him.
- In the joint criminal cases where other joint criminals in the same case have entrusted defenders, the people's court may notify a legal aid agency to designate a lawyer to defend him, if he has not retained a defender.
- In the cases where there is significant social influence, such as the defendant who has foreign nationality, the people's court may notify a legal aid agency to designate a lawyer to defend, if the defendant has not retained a defender.
- In the cases where the people's procuratorate has raised a protest, the people's court may notify a legal aid agency to designate a lawyer to defend the defendant, if he has not retained a defender.
- In the cases where the defendant might not be guilty, the people's court may notify a legal aid agency to designate a lawyer to defend, if the defendant has not retained a defender.
- In other situations where the people's court believes that it is necessary to designate a lawyer to defend, the people's court may notify a legal aid agency, if the defendant has not retained a defender.

553. Cases of first instance in a people's court shall be heard in public, except for those where no public hearing is permitted in the law (*supra*, paragraph 431).

The reason for not hearing a case in public shall be announced in court.

The circumstances of the proceedings in preparing an opening of a court session shall be entered in the written record, which shall be signed by the judge and the court clerk.

554. The people's procuratorate shall send its prosecutors to the court to support the public prosecution, when the case is being tried in a people's court, even when such case is conducted as a summary procedure (*supra*, paragraphs 464 et seq.).

§3. The Proceedings in Court

I. General Description

555. In accordance with the provisions of the CCP, the proceedings in court are composed of five stages:

- the opening of a court session;
- investigation in court;
- debate in court;
- the defendant's last statement;
- deliberation and announcement of the judgment.

556. If one of the following situations occurs during a trial, which affects the conduct of the trial, a hearing may be postponed in accordance with Article 198 of the CCP:

- if it is necessary to summon new witnesses, obtain new material evidence, make a new expert evaluation or hold another inquest;
- if the procurators find that a case for which public prosecution has been initiated requires supplementary investigation, and they make a proposal to that effect. However, the people's procuratorate shall complete its supplementary investigation within one month (Article 199); or
- if the trial cannot proceed because of an application for the withdrawal of a judicial officer.

Based upon special reason, the particularly grave and complex cases, which are not appropriate for trial even within a relatively long period of time, may have their hearings postponed with the approval of the Standing Committee of the NPC (Article 155 of the Criminal Procedure, *supra*, paragraph 528, item 3).

Postponement of a hearing is different from suspension of the proceedings, which principally applies to the following situations, when:

- during the phase of investigation, the possible investigation is done but the whereabouts of the criminal suspect is unknown and the conditions for issuing a wanted order are not yet fulfilled;
- during the phases of investigation, prosecution and trial in court, the criminal suspect or the defendant is so ill of mental disease or other serious diseases that he cannot stand for interrogation and trial;
- during the trial at court, the defendant escaped;
- during the trial at court, the defendant has justifiable reason to suspend the trial and the judicial organs agree.

In the CCP, the circumstances for suspension of proceedings are provided in Article 200 as follows:

- the defendant is unable to appear before court due to his suffering of a serious illness;
- the defendant has escaped;
- the private prosecutor is unable to appear before court due to his suffering of a serious illness and the defendant has not retained a litigation representative to appear before court; or
- there is any irresistible reason.

When the situations leading to the suspension of a trial disappear, the proceedings shall then be resumed. The time of suspension of a trial shall not be counted in the period of trial.

Postponement of a hearing is different from termination of proceedings, which applies to the situations specified in Article 15 of the Criminal Procedure (*supra*, paragraph 435).

557. A people's court shall pronounce judgment on a case of public prosecution within two months or, three months at the latest, after accepting it. For a case with the possibility of a death penalty, a case with an incidental civil action or under any of the circumstances as set forth in Article 156 (below, and *supra*, paragraph 528, item 4), the period of trial may be extended for three months with the approval of the people's court at the next higher level. If more extension is needed under special circumstances, the extension shall be reported to the SPC for approval (Article 202).

Under one of the following situations listed in Article 156 (*supra*, paragraph 528, item 4), however, the period may be extended by one month upon approval or decision by the higher people's court at the provincial level:

- grave and complex cases in outlying areas where traffic is most inconvenient;
- grave cases that involve criminal gangs;
- grave and complex cases that involve people who commit crimes from one place to another; and
- grave and complex cases that involve various quarters and for which it is difficult to obtain evidence.

If a people's court alters its jurisdiction over a case, the time limit for handling the case shall be calculated from the date when another people's court receives the case after the alteration.

For the case a people's procuratorate has to conduct supplementary investigation, the people's court shall start to calculate anew the time limit for handling the case after the supplementary investigation has been completed and the case has been transferred to it.

II. Opening a Court Session

558. In the Chinese court, it is the clerk's work to do the following jobs prior to the opening of a court session:

- make sure that the public procurator, parties, witnesses and other participants in the criminal proceedings have appeared in court;
- read out the Rules of the Court;
- announce the presiding judge and other judges or people's assessors as they come into the court session.

559. During a court session, everyone shall observe the rule of the court.

If any participant in the proceedings of a trial or by-stander violates the order of the courtroom, the presiding judge shall warn him to desist.

If any person fails to obey, he may forcibly be taken out of the courtroom.

If the violation is serious, the person shall be fined not more than CNY 1,000 or detained not more than fifteen days. The fine or detention shall be subject to approval of the president of the court.

If the person under punishment is not satisfied with the decision on the fine or detention, he may apply to the people's court at the next higher level for reconsideration. However, the execution of the fine or detention shall not be suspended during the period of reconsideration.

Whoever assembles a crowd to make an uproar, charges into the courtroom, or humiliates, slanders, intimidates or beats up judicial officers or participants in the proceedings, thereby seriously disturbing the order of the courtroom, which constitutes a crime, shall be investigated for criminal responsibility according to law (Article 194 of the CCP).

560. In accordance with Article 185 of the CCP, the presiding judge shall follow the following procedures for opening a court session:

- to ascertain if all the parties have appeared in court and announce the subject matter of the case;
- to announce the roll, naming the members of the collegial panel, the court clerk, the public prosecutor, the defender, agent *ad litem*, the expert witnesses and the interpreter;
- to inform the parties of their right to apply for withdrawal of any member of the collegial panel, the court clerk, the public prosecutor, any expert witnesses or the interpreter; and
- to inform the defendant of his right to defence.

561. Any member of the judicial, procuratorial or investigatory personnel, as well as court clerks, interpreters and expert witnesses, shall voluntarily withdraw and parties to the case and their legal representatives shall also have the right to demand such withdrawal, in any of the following situations:

- if he is a party or a near relative of a party to the case;
- if he or a near relative of his has an interest in the case;
- if he has served as a witness, expert witness, defender or agent *ad litem* in the current case;
- if he has any other relations with a party to the case that could affect the impartial handling of the case;

- if he accepted invitations to dinner or presents from the parties to a case or the persons entrusted by the parties and violated the regulations to meet with the parties to a case or the persons entrusted by the parties. The one who violates this regulation shall be investigated for legal responsibility.

The withdrawal of a judge, procurator and investigator shall be determined respectively by the president of the court, the chief procurator, and the head of a public security organ. The withdrawal of the president of the court shall be determined by the court's judicial committee, and the withdrawal of the chief procurator or the head of a public security organ shall be determined by the procuratorial committee of the people's procuratorate at the corresponding level.

An investigator may not suspend investigation of a case before a decision is made on his withdrawal. If a decision has been made to reject his application for withdrawal, the party or his legal representative may apply for reconsideration.

Defenders and litigation representatives may request withdrawal and apply for a reconsideration according to law (Articles 28–31 of the CCP).

III. Investigation in Court

562. Investigation in court shall be carried out according to the following procedures:

(1) The public prosecutor reads out the bill of prosecution.
(2) The defendant and the victim present statements regarding the crime accused in the bill of prosecution.
(3) The victim, the plaintiff and defender in an incidental civil action and the agents *ad litem* may put questions to the defendant with the permission of the presiding judge.
(4) The judge may interrogate the defendant.
(5) After the judges instruct the witness to give testimony truthfully and explain to him the legal responsibility for intentionally giving false testimony or concealing criminal evidence, the witness shall give testimony.
(6) The public prosecutor, the parties, the defenders and agent *ad litem* may question the witnesses and expert witnesses with the permission of the presiding judge; however, if the presiding judge considers any questioning irrelevant to the case, he shall stop it.
(7) If the public prosecutor, a party, the defender o agent *ad litem* raises any objection to a witness statement which has a material effect on the conviction and sentencing of a case, the witness shall testify before the court if the people's court deems it necessary. This rule shall also apply to policemen who testify before court regarding a criminal situation which he witnessed in his line of duty. This rule shall also apply to the expert opinion, the identification and the evaluation experts. If the identification or evaluation expert refuses to appear in court after being notified by the people's court, the expert opinion may not be used as a basis for deciding the case. However, if a witness refuses to testify before court without justifiable

reasons after being notified by a people's court, the people's court may force the witness to appear before court, unless the witness is the spouse, a parent, or a child of the defendant. A witness who refuses to appear before court or refuses to testify after appearing before court without justifiable reasons shall be admonished or, if the circumstances are serious, the witness may be detained for not more than ten days with the approval of the president of the people's court. Against the detention decision, the detainee may apply to the people's court at the next higher level for reconsideration but the execution of the detention decision shall not be suspended pending reconsideration.

(8) The judge may question the witnesses and expert witnesses after informing them of the requirement of truthfully providing testimony and the legal liability for perjury or concealing criminal evidence.

(9) The public prosecutor and the defenders shall show the material evidence to the court for the parties to identify. Any records of testimony of witnesses who are not present in court, any conclusion of expert witnesses who are not present in court, any records of inquests and other documents serving as evidence shall be read out in court. The judges shall heed the opinions of the public prosecutor, the parties, the defenders and the agents *ad litem*.

(10) During a court hearing, the parties, the defenders and agents *ad litem* shall have the right to request new witnesses to be summoned, new material evidence to be obtained, a new expert evaluation to be made, and another inquest to be held. The court shall make a decision whether to grant these requests.

(11) The public prosecutor or a party or the defender or agents *ad litem* may request the court to call a person with expertise to appear before court to offer an opinion on the expert opinion of an identification or evaluation expert. The court shall make a decision whether to grant these requests.

(12) During a court hearing, if the collegial panel has doubts about the evidence, it may announce an adjournment, in order to carry out investigation to verify the evidence. When carrying out investigation to verify evidence, the people's court may conduct inquest, examination, seizure, expert evaluation, as well as inquiry and freezes (Articles 186–192 of the CCP).

IV. Debate in Court

563. In accordance with Article 193 of the CCP, any fact or evidence related to conviction or sentencing shall be investigated and debated in a court session. The public prosecutor, the parties, the defenders and the agents *ad litem* may, with permission of the presiding judge, state their views on the evidence and the case, and they may debate with each other.

Accordingly, the debate in court actually begins from the time when evidence is shown in the court. Therefore, this provision is different from that in the Criminal Procedure of 1979, which explicitly provides that the debate in court shall begin after the investigation in court.

However, there is a stage for debate in court after investigation in court in the proceedings of first instance stipulated in the CCP. It is theoretically called 'conclusive debate', providing an opportunity for the accusing side and the accused side to present their conclusive opinions over the case.

564. In the legal practice, debate in court shall begin with the speeches of the public prosecutor, the victim and his agent *ad litem*, and then by the statement of the defendant and the defence of the defender. After the first round, there might be second and third rounds, until the presiding judge believes that the facts of the crime, the nature of the crime and the criminal responsibility are clear or the opinions of both sides have been fully presented.

Before announcing the end of the debate, the presiding judge will usually ask if the defendant and his defender have any new opinions.

V. The Defendant's Last Statement

565. It is a legal requirement that the defendant shall have the right to present a final statement after the presiding judge declares conclusion of the debate (Article 193).

This is an important procedural right of the defendant, which shall not be mixed up with debate in court, though the defendants often make use of this opportunity to give their confessions. It is also not uncommon that the defendant provides new evidence which shall lead the proceedings back to the investigation in court or even an adjournment of the court session.

VI. Deliberation and Announcement of Judgment

566. After a defendant makes his final statement, the presiding judge shall announce an adjournment and the collegial panel shall conduct its deliberations and, on the basis of the established facts and evidence and in accordance with the provisions of relevant laws, render one of the following judgments:

- if the facts of a case are clear, the evidence is reliable and sufficient, and the defendant is found to be guilty according to law, he shall be pronounced guilty accordingly;
- if the defendant is found to be innocent according to law, he shall be pronounced innocent accordingly;
- if the evidence is insufficient and thus the defendant cannot be found guilty, he shall be pronounced innocent accordingly on account of the fact that the evidence is insufficient and the accusation unfounded (Article 195 of the CCP).

567. Judgments shall be pronounced publicly in all cases.

If the judgment on a case is pronounced in court, a written form of the judgment shall be delivered within five days to the parties and the people's procuratorate that initiated the public prosecution.

In cases where the judgment is pronounced later on a fixed date, a written form of the judgment shall be delivered immediately after the pronouncement to the parties and the people's procuratorate that initiated the public prosecution. At the same time, a written sentence shall be served upon the defender and litigation representative (Article 196).

568. In accordance with the CCP, the court clerk shall make a written record of the whole court proceedings, which shall be examined by the presiding judge and then signed by him and the court clerk. The record of the testimony of witnesses shall be read out in court or given to the witnesses to read. After acknowledging that the record is free of error, the witnesses shall sign or affix their seals to it. The courtroom record shall be given to the parties to read or shall be read out to them. The parties shall have the right to request additions or corrections on it. After acknowledging the correctness, they shall sign or affix their seals to it (Article 201).

The written judgment shall be signed by the judges and the court clerk, and the time limit for appeal and the name of the appellate court shall be clearly indicated therein (Article 197).

Chapter 4. The Procedure of Legal Remedies and Special Procedures

569. It is true that the second instance is final in dealing with appellate matters (Article 10 of the CCP and *supra*, paragraph 40). In the Chinese judicial system, however, there are other procedures: the procedure for the review of the death sentence, the procedure for trial supervision when there is for the definite error in the determination of facts or application of the law in a legally effective judgment or order.

The CCP provides new special procedures, which are procedures for juvenile criminal cases, procedures for public prosecution cases where parties have reached settlement, confiscation procedures for illegal income in cases where a criminal suspect or defendant escapes or dies, and procedures for the involuntary medical treatment of mental patients who are legally exempted from criminal liability (*supra*, paragraph 490).

§1. The Procedure of Second Instance

570. The procedure of second instance shall be brought by an appeal or a protest against the judgment or ruling of the first instance which is not yet legally effective.

The procedure of second instance can be theoretically divided into two phases: the procedure to bring the appellate procedure and the procedure to try the appellate case.

I. The Procedure to Bring the Appellate Procedure

571. The procedure of second instance can be triggered by appeal and protest.

It is the right of a defendant to appeal. A defendant shall not be deprived on any pretext of his right to appeal.

572. In accordance with the CCP, an appeal can be brought by the following persons:

- defendant, private prosecutor or their legal representatives;
- defender or the near relatives of the defendant may file appeal with the consent of the defendant;
- a party to an incidental civil action or his legal representative may file an appeal against the part of a judgment or ruling that deals with the incidental civil action (Article 216).

A protest can be brought by the following organ and persons:

- If a local people's procuratorate at any level considers that there is some definite error in a judgment or ruling of first instant made by a people's court at the same level, it shall present a protest to the people's court at the next higher level.
- If the victim or his legal representative refuses to accept a judgment of first instance made by a local people's court at any level, he shall, within five days from the date of receiving the written judgment, have the right to request the people's procuratorate to present a protest. The people's procuratorate shall decide whether to present the protest or not and give him a reply within five days from the date of receiving the request made by the victim or his legal representative (Articles 217–218).

573. With respect to the reason, the form and the procedure, the CCP provides different requirements for appeal and protest.

With regards to the reason for appeal, there is no substantial restriction in the law. The persons who have the right to appeal may appeal in writing or orally, as long as they explicitly express that they refuse to accept the judgment or ruling of first instance and that they want to appeal. They do not need to explain why they refuse to accept the judgment or ruling, though they can do so or supplement the reason during the trial of second instance.

For a protest, it is the legal requirement that the local people's procuratorate shall believe that there is definite error in the judgment or ruling of first instance. If a local people's procuratorate protests against a judgment or ruling of first instance made by the people's court at the same level, it shall present a written protest through the people's court that originally tried the case and send a copy of the written protest to the people's procuratorate at the next higher level. The people's court which originally tried the case shall transfer the written protest together with the case file and evidence to the people's court at the next higher level and shall deliver duplicates of the written protest to the parties. If the people's procuratorate at the next higher level considers the protest inappropriate, it may withdraw the protest from the people's court at the same level and notify the people's procuratorate at the next lower level (Article 221).

The victim or his legal representative who refuses to accept a judgment of first instance cannot trigger the protest himself. He has to request the people's procuratorate to present the protest. So in practice, the victim or his legal representative has to provide their reasons to the people's procuratorate why they refuse to accept the judgment, so that the people's procuratorate can present the protest based upon them.

574. It is a legal provision of the Criminal Procedure that the time limit for an appeal or a protest against a judgment shall be ten days and the time limit for an appeal or a protest against a ruling shall be five days. The time limit shall be counted from the day after the written judgment or ruling is received (Article 219).

If a defendant, private prosecutor, a plaintiff or defendant in an incidental civil action files an appeal through the people's court which that originally tried the case, the people's court shall, within three days, transfer the petition of appeal together with the case file and the evidence to the people's court at the next higher level. Within the same time limit, it shall deliver duplicates of the petition of appeal to the people's procuratorate at the same level and to the other party.

If a defendant, private prosecutor, a plaintiff or defendant in an incidental civil action files an appeal directly to the people's court of second instance, the people's court shall, within three days, transfer the petition of appeal to the people's court which originally tried the case for delivery to the people's procuratorate at the same level and to the other party (Article 220).

II. The Procedure to Try the Appellate Case

575. In trying an appellate case, it is an important issue to consider whether the people's court of second instance shall form a collegial panel and open a court session to hear the case. In the Chinese Criminal Procedure of 1996, the regulation on this issue was to take opening as principle. However, there is an important revision on this point in the 2012 code. According to Article 223, a people's court of second instance shall form a collegial panel for certain appellate cases as follows:

- an appellate case where a defendant, a private prosecutor or the legal representative thereof has raised any objections to the facts and evidence determined in the trial at first instance, which may affect conviction and sentencing;
- an appellate case where the defendant is sentenced to death;
- a case protested by the people's procuratorate; and
- any other case which shall be heard in a court session.

Where a people's court of second instance decides not to hold a court session to hear a case, it shall arraign the defendant and hear the opinions of other parties, defenders, and litigation representatives.

576. It is an important characteristic of the Chinese criminal procedure that a people's court of second instance shall conduct a complete review of the facts determined and the application of law in the judgment of first instance and shall not be limited by the scope of appeal or protest. If an appeal is filed by only some of the defendants in a case of joint crime, the case shall still be reviewed and handled as a whole (Article 222).

However, the complete review can only cover the criminal part of the case. For the appeal or protest against a judgment of an incidental civil action, the error in the criminal part of the judgment cannot be corrected directly. It can only be done through the procedure of trial supervision if the party did not appeal against the criminal part of the judgment.

577. When a people's court of second instance opens a court session to hear a case of appeal or protest, it may do so in the place where the case occurred or in the place where the people's court which originally tried the case is located. The people's procuratorate at the same level shall send its procurators to the court for the cases protested by a people's procuratorate and cases of public prosecution tried by a people's court of second instance in a court session. The people's court of second instance shall, after deciding to hold a court session to hear a case, notify the people's procuratorate in a timely manner to consult the case file. The people's procuratorate shall complete their consultation of the case file within one month. The time for the people's procuratorate to consult the case file shall not be counted in the period of trial.

In accordance with Article 231 of the CCP, a people's court of second instance shall try cases of appeal or protest with reference to the procedure of first instance, except for those specified for the second instance, e.g., it is the appellant who shall present his speech first during the debate in court.

578. After hearing a case of appeal or protest against a judgment of first instance, the people's court of second instance shall handle it in one of the following manners in light of the different situations (Articles 225–229):

(1) If the original judgment was correct in the determination of facts and the application of law and appropriate in meting out of punishment, the people's court shall order rejection of the appeal or protest and affirm the original judgment (Article 225).
(2) If the original judgment contained no error in the determination of facts but the application of law was incorrect or the punishment was inappropriately meted out, the people's court shall revise the judgment. However, the people's court of second instance may not increase the criminal punishment on the defendant in the trial of the case appealed by a defendant, his legal representative, defender or near relative. The restriction that the punishment shall not be increased for appeal shall not apply to the cases protested by a people's procuratorate or cases appealed by private prosecutors (Articles 225 and 226).
(3) If the facts in the original judgment were unclear or the evidence insufficient, the people's court may revise the judgment after ascertaining the facts, or it may rescind the original judgment and remand the case to the people's court which originally tried it for retrial. However, in those cases where a defendant or the people's procuratorate appeals after the original trial court renders a sentence for a case remanded for retrial, the people's court of second instance shall render a sentence or ruling in accordance with law and may not remand the case again to the original trial court for retrial (Article 225).
(4) If a people's court of second instance discovers that when hearing a case, a people's Court of First Instance violated the litigation procedures prescribed by law in one of the following ways, it shall rule to rescind the original judgment and remand the case to the people's court which originally tried it for retrial:

    - violating the provisions regarding trial in public;
    - violating the withdrawal system;
    - depriving the parties of their litigation rights prescribed by law or restricting, such rights, which may hamper impartiality of a trial;
    - unlawful formation of a judicial organisation; or
    - other violations against the litigation procedures prescribed by law which may hamper the impartiality of a trial (Article 227).

    The people's court which originally tried a case shall form a new collegial panel for the case remanded to it for retrial, in accordance with the procedure of first instance. After the retrial, an appeal or protest may be lodged according to law (Article 228).

(5) After a people's court of second instance has reviewed an appeal or protest against a ruling of first instance, it shall order the rejection of the appeal or protest or rescind or revise the original ruling respectively according to the Criminal Procedure (Article 229, cf. items 1–4 above).

579. In accordance with the Criminal Procedure, a people's court of second instance shall conclude the trial of the appellate case within two months. For a case with the possibility of a death penalty or a case with an incidental civil action or under any of the circumstances as set forth in Article 156 (*supra*, paragraph 528, item 4), the period of trial may be extended by two months with the approval or decision of the higher people's court at the provincial level. If further extension is needed under special circumstances, the extension shall be reported to the SPC for approval. The period for the SPC to try an appellate case shall be decided by the SPC (Article 232).

580. All judgments and rulings of second instance and all judgments and rulings of the SPC are final.

After a judgment rendered by the people's court becomes effective, all the seized, impounded or frozen illicit money and goods as well as the fruits accruing therefrom, except those that are returned to the victim according to law, shall be confiscated and turned over to the State Treasury. The sentence of a people's court shall include the disposal of the seized, impounded, or frozen property and the fruits thereof (Articles 197 and 198 of the CCP).

§2. The Procedure for Review of Death Sentences

581. This is a special procedure solely contained in the Chinese criminal proceedings.

It is true that the system whereby the second instance is final is the system the people's court shall be used in trying cases involving death sentences. However, if the court sentences the defendant to death, the final judgment shall not become effective until the procedure for review of death sentences has been exhausted, even though the defendant has gone through the procedure of second instance.

This procedure is an important restriction on the application of death penalty (*supra*, paragraph 315).

This procedure applies to the case of the death penalty with immediate execution and the case of the death penalty with a suspension of execution.

582. Death sentences shall be subject to approval by the SPC, except for those otherwise specified in law (*supra*, paragraphs 291 et seq.).

I. The Procedure for the Immediate Death Penalty

583. In the CCP, Article 236 provides that:

> A case of first instance where an intermediate people's court has imposed a death sentence and the defendant does not appeal shall be reviewed by a higher people's

court and submitted to the Supreme People's Court for approval. If the higher people's court does not agree with the death sentence, it may bring the case up for trial or remand the case for retrial.

Cases of first instance where a higher people's court has imposed a death sentence and the defendant does not appeal, and cases of second instance where a death sentence has been imposed shall all be submitted to the Supreme People's Court for approval.

584. The cases of death sentence submitted to the SPC for approval shall be handled in the following ways:

- A case of first instance where an intermediate people's court has imposed a death sentence and the defendant does not appeal or the people's procuratorate does not protest shall be submitted to the higher people's court for review within ten days after the period of appeal expires. If the higher people's court approves the death sentence, the case shall be submitted to the SPC for verification within ten days after the approval was granted. If disapproved, the higher people's court may bring the case up for trial or remand the case for retrial. The judgments of death sentence with a suspension of execution revised by a higher people's court after its examination or trial shall be final and do not need to go through the procedure of review again.
- A case of first instance where an intermediate people's court has imposed a death sentence and the defendant does appeal or the people's procuratorate does protest, which a higher people's court maintains the death sentence as the final judgment, shall be submitted to the SPC for verification within ten days after the approval was granted. If the higher people's court disapproves the judgments of death sentence and revises the judgment to the death sentence with a two-years suspension of execution, that judgment is also a final one and does not need to go through the procedure of review anymore.
- A case of first instance where a higher people's court has imposed a death sentence and the defendant does not appeal or the people's procuratorate does not protest shall be submitted to the SPC for review within ten days after the period of appeal expires.
- With respect to the criminal who is sentenced to death in the case which shall be approved by the SPC, if he is verified to have committed an intentional crime during the period of the suspension, the execution of death penalty shall be submitted by the higher people's court to the SPC for verification.

585. The SPC reviewing a death sentence shall make a ruling to approve or disapprove the death sentence. If the death sentence is disapproved, the SPC may remand the case for retrial or render a new sentence (Article 239).

The SPC reviewing a death sentence shall question the defendant and, if the defence lawyer files a request for presenting an opinion, hear the opinion of the defence lawyer. During the review of a death sentence, the Supreme People's Procuratorate may present an opinion to the SPC. The SPC shall notify the Supreme People's Procuratorate of the review result (Article 240).

II. The Procedure for Suspending Death Penalty

586. Article 237 of the CCP provides that:

> a case where an intermediate people's court has imposed a death sentence with a two-year suspension of execution shall be subject to approval by a higher people's court.

Accordingly, the death sentence with suspension of execution shall be handled in the following ways:

- A case of first instance where an intermediate people's court has imposed a death sentence with a suspension of execution and the defendant does not appeal or the people's procuratorate does not protest shall be submitted to the higher people's court for verification. The higher people's court shall question the defendant before making the verification. If the higher people's court approves the death sentence with a suspension of execution, it shall make the ruling of verification for it. If it disapproves, it may revise the sentence directly. If it thinks that the defendant shall be sentenced to death with immediate execution, the case shall be remanded back to the intermediate people's court for retrial. The judgment of the retrial may be appealed and protested.
- With respect to a case of first instance where an intermediate people's court has imposed a death sentence with a suspension of execution and the defendant does appeal or the people's procuratorate does protest, if a higher people's court agrees to the death sentence with a suspension of execution in the procedure of second instance, it shall make the ruling to maintain the original judgment. If it disagrees, it may revise the sentence directly or remand the case for retrial.

587. Reviews by the SPC of the cases involving death sentences and reviews by a higher people's court of cases involving death sentence with a suspension of execution shall be conducted by collegial panels each composed of three judges (Article 238 of the CCP).

§3. The Procedure for Trial Supervision

I. Concept

588. The procedure for trial supervision is a special procedure in the Chinese criminal process. It refers to the procedure of re-hearing brought by the people's court and the people's procuratorate, with their powers and functions, if they find a definite error in the facts ascertained or the law applied in a legally effective judgment and ruling, and through which the case is retried by the people's court.

The different aspects between the procedure of second instance and that for trial supervision can be found in followings:

- the former is for the cases whose judgment and ruling are not yet legally effective, the latter is for the cases whose judgment and ruling are already legally effective, including those that are executing and have already been executed;
- the former can be triggered by the appeal of the defendant and the relevant persons or by the protest of the people's procuratorate at the same level (*supra*, paragraphs 548 et seq.), the latter can only be triggered by special persons and organs (*infra*, paragraph 590);
- there is no requirement for maintaining specific reasoning for triggering the former, however, the bringing of the latter shall be subject to strict restriction (*infra*, paragraphs 566);
- there is a legal limit of time for the former (*supra*, paragraph 574) but no such time limit for the latter. However, if the person who was found innocent shall be resentenced as a guilty person in the procedure for trial supervision, it shall be subject to limitations (Article 88 of the 1997 CCC, *supra*, paragraphs 360 et seq.);
- the people's court in the former procedure can only be the people's court at the next higher level; that in the latter procedure maybe either the people's court that originally tried the case or any people's court at the higher level;
- in the former procedure, it shall strictly observe the principle of 'no increased punishment for appellant' (*supra*, item 2 in paragraph 578), but there is no such requirement in the latter procedure.

II. Petition

589. It is the right of a party, his legal representative or his near relative to present a petition to a people's court or a people's procuratorate regarding a legally effective judgment or ruling, though this petition will not suspend the execution of the judgment or ruling (Article 241 of the CCP).

In accordance with the Criminal Procedure, if a petition presented by a party, his legal representative or his near relative conforms to any of the following conditions, the people's court shall retry the case:

- there is new evidence to prove that the facts in the original judgment or ruling were erroneously determined, which may affect conviction and sentencing;
- the evidence upon which the conviction and the sentence were made is unreliable and insufficient in which case the evidence shall be excluded in accordance with law, or the major pieces of evidence for supporting the facts of the case contradict each other;
- the application of law in making the original judgment or ruling is definitely incorrect;

- the statutory procedures were violated, which may have affected the provision of a fair trial; or
- the judges in trying the case committed acts of embezzlement, bribery, malpractice for personal gain, or bended the law in making the judgment (Article 242).

Petitions are one of the important sources that may initiate the procedure for trial supervision. The following are other important sources in the Chinese legal practice:

- opinions and reports of relevant organs, units and citizens; these are from sources such as: public media, state supervision organs, enterprises, and the disciplinary organ of the Chinese Communist Party;
- proposals regarding the correction of a wrong case brought by representatives of the people's congresses at various levels;
- the wrong cases discovered by the people's court and the people's procuratorate.

III. Subject

590. The procedure for trial supervision can only be triggered by definite errors in the facts ascertained, including the facts of the case and the evidence confirmed, and the law applied, including the substantial law governing the nature of the crime and the sentence of punishment as well as the procedural law.

However, the procedure for trial supervision can only be triggered by the following specific persons and organs in accordance with the Criminal Procedure:

- if the president of a people's court at any level finds some definite error in a legally effective judgment or ruling of his court as to the determination of facts or application of law, he shall refer the matter to the judicial committee for handling;
- if the SPC finds some definite error in a legally effective judgment or ruling of a people's court at any lower level, or if a people's court at a higher level finds some definite error in a legally effective judgment or ruling of a people's court at a lower level, it shall have the power to bring the case up for trial itself or may direct a people's court at a lower level to conduct a retrial;
- if the Supreme People's Procuratorate finds some definite error in a legally effective judgment or ruling of a people's court at any level including the SPC, of if a people's procuratorate at a higher level finds some definite error in a legally effective judgment or ruling of a people's court at a lower level, it shall have the power to present a protest to the people's court at the same level against the judgment or ruling in accordance with the procedure for trial supervision (Article 243).

IV. Trial

591. For the case protested by a people's procuratorate, the people's court that accept the protest shall form a collegial panel for retrial. If the facts, on the basis of which the original judgment was made, are not clear or the evidence is not sufficient, it may direct the people's court at the lower level to try the case again (Article 243 of the CCP).

A people's court shall form a new collegial panel for the retrial of a case in accordance with the procedure for trial supervision if the retrial is conducted by the original trial court. If the case was originally one of first instance, it shall be tried in accordance with the procedure of first instance and the new judgment or ruling may be appealed or protested. If the case was originally one of second instance or was brought up for trial by a people's court at a higher level, it shall be tried in accordance with the procedure of second instance and the judgment or ruling rendered shall be final.

When a people's court retries a case in a court session, the people's procuratorate at the same level shall send procurators to appear before the court.

For the cases where a people's court at a higher level orders a people's court at a lower level to retry a case, it shall order a people's court at a lower level other than the original trial court to try the case. However, if it is more appropriate for the case to be retried by the original trial court, it may order the original trial court to retry the case (Article 244).

For a case retried by a people's court in accordance with the procedure for trial supervision, it shall conclude the trial within three months from the day on which it makes the decision to start the trial of a case or on which the decision is made for it to retry the case. If it is necessary to extend the time limit, the period shall not exceed six months.

For the trial of a protested case, the people's court that accepts it shall follow these provisions of time limit.

For a case which a people's court decides to retry, any necessary compulsory measure against a defendant shall be decided by the people's court. For a case to be retried upon appeal of a people's procuratorate under the trial supervision procedures, any necessary compulsory measure against a defendant shall be decided by the people's procuratorate. For a case tried under the trial supervision procedures, a people's court may decide to suspend the execution of the original sentence or ruling (Article 246).

Where it is necessary to direct a people's court at a lower level to try a protested case again, the decision to such an effect shall be made within one month from the date when the protested case is accepted. The trial of the case by the people's court at the lower level shall observe the time limit mentioned in the first paragraph (Article 247 of the Criminal Procedure).

§4. Special Procedures

592. After 1996, the Chinese criminal procedure has been exploring better ways to deal with the most specific matters. In 2012, the Chinese Criminal Procedure added a whole 'Special Procedures' section. These special procedures include: the procedure for juvenile criminal cases, procedures for public prosecution cases where parties have reached settlement, confiscation procedures for illegal income in cases where a criminal suspect or defendant escapes or dies, and procedures for involuntary medical treatment of mental patients legally exempted from criminal liability.

I. Procedures for Juvenile Criminal Cases

593. Procedures for juvenile criminal cases not only include the 'old' provisions for dealing with the juvenile delinquent cases in the Criminal Procedure but also provide new regulations, so that the guiding line, principles and special regulations are provided as follows:

- For juvenile criminals, the policy of education, reformation, and redemption shall apply, and the principle of education assisted by punishment shall be followed. So, a people's court, a people's procuratorate, and a public security authority shall assign judges, prosecutors and investigators who are familiar with the physical and psychological characteristics of juveniles to handle the juvenile criminal cases and to notify a legal aid agency to assign a lawyer to defend the juvenile criminal suspect or defendant who has not retained a defender, so that the juveniles shall be able to exercise their procedural rights (Article 266).
- In dealing with the juvenile criminal cases, the protection of minors shall be careful. An arrest of a juvenile criminal suspect or defendant shall be under strict control. Before adopting an arrest, a people's procuratorate or a people's court shall question the juvenile criminal suspect or defendant and hear the opinion of his or her defence lawyer. After being detained, arrested or being given criminal penalties, the juvenile shall be held in custody, managed, and educated separately. The criminal history of the juvenile shall be investigated, including his growth, cause of crime, guardianship, education and other aspects. However, the criminal files and records shall be sealed for preservation if a juvenile has not reached the age of eighteen when committing a crime and is sentenced to fixed-term imprisonment of five years or a lighter punishment (Article 275). The juvenile's procedural rights shall be strictly protected (Articles 268–270).
- It is very significant to establish a non-prosecution system for the juvenile criminal cases. When a juvenile is involved in an offence in Chapter IV (Crimes Infringing upon Citizens' Civil and Democratic Rights, *supra*, paragraph 285), V (Property Crimes, *supra*, paragraph 286), or VI (Crimes Obstructing the Administration of Public Order, *supra*, paragraph 287) of the Specific Provisions of the Criminal Law, a people's procuratorate may make a conditional, non-prosecution decision after consulting the public security organ and the victim. This will occur if the prosecution conditions have been met and the juvenile could have been sentenced to fixed-term imprisonment of one year or a lighter punishment but the juvenile suspect has shown repentance. When the victim does not agree, he may ask for reconsideration at the next higher level but according to the legislative explanation of 2014, the victim cannot raise a lawsuit in a people's court according to Article 176 (*supra*, paragraph 544). Only when the juvenile criminal suspect or his legal representative raises an objection to the conditional non-prosecution decision of the people's procuratorate shall the people's procuratorate make a decision to

initiate a public prosecution (Article 271). The probation period for conditional non-prosecution shall range from six months to one year, starting from the day when the people's procuratorate makes a conditional non-prosecution decision. During the probation period for conditional non-prosecution, a people's procuratorate shall supervise and inspect a juvenile criminal suspect who is not prosecuted but is under conditions (Article 272).

II. Procedures for Settlement

594. Procedure for settlement refers to the procedures for public prosecution cases where parties have reached settlement. Settlement is a way to conclude the private prosecution (*supra*, paragraphs 380, 461, especially 463). In order to regulate the expansion of settlement into the public prosecution, the CCP provides the regulations as follows:

- In the public prosecution, only two groups of cases may be concluded by settlement if the criminal suspect or defendant has showed genuine repentance and obtained forgiveness from the victim by making compensation or an apology to the victim. The first group of the cases is involved in a case regarding a crime which arises from civil disputes as described in Chapter IV (Crimes of Infringing upon Citizens' Civil and Democratic Rights, *supra*, paragraph 285), or V (Property Crimes, *supra*, paragraph 286) of the Specific Provisions of the Criminal Law and is punishable by fixed-term imprisonment of three years or less. The second group of the cases refers to a case regarding a negligent crime, other than a crime of malfeasance, which is punishable by fixed-term imprisonment of seven years or less. However, the procedures in this Chapter shall not apply, if a criminal suspect or defendant has committed any intentional crime in the past five years (Article 277).
- After both parties have reached a settlement, a public security authority, a people's procuratorate or a people's court shall ask the opinions of the parties and other relevant persons, examine whether the settlement has been reached voluntarily and legally, and preside at the preparation of a settlement agreement. However, Chinese settlement in a public prosecution shall not automatically exempt individuals from criminal punishment. In a case where a settlement agreement is reached, a public security authority may provide a leniency suggestion to the people's procuratorate. A people's procuratorate may provide a leniency suggestion to the people's court. If the circumstances of a crime are minor and no criminal punishment is necessary, the people's procuratorate may make a decision not to initiate a public prosecution. A people's court may render a lenient sentence to a defendant in accordance with law (Articles 278 and 279).

III. Confiscation Procedures

595. Confiscation procedure refers to the confiscation procedures for illegal income in cases where a criminal suspect or defendant escapes or dies. The stipulation of the confiscation procedure is to meet the requirement of anti-corruption and to build the links with the requirements of the international convention on anti-corruption and anti-terrorism. This new procedure in the CCP includes the following provisions:

- A people's procuratorate may file an application with a people's court for confiscation of illegal income for those cases regarding a serious crime such as embezzlement, bribery, or terrorist activities, if a criminal suspect or defendant escapes and cannot be present in court after being wanted for a year, or if a criminal suspect or defendant dies and his or her illegal income and other properties are involved in the case, it shall be recovered in accordance with the Criminal Law. If a public security authority deems that there are such circumstances, it shall prepare a written opinion on the confiscation of illegal income and transfer it to a people's procuratorate (Article 280).
- The jurisdiction of the application for confiscation of illegal income shall belong to the intermediate people's court at the place of the crime or the place of residence of a criminal suspect or defendant, which shall form a collegial panel to hear the application. After a public announcement for six months, the people's court shall hold a court session to hear the application. The close relatives of a criminal suspect or defendant and other interested parties shall have the right to apply for participating in the procedure, and may retain litigation representatives to participate in the procedure (Article 281).
- In the case where the application is confirmed, the people's court shall render a ruling to confiscate illegal income and other properties involved, except for those legally returned to the victims. If not confirmed, a ruling to dismiss the application shall be granted and any seizure, impound, or freezing measures taken, shall be terminated immediately. Against these rulings, the close relatives of a criminal suspect or defendant, other interested parties, or the people's procuratorate may appeal (Article 282).
- If a fugitive criminal suspect or defendant voluntarily surrenders himself or is captured during the trial period, a people's court shall terminate the trial. In addition, where the property of a criminal suspect or defendant is erroneously confiscated, such property shall be returned, and compensation shall be made (Article 283).

IV. Procedures for Involuntary Medical Treatment

596. Procedures for involuntary medical treatment refer to the procedures for involuntary medical treatment of mental patients who are legally exempted from criminal liability. In accordance with the Chinese Criminal Code, a mental patient without the capacity to recognise or control his own conduct shall not bear criminal responsibility (Article 18 of the 1997 CCC, *supra*, paragraph 154). It is the responsibility of his family or his guardian and, when necessary, the government to subject him to strict surveillance and arrange for his medical treatment. The CCP provides the procedure for this kind of medical treatment.

- A procedure for the involuntary medical treatment of a mental patient shall be applied by the people's procuratorate for those who have committed any violent behaviour endangering public security or seriously endangering the personal safety of citizens and will be legally exempted from criminal responsibility after identification under statutory procedures, if the mental patient may continue to endanger the society. If a public security authority discovers that a mental patient meets the conditions for involuntary medical treatment, it shall prepare a written opinion and transfer it to the people's procuratorate for application. Before a people's court makes the decision, a public security authority may take interim protective restraint measures (Articles 284, 285).
- The people's court shall form a collegial panel to try the case of involuntary medical treatment. Before the trial, a people's court shall notify the legal representative of the respondent or defendant to be present. If the respondent or defendant has not retained a litigation representative, the people's court shall notify a legal aid agency to assign a lawyer to provide legal assistance for him. The people's court shall make a decision within one month and against an involuntary medical treatment decision, the person subject to involuntary medical treatment as decided, the victim, the legal representative or close relative thereof may apply to the people's court at the next higher level for reconsideration, if he refuses to accept the decision (Articles 286, 287).
- Involuntary medical treatment institutions shall regularly diagnose and assess persons subject to involuntary medical treatment. For those who are no longer dangerous to personal safety and no longer need this type of medical treatment, involuntary medical treatment institutions shall prepare opinions on termination of involuntary medical treatment timely and report such opinions to the people's courts which made the involuntary medical treatment decisions for approval. Persons subject to involuntary medical treatment and their close relatives have the right to apply for termination of involuntary medical treatment. The people's procuratorate shall oversee decisions and execution of involuntary medical treatment (Articles 288, 289).

Part III. Execution and Extinction of Sanctions

Chapter 1. Sources of Penitentiary Law and Nature of Regulations

597. The Chinese penitentiary law was used to refer to the laws of reform through labour. It was named from the 'Regulations of Reform through Labour of the People's Republic of China' adopted on 26 August 1954.

The Prison Law of the PRC (hereafter the CPL) was adopted at the 11th Meeting of the Standing Committee of the Eighth NPC on 29 December 1994 and revised at the 29th Session of the Standing Committee of the Eleventh NPC on 26 October 2012. The Prison Law is the basic law of the Chinese penitentiary law.

598. The sources of the Chinese penitentiary law are as follows:

- The Constitution provides the fundamental basis for the Chinese penitentiary law. In the Chinese Constitution, Article 28 provides the direct basis for the CPL, in which it is stipulated 'to punish and to reform criminals'. In the Constitutional Amendment of 2004, the article was added that the State respects and protects human rights, which shall also apply to the protection of prisoner's human rights.
- The Prison Law of the PR China, which was adopted in the Standing Committee of the NPC on 29 December 1994 and amended in 2012. The Prison Law is the most important part in the legal source for the Chinese penitentiary law. This law is composed of seven chapters with seventy-eight articles and divided into a General Part and some specific regulations. In the General Part, there are guiding principles and a legislative basis, the nature and task of prisons, basic principles and the methods of punishment in prison and reformation of criminals, the legal status of people's policemen in prisons, the rights and obligations of prisoners and the guarantee of a prison's budget and investments. In the specific regulations, there are articles concerned about the establishment of prisons, the duty of the people's policemen in prisons, the execution of criminal punishment, prison administration, education and the reform of prisoners and reform through education for juvenile delinquents. The supplementary provision follows last.
- The relevant provisions in the Criminal Code, Criminal Procedure and the People's Police Law are also the major sources of the Chinese penitentiary law. In the Chinese Criminal Code, commutation of punishment (*supra*, paragraphs 351 et

seq.) and parole (*supra*, paragraphs 355 et seq.) are closely linked with the execution of criminal punishment. In the Chinese Criminal Procedure, there is even a special part for execution (Part Four of the Criminal Procedure).

- Administrative regulations and local administrative regulations shall be deemed as part of the source of the Chinese penitentiary law. In the Chinese legal system, the administrative regulations enacted by the State Council, the rules made by ministries and commissions within the State Council and the local regulations enacted by the local legislature may be deemed as penitentiary law. For example, the Disciplinary Sanction against Misconducts of the People's Policemen for Violating Laws or Disciplines in Prisons and Organs in Charge of Reeducation through Labour, which was jointly issued in 2012 by the Ministries of Supervision, Human Resources, Social Security and the Ministry of Justice, is obviously linked with the execution of criminal punishment in prisons.
- Legal explanations, including legislative explanations, judicial explanations and administrative explanations (cf. *supra*, paragraphs 59 et seq.) are also a kind of legal sources. The judicial explanations issued by the SPC and the Supreme People's Procuratorate are commonly deemed to be within the category of prison law, at least in the broad sense, as long as they are involved in the detailed administrative work in prisons.
- International treaties concerning the management of prisons and the treatment of inmates, which have been concluded, participated or acceded by the PRC, are also sources of the Chinese penitentiary law, except for those where the PRC has its reservations. In the past three decades, the Chinese legislature has approved the accession to of a series of international human rights conventions. Among these international treaties, the Convention on the Protection of All Persons from Being Subjected to Torture and Other Cruel, Inhuman or Degrading Treatment of Punishment, which was accepted into the PRC by the approval of the Standing Committee on 5 September 1988, is very significant to the Prison Law of the PRC. The international conventions cannot be directly applied in the Chinese legal system. However, Chinese law shall adhere to the principles of the international conventions as long as China has accepted them.

Chapter 2. General Principles Concerning the Prison Law

599. The principles concerning the prison law, or the work of reform through law at the earlier time in the PRC, has progressed for a long time, since the founding of the new China. There were four stages to this development.

The first stage began in the early 1950s. The principle reasons then motivating the work of reform through labour are 'three for', i.e., for reforming criminals, for resolving the difficulties of prisons and to prevent the criminal who had been sentenced to fixed-term imprisonment becoming idle. The criminals were organised for work in the fields of production and construction, specifically engaging in water conservancy, land reclamation, road-building and mining. Through this method, new China began its work to reform criminals. However, the method of reforming criminals in the early 1950s was burdened by 'the preference of labour to reform' and reality of the phenomenon that the prisoners had to be overburdened with work. In order to overcome these problems, the policy of 'reform first and production second' was introduced.

The second stage began after the Regulations of Reform Through Labour of the People's Republic of China (cf. *supra*, paragraph 40) were adopted on the 26 August 1954. Article 4 of this Regulation provides for a 'two combination policy', i.e., that the reform through labour, carried out by the organ of the reform through labour, shall implement the guiding principles of combining custodial punishment with ideological reform and combining productive labour with political education. During this time, the task of reforming criminals had been successful in many ways. Many serious criminals were successfully reformed and became persons harmless to others and good to the society. The most famous example of the Chinese reform work was the reform of Mr Aixinjueluo Puyi, who had been the last emperor of the Chinese ancient dynasty system and who was also the emperor of the puppet state of Manchukuo set up by the Japanese in WW II. Many war criminals of Japan and the Kuomintang/Nationalist Party who were captured during the Anti-Japanese Invasion and the civil war were all gradually released by 1975, after they received ideological education and reform through labour for a period of time. The Japanese war criminals organised the Union of Returnees from China after they returned home to Japan and become an important force in fighting against aggressive war, guaranteeing world peace and promoting Sino-Japanese friendship.

The third stage began in early 1980. A new policy was worked out to combat juvenile delinquency. Based upon the new characteristics of prisoners in early 1980s, the new Chinese policy required the system 'to educate, to reclaim and to save the juvenile delinquents with patience and meticulousness, just like a parent's attitude towards their children who might suffer infectious diseases, like medical doctors towards their patients or teachers towards their students who made mistakes'. After that, the Chinese work of reform through labour began to enter a new stage of reform in modernised prisons, the focus was upon of 'establishing special schools' and 'developing modern and civilized prisons'.

The fourth stage came with the promulgation of the Prison Law. Article 1 of the CPL of 1994 sets that the Law is formulated in accordance with the Constitution for the purpose of correctly executing criminal punishments, punishing and reforming prisoners, preventing and reducing crime. The concrete expression of the general principles is in Article 3 (*infra*, paragraph 604).

600. Article 3 (In this Part, all articles without mentioning the name of the law shall only refer to the CPL of 2012) defines the principles of the CPL as follows:

> a prison shall, with regard to prisoners, implement the principle of combining punishment with reform and combining education with labour, in order to transform them into law-abiding citizens.

Accordingly, the general principles of the CPL are the following two:

- the principle of combining punishment with reform;
- the principle of combining education with labour.

However, the principles for educating and reforming juvenile delinquents have their own characteristics, i.e., more stress on education (*supra*, paragraphs 42 and 576).

601. Because crime is the conduct harmful to society (*supra*, paragraph 28), the state has to punish the criminal according to law. Prisons are the place where punishments shall be executed. It is the basic function of prisons to punish criminals. However, the purpose of punishments in China is not only to inflict punishment upon criminals. Criminal punishment is only a method rather than a purpose. In the theories of the Chinese criminal law and prison law (the law of criminal enforcement), the purpose of criminal sanction is to reform and educate criminals through punishment, so that they can be transformed into law-abiding citizens and, by this punishment, potential criminals in society might be warned, i.e., the purposes of specific prevention and general prevention shall be achieved. Therefore, it is important for Chinese prisons to stress upon themselves the need for the reformation and transformation of criminals, pure punishment only of criminals in the Chinese prisons is not allowed.

Correctly, the Chinese prisons shall have two fundamental functions: punishment and education. Punishment is the legal result of criminal conduct and the pre-condition of reforming criminals, but transforming criminals into law-abiding citizen is the final purpose of Chinese prisons in executing the punishment.

602. Education and labour are the two fundamental methods for Chinese prisons to transform criminals. In order to transform criminals, the Chinese prisons and their personnel shall not only give all inmates education of ideology, culture and technology but also organise them in a way to allow them to do productive work which is constructive to a better society. Through education and labour, prisons and their personnel can help criminals become espoused to labour, cultivate habits of regular labour and learn how to make their living in the future by some productive skill.

603. The principles of combining punishment with reform, and education with labour are based upon the successful experiences of reforming criminals in China. These principles are the concentrated reflection of the socialist characteristics of the Chinese prison system.

Chapter 3. The Prison System

§1. Classification of Penitentiary Facilities

604. As mentioned above (*supra*, paragraphs 40 and 41), the Chinese penitentiary facilities used to be named 'labour reform organs', which includes prisons, the supervision teams of reform through labour, management and education houses for juvenile delinquents and jails. The authority for reform through labour was responsible not only for the implementation of the criminal punishment given to those who were convicted and sentenced, but also for the custody of the criminal suspects and the accused persons who had not yet been tried or sentenced.

After the CPL, the Chinese concept of prison was gradually refined and now refers only to prisons and administrative and educational houses for juvenile delinquency.

Prisons refer to the places where the adult prisoners sentenced to fixed-term imprisonment, life imprisonment and the death penalty with a two-year suspension are to be implemented. According to the regulations on separate custody and separate control stipulated in the CPL, Chinese prisons are roughly classified into three categories: those for felons who were sentenced to the death penalty with two-year suspension, life imprisonment and fixed-term imprisonment of more than ten years; those for normal prisoners who were sentenced to fixed-term imprisonments of less than ten years; and those only for female adult prisoners. By 2012, there were 681 prisons in China with 1.64 million prisoners, of whom 30% had been convicted and sent to prisons for felonies and 70% for other reasons. There were thirty female only prisons in China in 2003 and 93,051 female prisoners in 2011.

Administrative and educational houses for juvenile delinquency are also known as administrative and educational houses for minors or prisons for juvenile delinquents. They are the places for keeping in custody juvenile delinquents who have reached the age of 14 but who are not yet 18. Those who have reached the age of 18 with a remaining term of less than two years may stay in administrative and educational houses until their remaining term has been served. In administrative and educational houses for juvenile delinquency, the prisoners shall be separately organised by gender for separate custody and control. The population of juvenile inmates was 18,450 in 2010 and 16,701 in 2011.

With the abolition of the system of Education through Labour at the end of 2012, came closing of the houses for Education through Labour.

In the Chinese system of criminal punishment, criminal detention is a type of short-term punishment which shall be for more than one month but less than six months. According to the CCL, a criminal sentenced to criminal detention may be allowed to go home for one or two days each month during the period of punishment and consideration may be given, according to the circumstances. In cases where one lives far away from a prison, a criminal detention may be served in a jail. After many reforms, jails are no longer under the name of prisons. Today, there are two types of jail in China. One is detention house and the other is custody house, both of them are run by the public security organ which does not belong to prisons. Detention house (Ju Liu Suo) is to detain those who are subject to administrative detention given by the public security and people's courts. Custody house (Kan Shou Suo) is mainly for those who are arrested and detained by the public security. In addition, it shall also be available for those whose punishments or whose remaining punishments are not more than one-year imprisonment.

§2. Prison Administration

605. In accordance with the Prison Law, the establishment, abolition or moving of a prison shall be subjected to the approval of the department of judicial administration under the State Council (Article 11 and also cf. *supra.* paragraph 44).

A prison shall engage one warden, several deputy wardens, and set up necessary working organs and provide other administrative personnel in light of the actual needs (Article 12).

606. In a prison, the administrative personnel are the people's police. By 2012, the total number of the people's police who acted as prison administration was 300,000.

The Prison Law explicitly provides that the activities of the people's police in prison, the administration and execution of criminal punishment, and the education and reform of prisoners conducted according to law shall be protected by law and that the people's police of a prison shall strictly abide by the Constitution and the law, be loyal to their duties, enforce the law impartially, strictly observe discipline and be honest and upright.

In addition, the Prison Law stipulates also that the people's police shall not do as follows:

- to demand, accept or seize money or goods from prisoners or their relatives;
- to release a prisoner without authorisation or through dereliction of duty to cause a prisoner to flee from the prison;
- to use torture to coerce a confession, or to use corporal punishment, or to maltreat a prisoner;
- to humiliate the human dignity of a prisoner;
- to beat or connive at others to beat a prisoner;
- to utilise a prisoner to provide labour services for personal gains;
- to privately deliver a letter or an article for a prisoner in violation of regulations;
- to illegally surrender the functions and powers to supervise and control prisoners to another person; or
- other law-breaking acts.

If the people's police of a prison commit any of these acts and the case constitutes a crime, the offenders shall be investigated for criminal responsibility. If the case does not constitute a crime, the offenders shall be given administrative sanctions (Articles 12–14).

§3. Classification of Prisoners

607. If people compare the characteristics of prisoners in China now with that of prisoners in the past, they can see great changes which reflect the development of the country.

In the 1950s–1960s, the portion of counter-revolutionary prisoners in China was very high. These counter-revolutionary prisoners were middle or old age. They were traitors to China, most of whom had defected to the Japanese in the Anti-Japanese War, had conducted espionage, or were bandits and despots, heads of reactionary superstitious sects and secret societies, and war criminals who committed crimes against the society and the new government of the PRC.

In later 1970s and early 1980s, ordinary prisoners became the majority population in Chinese prisons. There were rare additions of new counter-revolutionaries who committed crimes which endangered national security. Prisoners also became younger but there was a large proportion of illiterate prisoners.

At present time, the characteristics of prisoners in Chinese prisons are as follows:

- young prisoners still make up the majority of the whole inmates. However, the proportion of the prisoners who are under 25 years old has shown decline, which indicates that the state, schools and society have stressed their works of education and protection on the youth;
- the proportion of illiterate prisoners is still very high but the proportion of illiterate has significantly declined, which shows that the National Obligated Education Plan has worked;
- the proportion of prisoners who have come from the countryside or are jobless is still increasing, while the proportion of the prisoners who are governmental officials, students and civil servicemen is declining;
- the proportion of prisoners who have committed crimes violating property or corruption, such as robbery, theft, fraud, embezzlement, bribery and extortion, is increasing;
- the proportion of prisoners who have committed serious crimes, such as violent crimes, drug related crimes and recidivists is also increasing;
- the foreign prisoners and the prisoners from Hong Kong, Macao and Taiwan are increasing.

The new characteristics of prisoners provide many new topics for the study of prisons.

608. Classification of prisoners shall depend on certain standards. According to different standards, prisoners can be classified into different classifications:

- according to sexual distinction, prisoners can be classified as male prisoners and female prisoners;
- according to age, prisoners can be classified as adult prisoners and juvenile delinquents;
- according to the time of sentence, prisoners can be classified as first offenders and recidivists;

- according to the seriousness of sentence, prisoners can be classified as seriously sentenced prisoners and lightly sentenced prisoners. Other classifications according to this standard may include those prisoners who have been sentenced to the death penalty, life imprisonment, and so on;
- according to the types of crime, prisoners can be classified as those who have committed the crime of murder, rape, theft, assault, and so on;
- according to religions and beliefs, prisoners can be classified as ordinary prisoners and the prisoners with firm beliefs.

609. It is true that the classification of prisoners is the basis for prison administration.

The Prison Law states that a prison shall carry out separate custody and separate control with respect to male adult prisoners, female adult prisoners and juvenile delinquents. In respect of the reform of juvenile delinquents and female prisoners, special consideration shall be given to their physiological and psychological characteristics.

With respect to prisoners, a prison shall carry out separate custody and varied control on the basis of their types of crimes and punishments, terms of sentences and performances of reform.

Female prisoners shall be under the direct control of the people's policewomen (Articles 39–40).

610. In practice, Chinese prisons usually carry out 'three separations', i.e., separate custody, separate control and separate education, according to the motivation, purpose and method of committing crimes. The common classifications are as follows:

- crimes violating property;
- crimes which are sexual in nature;
- violent crimes;
- negligent crimes and crimes of dereliction of duty; and
- other crimes.

Chapter 4. The Penitentiary Regime

§1. Introduction

611. Briefly speaking, prison in China shall undertake the following tasks:

- to guarantee the correct execution of punishment imposed upon criminals;
- to maintain the safety of the penitentiary places;
- to create a good environment for reform; and
- to manage the standards of prisoners' living and sanitation.

In China, it is generally agreed that prisons have three functions:

- to punish;
- to correct and to cultivate; and
- to guarantee.

It is evident that all the tasks and functions of the Chinese prison shall be carried out by lawful management, strict management, scientific management and direct management.

In order to ensure that prisons shall be able to fulfil their tasks and functions, Article 8 of the Prison Law states that:

> the state shall ensure the expenditures of a prison for the reform of prisoners. The prisons' expenditures for the people's police, for the reform of prisoners, for the living expenses of prisoners, for the administration and installations of the prisons, and other special expenses shall be included into the state budget.

§2. Guard

612. The guard of prisons in China is taken by the PAPFs. The people's armed police is responsible for the external safety of prisons and shall not be involved in the internal administration of prisons.

However, the whole guarding system around a prison is composed of three lines of defence.

The first line is the guarding line of the prison area. Behind this line is the inner part of a prison which shall be guarded by the personnel of the prison. The principal tasks behind this line are as follows:

- to manage all prisoners within this area, including the management of the time for work and rest and to keep all prisoners under control;
- to control the entrance of a prison, including the checks of permits and registration; and

– to manage the confinement room.

The second line is beyond the first line. This is the area where no ordinary people are allowed to enter and which is guarded by the people's armed police. Article 43 of the Prison Law provides that a prison shall set up guard installations according to the needs of supervision and control. The guard segregation zone around a prison shall be restricted. No one shall enter into such zone without permission. The principal tasks within this area are as follows:

– to guard prisoners when they are working or transferred under escort;
– to guard the gate of a prison;
– to report and to catch the escaped prisoners;
– to suppress any disturbance or riot in prison;
– to rescue prisoners and the property of the prison in the occurrence of natural calamities or incidents;
– to defend against illegal attack from outside.

The third line is commonly called the people's supervision, which means that the organisations, enterprises and institutions as well as the people around or near a prison shall be encouraged or organised to assist the prison in the maintenance of its safety and guard. Article 44 of the Prison Law stipulates that state organs, public organisations, enterprises, institutions and grass-roots organisations in the neighbourhood of a prison or its operation areas, shall assist the prison in its security work.

Generally speaking, these guarding systems work well in practice.

613. The Prison Law permits a prison to use restraint implements under any of the following circumstances:

– if a prisoner commits any attempt of escape;
– if a prisoner commits any acts of violence;
– if a prisoner is being escorted; or
– if a prisoner commits other dangerous acts against which it is necessary to take precautions.

However, restraint implements shall not be used after the circumstance returns to normal (Article 45).

614. The Prison Law permits the personnel on duty of the people's police or the PAPF to use weapons according to the relevant regulations of the state under any of the following circumstances, which cannot be rectified without the use of weapons:

– if any prisoner is assembling a crowd to start a riot or rebellion;
– if any prisoner is escaping or resisting arrest;
– if any prisoner is committing physical assault or destruction with a lethal weapon or other dangerous articles to endanger the safety of another person's life or property;
– if any prisoner is being seized and rescued by force; or
– if any prisoner is seizing a weapon by force.

When using weapons, the policemen should keep the crimes and violations under control and minimise the losses of injury, life and property. It is also a legal requirement for the personnel who have used their weapons to report those situations, according to the relevant regulations of the state (Article 46).

615. A confinement room may be set up by prisons to punish a prisoner who has seriously violated the rules and disciplines of the prison (Article 58).

The confinement room shall be not smaller than $3m^2$, lower than 3m and the window shall not be smaller than $0.8m^2$.

According to the Prison Law, the confinement room shall only be applied to the following prisoners when the misconducts are serious but not yet constitute a type of new crime (Article 58):

- assembling a crowd to disturb the order of the prison;
- abusing or beating the people's police; bullying other prisoners; stealing, gambling, coming to blows, or stirring up fights and causing troubles;
- refusing to do work without sound reasons and refusing to mend his ways even after education; escaping from doing work by means of self-injury or self-mutilation; intentionally violating the operation rules in productive work or intentionally destroying tools of production;
- other acts violating the rules and discipline of the prison.

The confinement room for the prisons are usually seven to fifteen days.

§3. Visits, Correspondence and Request for Leave

616. Correspondence is one of the rights a prisoner can have in prison.

In accordance with the Prison Law, a prisoner may correspond with others during the service of his sentence but said correspondence shall be examined by the prison. If the prison discovers that the contents of a letter present a hindrance to the reform of the prisoner, the prison may detain the letter. Letters from a prisoner to the higher authorities of the prison or to the judicial organs shall be free from examination (Article 47).

In practice, a prisoner is generally allowed to send one letter per month. Under special circumstance, he may send more with the permission of the prison.

The correspondence of prisoners shall not be allowed to use the name of the prison in the letter or on the envelope and shall only use a special number of mail box.

Prisoners were usually not allowed to use the telephone in prison but recent developments have changed this situation. Now, prisoners will be allowed to call persons outside of the prison with the approval of the prison authority. This new policy brings the prisoners closer with their family and enhances the effect of education and reform.

617. It is stipulated in the Prison Law that a prisoner may meet with his relatives and guardians during the service of his sentence (Article 48). However, other people are usually not allowed to meet a prisoner.

Usually, a prisoner may meet with relatives and guardians once or twice in a month and each time shall not be longer than one hour. The prisoner who is being held in the confinement room is not generally allowed to meet his relatives and guardian.

Any things given by visitors to a prisoner shall be permitted but examined by the prison. Cash shall be deposited in a bank and can be used by the prisoner for due purpose. All property will be returned to the prisoner when he is released.

The visitors from out of town will be housed by the prison. Usually, the personnel of the prison shall actively inform them about the rule for visitors, as well as the performance of the prisoner, so that the relatives and guardian may help the prison to give the prisoner good advice and education. There were some experiments in Chinese prisons which allowed prisoners who had good performance to stay overnight with their spouses in the prison's guest houses. However, this practice is under strict control.

618. Article 49 of the Prison Law states that goods or money to be received by a prisoner shall be subject to the approval and examination of the prison.

619. In principle, prisoners are not allowed to leave the prison for home when serving their sentence. New reform has taken place since early 1990s and so, today, in accordance with the Prison Law, prisoners who have been sentenced to fixed-term imprisonment may under special circumstances (*infra*, paragraph 629) leave the prison for the purpose of visiting family members or relatives, if they have served more than half of the original term of their sentence, has always shown good performances during imprisonment and if their leaving the prison will no longer endanger the society (Article 57).

In practice, in the following situations, prisoners shall usually not be allowed to visit home:

- the crime committed by the criminal were those endangering national security;
- the prisoner whose sentence is the death penalty with a suspension of execution.

The common examples of the events allowing a prisoner to go home are as follows:

- the direct relatives of a prisoner are terminally ill such as one's husband or wife, father, mother, sons and daughters;
- the direct relatives of a prisoner are dying or dead;
- other substantial circumstances.

620. The term of a prisoner to go home is usually three to five days and can be a maximum of seven days. When a prisoner applies to go home, he shall show the certificate issued by the people's government at the level above the township or the public security organ. He cannot go home without the permission of the warden.

The prisoner shall pay the travel expenses himself. When he cannot afford that, the prison may give him some expenses.

§4. Life and Health

621. The life and health of a prisoner shall be managed by the following systems in the prison:

- management system of work and rest;
- management system of food;
- management system of clothing;
- management system of house; and
- management system of medical care and sanitation.

622. In accordance with Article 71 of the Prison Law, a prison shall make reference to the state's relevant regulations on working hours with regard to the working hours of prisoners. Under special circumstances such as seasonal production, the working hours may be readjusted. Prisoners shall have the right to rest on statutory festivals and holiday.

Usually, prisoners shall work for eight hours and study for two hours on a weekday. The juvenile delinquents shall only work half days but also study for half the day.

623. Article 50 of the Prison Law provides that the living standard of prisoners shall be measured by the quantity of material objects, and it shall be set by the state.

Accordingly, prisons shall provide enough drinking water, water for washing in dining rooms, living houses and working places. The living habits of those prisoners who belong to a minority nationality shall be cared for. The special habits and customs of prisoners of minority ethnic groups shall be given consideration (Article 52). Prisoners will be selected in order to form a committee which will assist the prison in managing foods. The mass accounts shall be published every month.

624. Article 51 of the Prison Law provides that the bedding and clothing of prisoners shall be uniformly rationed and provided by the prison. But the words 'criminal' or 'prisoner' is forbidden to be printed on the clothes.

625. Article 53 of the Prison Law requires that the wards of a prison are solid, ventilated, clean, warm and have the possibility for natural light to come in. Usually, a prisoner shall have a living area of not less than $3m^2$.

626. In accordance with the Prison Law, a prison shall set up medical organs and living and sanitary facilities, and institute regulations on the life and sanitation of prisoners. Medical and health care of prisoners shall be put into the public health and epidemic prevention programme of the area in which the prison is located (Article 54).

When a criminal is handed over for the execution of his criminal punishment sentence, the prison shall give him a physical examination. A criminal sentenced to life imprisonment or fixed-term imprisonment may, after physical examination, temporarily not be put into prison under either of the following circumstances:

- if he is seriously ill and needs to be released on parole for medical treatment; or
- if she is pregnant or a woman who is breastfeeding her own baby (Article 17).

A criminal may not bring his or her child with him or her to serve sentence in prison (Article 19).

627. If a prisoner dies during imprisonment, the prison shall immediately inform the prisoner's family members, the people's procuratorate and the people's court. If a prisoner dies from a disease, the prison shall make a medical appraisal. If the people's procuratorate is suspicious of the prison's medical appraisal, it may make an appraisal anew on the cause of the death. If the family members of the prisoner are suspicious of the prison's medical appraisal, they may raise their suspicion to the people's procuratorate. If a prisoner dies an abnormal death, the people's procuratorate shall immediately conduct examinations and make an appraisal on the cause of the death (Article 55 of the Prison Law).

§5. Disciplinary Measures

628. The Prison Law requires that a prison shall establish a routine check-up system for prisoners. The result of such check-ups shall be taken as the basis for awarding or punishing prisoners (Article 56).

Accordingly, the routine check-up system for prisoners has been popularly established in prisons. The principal methods of the system are the following:

- combining the checks in normal time with that at regular intervals. In Chinese prisons, checks shall be done daily, weekly, monthly, quarterly, half yearly and annually;
- combining the checks by the personnel of the prison with the appraisals made by other prisoners;
- combining the analysis of nature with the checks based upon points.

The checks are based upon the so-called system of prisoner evaluation by points. This system is closely guided by the Code of Conduct for the Prisoners (*infra*, paragraph 646). The performance of each prisoner will be dispersed into various detailed indicators and each indicator shall be given a reasonable point. The system is formed by this set of quantitative indicators of assessment and shall be used to evaluate the performance/behaviour of prisoners while in custody. This system shall completely cover the whole conduct of a prisoner in a prison, which can be generally divided into two parts: ideological reform and labour reform. The points shall be allocated about 55% for former and 45% for the latter. Ideological reform refers to the conducts such as such as admitting the guilt, obeying the rules and disciplines of the prison, education of politics, culture and productive skills, living sanitation, attitude toward labour, costs of production, labour discipline, and safe production. Labour reform refers to those conducts such as: working actively, limiting the cost of material under the standard, increasing production, practising efficiency and avoiding production accidents. Each item shall be affixed by a certain amount of points and the total is 100. A prisoner will earn or lose certain points in each aspect. Of course, the more points a prisoner obtains, the better it indicates his performance is in the prison. If a prisoner disagrees with a result of the checking, he shall have the right to defend himself. For those who have reached a certain amount of points, the prison shall give him punishment or reward, and may even provide the suggestion of parole or commutation of punishment.

629. In accordance with the Prison Law, the prison may command or award a prisoner, or record a merit for him, if it is under one of the following circumstances:

- if a prisoner observes the rules and discipline of the prison, studies hard, takes an active part in labour and shows admission of guilt and acceptance of the judgment;
- if a prisoner has stopped any law-breaking or criminal activities;
- if a prisoner has over fulfilled his production quota;
- if a prisoner has made achievements in saving on raw materials or caring for public property;
- if a prisoner has achieved certain success in technical renovation or passing on his production skill;
- if a prisoner has made contributions in preventing or removing a disastrous accident; or
- if a prisoner has made other contributions to the state and the society (Article 57).

630. The Prison Law also states that if a prisoner has committed one of the following acts obstructing the order of supervision and control, the prison may give him a warning, demerit-recording or solitary confinement:

- assembling a crowd to disrupt the order of the prison;
- abusing or beating the people's police;
- bullying other prisoners;
- stealing, gambling, coming to blows, or starting fights and causing troubles;
- refusing to do labour though he has the ability to work or slacking in work and refusing to mend his ways even after education;
- escaping from doing labour by means of self-injury or self-mutilation;
- intentionally violating the operation rules in productive labour or intentionally destroying tools of production; or
- other acts violating the rules and discipline of the prison.

The term of solitary confinement imposed on a prisoner shall be from seven to fifteen days.

If a prisoner has committed any act mentioned above during his service of the sentence, and if the case constitutes a crime, he shall be investigated for criminal responsibility according to law (Article 58). If a prisoner intentionally commits a crime during the service of his sentence, he shall be given a heavier punishment according to law (Article 59).

A criminal act committed by a prisoner in the prison shall be investigated by the prison. On the conclusion of the investigation, a recommendation for prosecution or a recommendation for exemption from prosecution written by the prison together with the case file and the evidence shall be handed over to a people's procuratorate (Article 60).

§6. Prison Labour

631. In accordance with Article 3 of the Prison Law (*supra*, paragraph 604), prison labour is the fundamental method to reform criminals in China. Labour includes physical labour and mental work. Prison labour usually is physical labour and mental work is very rare. Article 69 also requires that any able-bodied prisoner to do labour.

In order to maintain prison labour, Article 8 of the Prison Law states that the state shall provide production facilities and production expenses necessary for prisons to do labour.

632. The functions of prison labour are as follows:

- to reform the ideology of criminals;
- to correct the wrong habits of prisoners and to cultivate the right one;
- to keep prisoners in good health;
- to help prisoners learn a type of productive skill which can be useful to them after they are released from the prison;
- to create certain property for the society.

In practice, prison labour shall observe the following principles:

- to be conducive to reforming criminals;
- to combine labour with education;
- to follow the economic rule to produce;
- to organise prison labour according to the characteristics of prisoners.

It is also a legal requirement that a prison shall, in light of the individual conditions of prisoners, rationally organise them to do labour so as to correct their bad habits, to cultivate habits of working, to acquire production skills and to create conditions for employment after their release (Article 70). China has strictly prohibited anyone from organising prisoners to do labour which is poisonous, contaminating, flammable or explosive and it has sped up steps to withdraw prisoners from dangerous enterprises such as coal mining. Chinese prisons have gradually reached their reform goal is 'to separate prisons from enterprises' and the approval system for the prisoners' work programmes, has been further strengthened. During labour, prisoners are entitled to the right of safe working conditions and the right to rest, by reference to the State's regulations on working hours.

633. It is quite common in Chinese prisons for the system of education and reform to be organised as five days work, one day of classroom education and one day of rest each week. Chinese prisons always carry out a system of paid labour for prisoners. The Prison Law requires that prisons pay a remuneration to the prisoners who take part in labour according to the relevant regulations and implement relevant regulations on labour protection. However, prisoners' labour is compulsory. The labour is particularly different from normal labour in society in terms of organisation, contents of work and standards of compensation. Furthermore, the compensation the prisoners earn from their work cannot be spent freely in prison, except for a part approved for prison use, the rest is to be deposited into a bank and will be given back to the prisoners when they are released.

§7. Prison Education

634. Prison education refers to the education of ideology, culture and productive skill. This is an important part in the education and reform of prisoners. Compared with the normal education, prison education has the following characteristics:

- it is carried out or organised by penitentiary facilities;
- it is only for prisoners;
- it is to correct the ideology and behaviour of prisoners, in order to prevent and reduce crime;
- it will be focussed on ideology, culture and productive skill;
- it is a kind of compulsory education and shall be combined with prison labour.

635. The Prison Law requires that in the education and reform of prisoners, the principle of suiting education to different persons and cases, persuading prisoners through reasoning shall and the method of combining collective education with individual education and combining education by the prison with education by the society shall be adopted (Article 61).

636. A prison shall carry out ideological education among prisoners in the context of legality, morality, current situations, policies and outlook on their future, in accordance with Article 62 of the Prison Law. The purposes of ideological education are as following:

- to cultivate prisoners' views on obeying laws by teaching them the basic legal knowledge of daily life in terms of criminal law, criminal procedure, civil law and marriage law, etc.;
- to gradually improve the prisoners' moral character and behaviour by giving them guidance of the right patterns of morality and behaviour and correcting their immoral and uncontrolled conduct over time;
- to encourage prisoners to lead to a new life and a bright future by piloting them to understand the state's important policy, current political and economic situation, and the state's policy in reforming criminals, in order to inspire them to understand the relations between their personal futures and the national future and the reasons why a person's individual pursuit shall be in line with the rule of social development.

637. In China, illiteracy is one of the main cause of crimes. Therefore, the Prison Law provides that a prison shall carry out literacy education, primary education and junior secondary education in light of different conditions of prisoners. If a prisoner has passed due examinations, the educational department shall issue him the corresponding certificate of education (Article 63). Meanwhile, prisoners are encouraged to study the courses at a university or college level, if they are qualified.

638. In order to help prisoners have a productive skill after being released, the Prison Law provides that a prison shall carry out occupational and technical education among prisoners in accordance with the needs of production in the prison and of employment after their release. If a prisoner has passed due examination and verification, the labour department shall issue him the corresponding certificate of technical grade (Article 64).

Literacy education and the occupational and technical education of prisoners shall be integrated into the local education programmes.

639. A prison shall encourage prisoners to study on their own. If a prisoner has passed due examinations, the relevant department shall issue him the corresponding certificate (Article 65 of the Prison Law).

640. In order to help prisoners to study, the Prison Law requires that the cultural, occupational and technical education of prisoners shall be included into the educational plan of the area where the prison is located.

A prison shall have necessary educational facilities such as classrooms and reading rooms (Article 66).

A prison shall organise prisoners to conduct proper sport activities and cultural recreations (Article 67).

The work of educating and reforming prisoners is usually conducted though methods which combine collective education (collective classes) with individual education (individual tutorials), uniting prison education with local education. The prison will invite social workers to give lectures or to have discussions with prisoners, while combining formal education (formal classes) with supplementary education (blackboard information, wall newspapers, culture and sports activities, etc.). Various methods of education and reform have been invented by the working staff in prisons and they often work well in practice.

641. State organs, public organisations, units of armed forces, enterprises, institutions, personage of various circles and family members or relatives of prisoners shall assist prisons in doing a good job in the education and reform of prisoners (Article 68 of the Prison Law).

From 2008 to 2012, Chinese prisons completed literacy education and compulsory education for more than 1.25 million prisoners, of whom 98.1% received a certificate of qualification for popular legal education and about 5,800 received certificates of graduation from qualifications above the level of college education. Meanwhile, there were more than 30,000 programmes of various types of technical training held in prisons and 77.3% of the prisoners who participated in the training obtained various types of occupational and technical certificates.

§8. Education and Reform of Juvenile Delinquents

642. Juvenile delinquents have been different from adult prisoners in many ways, so the Prison Law contains a specific chapter for their education and reform (Chapter 6).

643. Juvenile delinquents shall not be kept in custody with adult prisoners. It is the legal requirement that the criminal punishment of juvenile delinquents shall be executed in the reformatories for juvenile delinquents (Article 74). If a juvenile delinquent has reached the age of 18 and the remaining term of his sentence does not exceed two years, he may still be kept in the reformatory for juvenile delinquents for the execution of the remaining term of his sentence (Article 76).

644. The execution of punishment for juvenile delinquents shall also differ from that of adult prisoners. The focus in the execution of criminal punishment for juvenile delinquents shall be on education and reform. Labour for juvenile delinquents shall conform to the characteristics of minors and its main objectives shall be to help the juvenile delinquents to acquire an elementary education and production skills. A prison shall co-ordinate with the state, society and educational institutions, such as schools, in providing necessary conditions for juvenile delinquents to receive compulsory education (Article 75 of the Prison Law).

645. In the Outline of Education and the Reform of Prisoners, compiled by the Chinese Ministry of Justice, it is stipulated that the juvenile delinquents under the age of 16 shall not participate in Education through Labour. In addition, while the teaching hours for adult prisoners are not less than 500 class hours per year, the teaching hours for the minors' ideological, cultural and technical education shall not be less than 1,000 class hours per year. In practice, Chinese prisons will, in the light of the characteristics of juvenile delinquents, pay special attention to encourage the community, especially the family of the juvenile delinquents, to jointly care, help and support the work of education and reform for the juvenile delinquents. These programmes work well; during the period of 2002–2012, the recidivist rate of juvenile delinquents was generally controlled by 1%–2%. Since 2010, the criminal cases of juvenile delinquency have declined and the number of juvenile delinquents has been limited to around 6% of all criminals.

§9. PRISONER'S RIGHTS AND DUTIES

646. A prisoner, as a citizen of the PRC, can still enjoy certain types of rights. However, in comparison with the ordinary citizen a prisoner has the following rights:

- A prisoner's rights are incomplete, i.e., his personal freedom has been lawfully deprived and those prisoners whose political rights have also been deprived cannot enjoy these rights during the term when they are in prison and for a certain term after being released.
- The exercise of a prisoner's rights is limited. For example, the prisoners whose political rights were deprived may not exercise the rights of freedom of speech, of the press, of assembly, of association, of procession and of demonstration in a prison, however, he can still enjoy the right of election.
- A prisoner has specific rights and duties, e.g., the rights to meet his family members regularly and to receive commutation of punishment or parole and the duties to observe the rules and regulation of the prison and to accept the education and reform.
- The duties of a prisoner are compulsory. Article 7 of the Prison Law stipulates that a prisoner must strictly observe laws, regulations, and rules and discipline

of the prison, subject himself to control, accept education and take part in labour. The Code of Conduct for the Prisoners (hereinafter: the Code of Conduct) issued by the Chinese Ministry of Justice in 2004 has provided a unified standard for the assessment and judgment of the prisoners' performance/behaviour in prisons. The Code of Conduct is composed of five chapters with thirty-eight articles, including a general standard and the standards of life, study, labour and civilised manners. Together with other disciplines issued by prisons, this Code of Conduct shall play a very positive role in encouraging the prisoners to carry out their reformation/rehabilitation.

647. In accordance with the Prison Law, the human dignity of a prisoner shall not be humiliated, and his personal safety, lawful properties, and rights to defence, petition, complaint and accusation as well as other rights which he has not been deprived or restricted of according to law, shall not be violated (Article 7). According to the Chinese Constitution, Criminal Law, Criminal Procedure, Prison Law and other legal regulations, the main rights a prisoner shall enjoy are as followings:

- right of personality against humiliation;
- right of personal safety against violation;
- right of lawful property against violation;
- right of defence;
- right to make complaints, charges or reports;
- right of the material treatment necessary in their daily lives;
- right of communication and meeting with a defender, guardian and relatives;
- right to receive education;
- right of safety in labour;
- right to rest;
- right to receive commutation or parole or other awards;
- right of freedom of religious belief;
- right of lawful marriage against interruption of destroying.

In addition, a prisoner might be entitled to rights which are not legally deprived or restricted. For example, a prisoner shall have the right of election if he was not sentenced to deprivation of political rights as a supplementary punishment.

Besides all that, Article 38 of the CPL states that a person released after serving his sentence shall enjoy equal rights with other citizens in accordance with the law.

648. If a prisoner is not satisfied with the effective judgment, he may file a petition. A prison shall transfer without delay the petitions, complaints and accusations made by prisoners and shall not withhold them. A people's procuratorate or a people's court shall without delay handle the petitions filed by prisoners. The public security organ or the people's procuratorate shall inform the prison of the result (Articles 21–23).

Chapter 5. Release and Resettlement

§1. Early Release

649. A prisoner may legally leave the prison where he serves his sentence before he has completed his term of sentence, temporarily or finally.

Strictly speaking, the request for leave (*supra*, paragraph 619) is not a kind of release, though the prisoner does temporarily leave a prison for home.

650. Generally, execution outside prison is not a kind of early release in China, though the criminal goes home too after he is sentenced.

In accordance with Article 254 of the Criminal Procedure of 2012, a criminal sentenced to fixed-term imprisonment or criminal detention, under one of the following conditions, may be permitted to temporarily serve his sentence outside prison:

- if the criminal is seriously ill and needs to be released on parole for medical treatment;
- if the criminal is pregnant or is breastfeeding her own baby. This condition shall also apply to the female criminal who has been sentenced to life imprisonment who is pregnant or is breastfeeding her own baby;
- if the criminal cannot live alone by himself and will not cause any danger to the society by temporarily serving his term outside prison; or
- if the criminal is seriously ill and needs to be released on bail for medical treatment with a certification document given by a hospital designated by the people's government at the provincial level after diagnosis.

Besides that, those who have reached the age of 60, suffer from illness and have lost the likelihood to harm society and those who have lost the ability to labour due to a physical disability, may be allowed to temporarily serve their sentences outside prison in practice.

However, the Chinese Code of Criminal Procedure of 2012 explicitly provides that those convicted persons may not be released on bail for medical treatment, if they may cause any danger to the society or they may intentionally inflict injury or disability to themselves (Article 254 of the CCP).

Execution outside prison may be decided by the people's court or by the administrative organ of prisons at the provincial level. According to the legislative explanation of 2014, the people's court shall be responsible for organising the relevant disease diagnosis, pregnancy check or evaluation of inability to take care of oneself for those who have not yet been delivered to a prison for the execution of a sentence, if a convict files an application to be able to temporarily serve his or her sentence outside prison in accordance with the law. The people's court may also directly decide to allow an execution outside prison in the judgment if it discovered that the defendant fulfilled the legal conditions for this execution outside prison before the judgment is made. A prison may submit its report to the administrative organ of prisons at the provincial level, if it discovered that a prisoner in the prison fulfils the legal conditions while he is serving his sentence.

Those who are allowed to temporarily serve their sentences outside prison shall be subject to community correction, which is the responsibility of the local station of the justice administration.

In accordance with the Criminal Procedure of 2012, as soon as the conditions under which a criminal is permitted to serve his sentence outside prison temporarily cease to exist or the criminal seriously violates the regulations of supervision and management, he shall be taken back to prison without delay, if his term of sentence has not expired (Article 257 of the 2012 CCP). According to the legislative explanation of 2014, it is the public security organ who shall be responsible to deliver the criminal to prison, if the people's court makes the decision to take him back into custody due to the requirement of Article 257 of 2012 CCP.

651. The real early release can only occur in the cases of commutation of punishment (*supra*, paragraphs 351 et seq.) and parole (*supra*, paragraphs 355 et seq.) in accordance with the Chinese laws.

§2. Release and Resettlement

652. Release and resettlement are not in the works of execution of sentence. However, they have very close relations with execution. Criminal punishments will have a great impact upon an individual. According to Chinese laws, for example, those who were sentenced to deprivation of political rights or, due to an intentional crime, a criminal punishment above a fixed-term imprisonment, cannot ever acquire or continue any qualification as a teacher. Those who were convicted and sentenced to criminal punishment cannot become policemen, judges, prosecutors and governmental officials, while those who were convicted of an intentional crime and sentenced to any kind of criminal punishment cannot practice as a lawyer. Those who received criminal punishment also cannot practice as a licensed medical doctor within two years after their terms are completed, and so on. Article 100 of the 1997 CCC sets that those who once received criminal punishment according to law shall factually report to the relevant units the penalties they had received without concealing any of them, whenever they join the military or seek employment. Only those who were younger than 18 when committing the crime and who had not received a criminal punishment of more than a five-year fixed-term imprisonment may be exempted from this obligation of reporting. The system of resettlement after completely serving the term of a sentence is a special system in which prisons together with other relevant governmental units and social organisations help the person released resolve the problems of residential registration and employment, so that they can begin their new lives and jobs.

In the Prison Law, there are some important provisions about this system. First of all, if a prisoner has completed the service of his sentence, the prison shall release him as scheduled and issue him a certificate of release (Article 35). Before release, the prison shall provide some education regarding release to the prisoners who will soon be completing their terms, then make an appraisal for performance during their time in prison, inform the public security authorities of the places where they will return, and co-ordinate with other units and organisations to resolve specific problems in the settlement and the education through assistance. For those who have seriously evil habits, who were not satisfactorily affected by the education and who therefore have recidivist tendencies, the prison shall alert the local public security of the necessity of careful management, so that these kinds of persons will not be out of supervision and control.

653. After a prisoner is released and on the strength of the certificate of release, the public security organ shall make residence registration for him (Article 36 of the Prison Law). At this point, the release is complete and resettlement begins (cf. *supra*, paragraphs 44 et seq.). After 2009 when the system of community correction was put into trial use nationwide, resettlement has become the most important part of that system in the local level. Various governmental agencies are involved: Labour offices shall provide them with employment guidance and skill training and issue doles, according to the regulations, to those who have participated in the programme of unemployment insurance. Offices of industrial and commercial administrations shall treat equally the applications submitted by those who want to open an individual business or other economic entity and protect their lawful interests as well as work with other organisations in order to ascertain the security responsibility system and to ensure their operations are complying with law. Offices of civil administration shall encourage the local economic entities to help with the settlement. Public security stations shall establish a responsibility system to help and educate the released persons. Prisons shall carry out a system of regular inspection and local feedback for those who are released during the first three years. China is trying to establish a system which is organised by prisons, local governments, employment units and the families of the released persons, so that they can receive better help and education.

654. With respect to a person released after serving his sentence, the local people's government shall assist him in resettling. If a person released after serving his sentence has lost his ability to labour, and has no statutory supporters or basic source of income, the local people's government shall offer him relief (Article 37 of the Prison Law). By 2011, there were 3.8 million released persons, of whom 1.95 million received help and education and 1.68 million were effectively settled. The recidivist rate of these persons is 0.9%.

655. A person released after serving his sentence shall enjoy equal rights with other citizens according to the law (Article 38 of the Prison Law).

Chapter 6. Extinction of Sentences

656. In accordance with the Chinese laws, extinction of sentences shall occur under one of the following circumstances:

- A sentenced punishment is completed.
- Upon the expiration of the probation period for sentence suspension, a criminal whose sentence is suspended does not commit a crime again or it is not discovered that he has committed another crime for which he is not sentenced before the judgment is pronounced. In addition, he does not seriously violate laws, administrative rules and regulations or regulations relating to supervision and control over suspension of sentence stipulated by the department of public security under the State Council.
- After commutation, there is no remaining punishment to be executed.
- Upon the expiration of the probation period for parole, a criminal who is granted parole is not found to have committed a new crime or it is not discovered that he has committed another crime for which he is not sentenced before the judgment is pronounced. In addition, he does not seriously violate laws, administrative rules and regulations or regulations relating to parole and control over parole stipulated by the department of public security under the State Council.
- He is pardoned.

657. It shall be noticed that the Chinese punishment system in the Chinese criminal law is composed of principal punishments and supplementary punishments (*supra*, paragraphs 275 et seq.). Therefore, if the sentenced punishments upon a criminal include a principal punishment and a supplementary punishment, they shall be finally extinct only when both principal and supplementary punishments are executed.

658. With respect to pardon, there are general pardons, which apply to all criminals, and special pardons, which apply to specific criminals.

In the Chinese legal system, only the Constitution of 1954 stipulated the powers of both the general pardon and special pardon. However, only the special pardon was exercised and the general pardon has never been practised. In the Constitutions of 1975, 1978 and 1982, there is only the provision for the special pardon and none for the general pardon.

To this day the special pardon has been issued seven times in the PRC:

- 17 September 1959, for the war criminals, counter-revolutionary criminals and ordinary criminals of Kuomingtang (Nationalist Party) Group and the puppet Manchuria Nation who did abandon evil and do good after reform through labour; this first special pardon was exercised to celebrate the tenth anniversary of the founding of the PRC;
- 19 December 1960 and 16 November 1961, for the war criminals of Kuomingtang (Nationalist Party) Group and the puppet Manchuria Nation who did abandon evil and do good after reform through labour;

- 30 March 1963, 12 November 1964 and 29 March 1966, for the war criminals of Kuomingtang (Nationalist Party) Group, the puppet Manchuria Nation and the puppet Mongolia-Xinjiang government who did abandon evil and do good after reform through labour;
- 17 March 1975, for all remaining war criminals.

All these special pardons were based upon the suggestions of the Central Committee of the Communist Party or the State Council, decided by the Standing Committee of the NPC and issued by the Order of Special Pardon by the President of the PRC (except for the time of 1975 when the PRC did not have a President).

According to the current Constitution of 1982, the power to decide special pardons belongs to the Standing Committee of the NPC. The Order of Special Pardon shall be issued by the President of the PRC. In practice, the execution organs for special pardon are the SPC and the higher people's courts and the concrete legal procedures for special pardon shall be handled by the prison authority.

So, the pardon mentioned in the Chinese law refers only to special pardon.

659. With respect to death penalty with immediate execution, the sentence may be extinct when it is executed or changed.

In accordance with the Criminal Procedure, when a judgment of the death penalty with immediate execution is pronounced or approved by the SPC, the President of the SPC shall sign and issue an order to execute the death sentence.

After receiving an order from the SPC to carry out the sentence, the People's Court at a lower level shall carry out the sentence within seven days. However, under one of the following conditions below the People's Court at a lower level shall suspend execution and immediately submit a report to the SPC for an order:

(1) if it is discovered before the execution of the sentence that the judgment may contain an error;
(2) if, before the execution of the sentence, the criminal exposes major criminal facts or renders other significantly meritorious services, thus creating a chance that the sentence may need to be revised; or
(3) if the criminal is pregnant.

If the reason given in (1) or (2) of the preceding paragraph which caused the suspension of the sentence disappears, the sentence may be executed only after a report is submitted to the President of the SPC for him to sign and issue another order for execution of the death sentence. If execution is suspended for the reason given in (3) of the preceding paragraph, a request shall be submitted to the SPC for it to alter the sentence according to law.

Before a people's court causes a death sentence to be executed, it shall notify the people's procuratorate at the same level to send an officer to supervise the execution. A death sentence shall be executed by such means as shooting or injection. After a death sentence is executed, the court clerk on the scene shall prepare a written record of it. The people's court that caused the death sentence to be executed shall submit a report on the execution to the SPC (Articles 210–212).

General Conclusion

660. The foregoing overview of substantial criminal law, criminal procedure and the execution of punishment may present you a general picture of the Criminal Justice System in the PRC.

After 1979 when China began to carry out the policy of opening up to the outside and reforming the old and out-of-date system, Chinese society has been progressing and flourishing. But at the same time, the demands for legal protection, including the protection of criminal law, are also increasing. The great expansion of economic crime, including crimes violating intellectual property, security fraud, etc. in the Criminal Code of 1997 is a good example. However, the theoretical structure of the Chinese criminal law has begun to change significantly, after a long-held desire for reform. It is a tough job for the leadership to correctly and appropriately protect this country, which has the largest population in the world and the longest history of criminal law, with criminal sanctions. There are still many fields to be improved. But maybe we can still say that the development of the Chinese criminal law does keep abreast of the times, at least in the direction the times require.

In respect of the criminal procedure law, the rights of a defendant and a victim are significantly improved now and the role of the defender, especially lawyers, is enhanced in the criminal process, compared with the Criminal Procedure of 1979 and 1996. We can also see that the Chinese criminal procedure is changing from the judge-guided system, which is one of many characteristics of inquisitorial system, into the judge-in-neutral system, which is more similar to the adversarial system. However, the reform of Chinese criminal procedure is not yet complete.

The trends in the execution of criminal sanctions in China seem not to have changed too much, though the law of reform through labour has been replaced by the Prison Law and the system of Education through Labour has been abolished. The focus of the execution is still on reform and education, while the function of punishment is still evident. The system of community correction has been established. The death penalty is gradually decreasing, both in the number in the law and in legal practice. The abolition of death penalty has actually begun. The embedment of resettlement of the prisoner who was released from prison after he had served his sentence into the system of execution does make the execution of the Chinese criminal sanction full of human sympathy and quite successful, though its practice will meet more new problems in a new society with a market economy.

Anyway, it is true that the Chinese Criminal Justice System is still under reform. It appears to have become more comparable to that of other countries in many respects while it retains many characteristics of China.

Selected Bibliography

I. Legislative References

The Legislative Commission of the Standing Committee of the National People's Congress of the People's Republic of China, *The Laws of the People's Republic of China* (in English), Foreign Languages Press, Beijing (since 1979).

Bureau of Legislative Affairs of the State Council of the People's Republic of China, *The Collection of the New Laws and Regulations of the People's Republic of China* (since 1988).

II. Official Documents

The Report of the Supreme People's Court of the People's Republic of China (since 1985).

The Report of the Supreme People's Procuratorate of the People's Republic of China (since 1987).

The Supreme People's Court, *The Judicial Explanation of the Supreme People's Court of the People's Republic of China* (Looseleaf), The Press of People's Court and the Press of Law, 1997.

III. Website

http://www.lawinfochina.com

IV. Books

Chen Guangzhong, Editor, *Science of Criminal Procedure (5th Edition), Textbook Series for 21 Century*, The Press of Peking University & Higher Education Press, 2013.

Compiling Committee of Peking University Encyclopedia, *Peking University Encyclopedia: Criminal Law, Criminology and Penology*, The Press of Peking University, 2003.

Gao Mingxuan & Ma Kechang, Editor, *Criminal Law (6th Edition), Textbook Series for 21 Century*, The Press of Peking University & Higher Education Press, 2014.

Kang Shuhua, Editor, *Criminology (3rd Edition)*, The Press of Peking University, 2011.

Lang Sheng, Editor, *Annotation of the Criminal Code of the People's Republic of China (5th Edition, including 8th Amendment of the Criminal Law)*, in the Series Books of the Criminal Law Department of the Legislative Affairs Committee of the Standing Committee of the National People's Congress, The Law Press, 2011.

Wang Guosu & Chen Yiyun, Co-editors, *Science of Criminal Procedure*, The Press of Peking University, 1990.

Wang Shizhou, *Modern Criminal Law (General Part)*, The Press of Peking University, 2011.

Yang Cunxi, General Editor, *Encyclopaedia of Criminal Law Science*, The Press of Nanjing University, 1990.

Yang Cunxi, Yang Dunxian & Guo Zili, Editors, *Chinese Criminal Law (5th Edition)*, The Press of Peking University, 2011.

Yang Diansheng, Editor, *Prison Law Science (2nd Edition)*, The Press of Peking University, 2008.

Zhao Guoling, Editor, *Science of Implementation of Criminal Punishment*, The Press of Peking University, 2014.

Zhou Daoluan & Zhang Jun, *Exact Explanation of the offences in the Criminal Law (4th Edition)*, The Press of the People's Court, 2013.

Zhou Mi, Kang Shuhua & Wang Shizhou, *Criminal Law, Supplement 21 People's Republic of China, International Encyclopaedia of Laws*, Roger Blanpain, Frank Hendrickx (General Editors); Frank Verbruggen, Vanessa Franssen (Volume Editors), Kluwer Law International, 2001.

Zhou Mi, Kang Shuhua, Wang Shizhou & Zhao Guoling, co-authors, *Criminal Law Supplement 3 People's Republic of China in International Encyclopaedia of Laws*, Roger Blanpain, Frank Hendrickx (General Editors); Frank Verbruggen, Vanessa Franssen (Volume Editors), Kluwer, 1994.

Zhou Mi, *The History of the Chinese Criminal Law*, The Press of the Peking University, 1998.

Index

The numbers here refer to paragraph numbers

Index

www.ingramcontent.com/pod-product-compliance
Lightning Source LLC
Chambersburg PA
CBHW071434230926
51846CB00001B/226
9789041195272